EXPLORATIONS IN A CHRIST...
OF PILGRIMAGE

Many Christians go on pilgrimage, whether to Jerusalem, Rome, Santiago, or some other destination, but few think hard about it from the perspective of their faith. This book fills that gap, looking at the biblical and theological elements in pilgrimage and asking how we could do pilgrimage differently.

Exploring the current resurgence of pilgrimage from a Christian viewpoint, this book seeks to articulate a theology of pilgrimage for today. Examination of pilgrimage in the Old and New Testaments provides a grounding for thinking through pilgrimage theologically. Literary, missiological and sociological perspectives are explored, and the book concludes by examining how such a theology could change our practice of pilgrimage today, raising such questions as how tourism to the Holy Land should reflect the situation in the region today. Pilgrims, students and all interested in contemporary pilgrimage will find this accessible book a valuable articulation of the different elements in a Christian theology of pilgrimage.

Dyrness, ... "... ... ..." Missions: Where Have We Gone Wrong?

Book: John ... Evangelism in ... ... "... God ... to those ... ... Approach"

Goldsmith, ... in a ... hungry World

Kirk, J. Andrew ... "What is Mission? ..." ... / Explorations"

We... and (eds.) "... ... ... Mission" ... ... A Reader

EXPLORATIONS IN A CHRISTIAN THEOLOGY
OF PLURALISM

Explorations in a Christian Theology of Pilgrimage

Edited by
CRAIG BARTHOLOMEW AND FRED HUGHES

ASHGATE

Published by
Ashgate Publishing Limited
Gower House
Croft Road
Aldershot
Hants GU11 3HR
England

Ashgate Publishing Company
Suite 420
101 Cherry Street
Burlington, VT 05401-4405
USA

Ashgate website: http://www.ashgate.com

British Library Cataloguing in Publication Data
Explorations in a Christian theology of pilgrimage
    1. Christian pilgrims and pilgrimages – Congresses
    2. Christian pilgrims and pilgrimages – History – Congresses
    3. Pilgrims and pilgrimages in the Bible – Congresses
    I. Bartholomew, Craig G., 1961- II. Hughes, Fred
263^1.041

Library of Congress Cataloging-in-Publication Data
Explorations in a Christian theology of pilgrimage / edited by Craig Bartholomew and Fred Hughes.
       p. cm.
    Includes bibliographical references.
    ISBN 0-7546-0855-7 (alk. paper) – ISBN 0-7546-0856-5 (pbk.: alk. paper)
      1. Christian pilgrims and pilgrimages. I. Bartholomew, Craig G., 1961- II. Hughes, Fred, 1946-

BX2323.E97 2003
263^1.041–dc22

                                    2003058324

ISBN 0 7546 0855 7 (HBK)
ISBN 0 7546 0856 5 (PBK)

Typeset in Times by Tradespools, Frome, Somerset and printed in Great Britain by MPG Books Ltd, Bodmin, Cornwall

Contents

PART III   Theological Perspectives on Pilgrimage

Preface

This book has been several years in the making, a process that has included a conference and a consultation. The book is the deposit from that journey, which has itself been a fascinating pilgrimage, which has far exceeded my expectations. Pilgrimage has turned out to be a far more fertile topic for theological exploration than I, with my Protestant Anglican background, had anticipated.

It remains to thank my fellow pilgrims for all their help in making this book possible. I am grateful to Dame Janet Trotter and the University of Gloucestershire for providing a context in which to do this sort of research. Canon Robert Llewelyn, who recently completed a doctorate here on pilgrimage, has been a source of inspiration and support throughout, as have Dr Fred Hughes and my colleagues here in Theology and Religious Studies. McCabe Pilgrimages and Robert Trimble generously sponsored the initial conference, for which we are very grateful. It has been a joy to work with Sarah Lloyd and Ashgate and I am thankful to them for taking on this project. Gert Swart, Istine Rodseth Swart and Craig Swart have developed a fine cover for our *Explorations* – many thanks indeed!

Craig Bartholomew, Pentecost 2003

Abbreviations

ANE	Ancient Near Eastern
EJT	European Journal of Theology
EKK	Evangelisch-Katholischer Kommentar zum Neuen Testament
ENG	English
EQ	Evangelical Quarterly
JBL	Journal of Biblical Literature
LW	Luther's Works
LXX	Septuagint
MT	Masoretic Text
NIV	New International Version
NRSV	New Revised Standard Version
NTS	New Testament Studies
PG	Preparation of the Gospel
REB	Revised English Bible
SBLSP	Society of Biblical Literature Seminar Papers
TynBul	Tyndale Bulletin
ZTK	Zeitschrift füer Theologie und Kirche

Contributors

Craig Bartholomew is Professor of Philosophy and Biblical Studies at Redeemer University College, Ancaster, Canada. He heads and is the series editor for the Scripture and Hermeneutics Seminar. He is the author of *Reading Ecclesiastes: Old Testament Exegesis and Hermeneutical Theory*, co-editor of *Christ and Consumerism, Praying By the Book: Reading the Psalms* and editor of *In the Fields of the Lord: A Calvin Seerveld Reader*.

Kenneth Cragg was Assistant Bishop in Jerusalem, 1970–1985 (partly in an honorary capacity). He is the author of books and papers on the Middle East, on Islam and on the relations between the monotheistic religions. Publications include *The Arab Christian, Readings in the Qur'an, To Meet and To Greet, Faith and Life Negotiate* and *The Lively Credentials of God*.

Dee Dyas is a director of Christianity and Culture (based at the University of York and St John's College Nottingham). Her main publications are *Images of Faith in English Literature, 700–1500* and *Pilgrimage in Medieval Literature*.

Fred Hughes was Head of Theology and Religious Studies from 1997 to 2003 at the University of Gloucestershire, where he is currently chair of the Academic Standards Committee in the Faculty of Arts and Humanities. His published writings are on Christian and religious education, for example, *What Do You Mean – Christian Education?* (Paternoster: 1992).

Andrew T. Lincoln is Portland Professor of New Testament at the University of Gloucestershire. He was previously Lord and Lady Coggan Professor at Wycliffe College, University of Toronto. His publications include *Paradise Now and Not Yet, Ephesians, Colossians* and *Truth on Trial*.

Robert Llewelyn retired in 1999 after 30 years' parochial ministry in the Diocese of Gloucester. In 2001 he completed a PhD thesis at the University of Gloucestershire on the Anthropology of Pilgrimage, with particular reference to the experiences of Anglican clergy on pilgrimage in the Holy Land. His current research interest is in places of pilgrimage throughout the world which have peace and reconciliation as their especial intention. These include St Paul's Chapel at Ground Zero in New York and St Ethelburga's Church in the City of London.

Gordon McConville read Modern Languages at Cambridge and Theology in Edinburgh, before doing a PhD in Old Testament at Queen's University, Belfast. He has taught at Trinity College, Bristol and Wycliffe Hall, Oxford, and is now Professor in Old Testament at the University of Gloucestershire. He has published mainly on Deuteronomy, including a recent commentary (Apollos: 2002). He is married to Helen, and they have four grown-up children.

Steve Motyer teaches New Testament and Hermeneutics at the London School of Theology (formerly London Bible College), where he also leads the Theology and Counselling course. His interests have focused on John and Paul, and in particular on their attitude towards Israel. Consequently the issue of 'sacred space' and its reconfiguration in Christ is of special interest to him.

Anthony O'Mahony is Director of Research and Lecturer in Theology, Centre for Christianity and Interreligious Dialogue, Heythrop College, University of London. His books include *Palestinian Christians: Religion, Politics and Society in the Holy Land*, *Christians and Muslims in the Commonwealth*, *Eastern Christianity: Studies in Modern History, Religion and Politics*, *The Christian Communities in Jerusalem and the Holy Land: Studies in History, Religion and Politics* and *World Christianity: Dialogues, Politics and Theology*.

Martin Robinson is a minister with Churches of Christ. Besides working as a minister in two congregations, one in inner-city Birmingham and the other in suburban Birmingham, he has worked for the Bible Society for 15 years, most recently as Director for Mission and Theology. He is currently the National Director for Together in Mission. Martin has written ten books on mission in a western context. These include *Planting Tomorrow's Churches Today* (with Stuart Christine), *The Faith of the Unbeliever* and *Winning Hearts, Changing Minds*. Martin is a visiting professor at Seattle Pacific University.

Peter Scott is Senior Lecturer in Theology and Academic Dean of the Faculty of Arts and Humanities at the University of Gloucestershire. Author of *Theology, Ideology and Liberation* and *A Political Theology of Nature*, co-editor of the *Blackwell Companion to Political Theology*, Dr Scott is a member of the Center of Theological Inquiry, Princeton, USA, and is on the editorial board of *Ecotheology*.

Derek Tidball has been Principal of London Bible College since 1995. Derek has degrees in sociology and theology and a doctorate in history. He has written widely, especially on the Bible and on Pastoral Theology. His *The Message of the Cross* appears in the Bible Speaks Today Series (IVP) and he has recently published *Discerning the Spirit of the Age* (Kingsway Publications).

Graham Tomlin is Vice Principal and tutor in Historical Theology and Evangelism at Wycliffe Hall, Oxford. He is a member of the Theology Faculty of Oxford University, where he teaches on the Reformation and on contemporary Mission. He is the author of *The Power of the Cross: Theology and the Death of Christ in Paul, Luther and Pascal, Walking in His Steps: A Guide to Exploring the Land of the Bible* (with Peter Walker), *The Provocative Church* and *Luther and his World*.

Peter Walker studied Classics at Cambridge University and then pursued doctoral research there on early Christian approaches to pilgrimage. After four years in Anglican parish ministry in Kent he was the New Testament postdoctoral research fellow at Tyndale House, Cambridge. Since 1996 he has been lecturing in New Testament, Biblical Theology and Preaching at Wycliffe Hall, an Anglican training college within the University of Oxford. His writings include: *Holy City, Holy Places? Fourth Century Christian Attitudes to Jerusalem and the Holy Land, Jesus and the Holy City* and *Walking in His Steps*, with G.S. Tomlin.

Introduction

Craig Bartholomew and Robert Llewelyn

Pilgrimage is a journey to a special or holy place as a way of making an impact on one's life with the revelation of God associated with that place. Pilgrimage is by no means confined to Christianity – it is utterly central to Islam, common among other religions and present in secular life too, as witness, for example, the popularity of visits to Gracelands, the home of Elvis Presley.[1]

In the Old Testament, pilgrimage to Jerusalem became mandatory once Israel was settled in the land of Canaan. Mount Zion in Jerusalem was where God lived among the Israelites, his 'address' as it were, and regular pilgrimage to Jerusalem was a vital way of embedding within Israelite consciousness their identity as the people of Yahweh. This is wonderfully captured in Psalm 84:5: 'Blessed are those whose strength is in you, in whose heart are the highways to Zion.' The dynamic of pilgrimage to Jerusalem is evoked, for example, in the psalms of ascent. Psalms 120–34 share the title 'A song of ascent', most probably because they are a 'pilgrim hymnal' for use by pilgrims en route to Jerusalem. It is moving to imagine pilgrims walking to Jerusalem and thinking, 'I lift my eyes to the hills – from where will my help come? My help comes from the LORD, who made heaven and earth' (Psalm 121:1).

Within Christianity there is a long tradition of pilgrimage. Indeed, at present, while mainline church attendance in Europe is in decline, the opposite is true of Christian pilgrimage. Western Europe's six thousand plus pilgrimage sites generate some 60 to 70 million religiously motivated visits each year.[2] Many of these visitors are North American. Total visitors at these shrines each year exceed 100 million. Indeed, 'The late twentieth century is, therefore, the latest epoch in a dynamic pattern of rise and decline in enthusiasm for pilgrimage that has characterised the European Christian tradition for nearly 2000 years.'[3]

Christians of all theological traditions participate in pilgrimage today. Within Roman Catholicism there was a resurgence of pilgrimage in the late 19th and early 20th centuries to sites such as Lourdes, Fatima, Knock (in Ireland), Santiago and Medjugorje. According to records at the *Bureau d'Accueil* in Santiago the numbers of pilgrims to Santiago de Compostela have increased dramatically in recent years. Santiago is connected with the apostle James, a connection dating from the 'miraculous' discovery of the tomb of James here in the 9th century. In 1985, 2490 pilgrims were recorded. This had grown in 2001 to 61 420. In the Holy Years – years in which the saint's day of

25 July falls on a Sunday – these numbers rise dramatically (99 400 in 1993 and 154 600 in 1999). These are the numbers of those who have travelled by foot or bicycle along the Camino and thus qualified to receive the Compostela, the authenticated certificate of such a journey. The numbers take no account of those who journey to Santiago by powered means.

The Protestant Reformation resulted in a decline in shrine formation and discouraged pilgrimage, for doctrinal reasons and because of its potential for abuse.[4] Today, however, the Evangelical descendants of Protestantism, while they may never dream of going to Lourdes or Santiago, flock to the 'Holy Land' when it is safe to visit.[5] In 2000, there were some four million visitors to Israel; the number has doubled since 1992, but has, of course, fallen away dramatically with the *Intifada*.[6] And the way in which charismatic Evangelicals from all over the world flocked to Toronto Airport Christian Fellowship in the 1990s bore the marks of postmodern-style pilgrimage seeking to connect with God's revelation of himself at this place.[7]

Amidst the current Evangelical recovery of spirituality, the holiness of certain places and the relevance of pilgrimage are being affirmed. Tom Wright connects his growing awareness that certain places are holy with pilgrimage to Israel. He describes how he was profoundly moved when in 1989 at the height of the *Intifada* he visited the Church of the Holy Sepulchre, built over and around the site of Calvary. Referring to the pain of the Middle East he writes,

> So much pain; so many ugly memories; so much anger and frustration and bitterness and sheer human misery. And it was all somehow concentrated on that one spot. And then, as I continued to reflect and pray, the hurts and pains of my own life came up for review, and they too all seemed to gather together with clarity and force in that one place. It was a moment – actually two or three hours – of great intensity, in which the presence of Jesus the Messiah, at the place where the pain of the world was concentrated, became more and more the central reality. I emerged eventually into the bright sunlight, feeling as though I had been rinsed out spiritually and emotionally, and understanding – or at least glimpsing – in a new way what it could mean to suppose that one act in one place at one time could somehow draw together the hopes and fears of all the years. I had become a pilgrim.[8]

These experiences caused Wright to rethink pilgrimage and in his *The Way of the Lord* he describes how he has come to see the value of Christian pilgrimage, not least to the Holy Land.

The current renaissance in Christian pilgrimage is receiving considerable academic attention, especially among historians and anthropologists. Consequently there is increasingly an excellent body of descriptive (historical and modern) work now available.[9] Amidst this resurgence however, there is a noticeable lack of a coherent *theology* of pilgrimage. There are various descriptive and historical accounts of pilgrimage, Christian and other, but theological analyses are rare. This book aims to contribute towards articulating the contours of a Christian theology of pilgrimage for today.

In January 2000, the School of Theology and Religious Studies at Cheltenham and Gloucester College of Higher Education (now the University of Gloucestershire) held a successful two-day conference on Christian perspectives on pilgrimage kindly sponsored by McCabe Pilgrimages. The conference included biblical, theological, historical, literary, anthropological and practical dimensions of pilgrimage. Since then we have held a further day consultation en route to the production of this book. In the process it was decided to focus this collection of essays firmly upon the theme of a Christian theology of pilgrimage. Several of the essays direct their attention to Jerusalem in particular, but the overall concern of this volume is with pilgrimage in general rather than Jerusalem in particular. All the contributions pose in one way or another the question of a Christian theology of pilgrimage for today.

Bishop Kenneth Cragg foregrounds the complex theological questions that surround pilgrimage to Jerusalem today. He does this via the notion of the 'sacrament of geography' that arises from 'the place of the Name' in the Old Testament, and its fulfilment in Jesus in the events of the Gospels. Cragg notes how the fulfilment in Jesus and its re-enactment in the Eucharist 'neutralizes' the OT particularity of Jerusalem. Cragg nevertheless still discerns a place for sacred geography; through associationism, pilgrimage to Jerusalem and the associated sites remains a legitimate Christian practice. However, he links this firmly to what he calls the 'Gentile offering'. Christian pilgrimage must be connected with the experience and needs of Christians (the living stones) in Israel, and this means it would have to take account of the complex and bitter political realities of the Middle East today.

The chapters that follow Cragg's masterful exposition examine the biblical, historical and theological strands that constitute a Christian theology of pilgrimage. Chapters 2 to 4 examine pilgrimage in the Bible. Gordon McConville looks at pilgrimage in the Old Testament, and Andrew Lincoln and Steven Motyer explore it from a New Testament perspective. Inevitably this raises the question of the relationship between the Testaments and how we are to construe them in relation to a theology of pilgrimage. For the Old Testament, pilgrimage is mandatory, whereas the rationale of pilgrimage appears to be radically undermined in the New Testament. Through their readings of key New Testament texts, Lincoln and Motyer arrive at different assessments of the implications of the New Testament for pilgrimage today.

The Christian practice of pilgrimage developed in particular after the rise of Constantine. Peter Walker outlines these early origins of Christian pilgrimage; Dee Dyas examines pilgrimage in the Middle Ages, and Graham Tomlin re-examines the Reformers' critique of pilgrimage to see if a positive, Reformed theology of pilgrimage for today might be possible. Anthony O'Mahony examines Louis Massignon's involvement in Christian–Muslim pilgrimage to Vieux-Marché.

Pilgrimage might be thought to be the reverse of mission, but Martin Robinson argues that modern missiology can help us to locate pilgrimage theologically. Peter Scott rightly discerns that pilgrimage raises the question of a theology of place and he explores pilgrimage via a sacramental theology of place. Theology is always done at a particular time and place, and Derek Tidball examines the relevance of pilgrimage today through a dialogue with Zygmunt Bauman's understanding of postmodernism.

The title of this volume deliberately begins, *Explorations in* .... There is no attempt to reach a final consensus among all the contributors. In his conclusion, Craig Bartholomew reflects upon the main issues that a theology of pilgrimage for today must address as he sees them, and he suggests a possible route for such reflection. Our hope is that this collection will provoke others to work further at a theology of pilgrimage for today.

Notes

1   See Reader and Walter, *Pilgrimage*.
2   Nolan and Nolan, *Christian Pilgrimage* 1.
3   Ibid., 3.
4   See Graham Tomlin's chapter in this respect.
5   For a recent Evangelical guide to pilgrimage to the Holy Land, see Walker and Tomlin, *Walking in His Steps*.
6   These figures do not distinguish between pilgrims and tourists. The difficulties of travelling to the Holy Land at present are resulting in pilgrimage tour companies redirecting tourists to sites such as those in Greece, Turkey, Rome, Assisi, Santiago, Fatima, and even Poland and Russia.
7   See Lyon, *Jesus*, 106–10 and Percy, 'The Morphology'.
8   Wright, *The Way*, 6,7.
9   In the mid-20th century the study of pilgrimage was given respectability by the studies of Victor and Edith Turner. Though his theories, especially of 'Communitas', have been largely discredited, they remain a benchmark for subsequent study. See Turner and Turner, *Image and Pilgrimage*. More recently the work of Eade and Sallnow, *Contesting the Sacred*, has established fresh agendas for pilgrimage, particularly as regards notions of 'contestation' at shrines and 'person, place and text' as a means of explicating the power of pilgrimage shrines. A good example of historical, descriptive study of pilgrimage is Sumption, *Pilgrimage*.

Bibliography

Coleman, S. and J. Elsner, *Pilgrimage Past and Present: Sacred Travel and Sacred Space in World Religions* (London: British Museum Press, 1995).
Davies, J.G., *Pilgrimage Yesterday and Today: Why? Where? How?* (London: SCM, 1988).
Eade, J. and M. Sallnow (eds), *Contesting the Sacred: Anthropology of Christian Pilgrimage* (London: Routledge, 1990).

Hilliard, A. and B.J. Bailey, *Living Stones Pilgrimage: with the Christians of the Holy Land* (London: Cassell, 1999).

Lyon, D., *Jesus in Disneyland: Religion in Postmodern Times* (Cambridge: Polity, 2000).

Nolan, M.L. and S. Nolan, *Christian Pilgrimage in Modern Western Europe* (Chapel Hill and London: The University of North Carolina Press, 1989).

Percy, M., 'The Morphology of Pilgrimage in the Toronto Blessing', *Religion*, 28 (1998), 281–8.

Peterson, E., *The Wisdom of Each Other: A Conversation Between Spiritual Friends* (Grand Rapids: Zondervan, 1998).

Reader, I. and T. Walter (eds), *Pilgrimage in Popular Culture* (Basingstoke: Macmillan, 1992).

Sheldrake, P., *Spaces for the Sacred* (London: SCM, 2001).

Sumption, J., *Pilgrimage* (London: Faber and Faber, 1975).

Turner, V. and E. Turner, *Image and Pilgrimage in Christian Culture* (New York: Columbia University Press, 1978).

Walker, P. and G. Tomlin, *Walking in His Steps: A Guide to Exploring the Land of the Bible* (London: Marshall Pickering, 2001).

Wright, N.T., *The Way of the Lord* (London: SPCK, 1999).

CHAPTER 1

Jesus, Jerusalem and Pilgrimage Today

Kenneth Cragg

I

That 'bowels move pilgrims' must sound in our ears as the oddest thing that John Bunyan ever said, but in the parlance of the 17th century 'bowels' were the seat of the heart's affections, the inner springs of emotion and feeling. The contemporary versions of the New Testament (Tyndale and Coverdale) used it to translate Paul's *splagchna* in writing to the Colossians and Philemon. These did not mean unhappy digestions responding to travelling ills in foreign climes.[1] In truth, 'the road to Jerusalem is in the heart' – an old saying with a nice ambiguity. For having it there argues no need to travel, yet will inspire every urge to do so. That paradox is at the core of the entire theme of Jerusalem in Christian mind and conscience.

As with electricity, the current has to 'go to earth'. Hence the earthing wires and the lightning conductors high on towers and steeples. Or, in the different idiom of time and place, meanings call for memories to be visited, if their 'when and where' remain accessible. For these are important for the 'what and why' within those happenings. If we use the word 'point' in its double sense, then 'the point of the event' – in this case the Christ-event – can be grasped (in some measure) at 'the point' of its eventuation. Or, as Augustine had it in a sermon (not preached in Galilee or Jerusalem): 'Christians worship in the place where Christ's feet trod.' He could only have meant that the Lord's 'feet-treading' was always imaginatively His people's territory and sanctuary, even in Milan, Rome or Thagaste. English William Blake, in his elusive way, may have had the same idea in picturing, if only with interrogation, 'those feet in ancient time ... on England's mountains green'.

What, with pilgrimage in mind, has been well called 'the sacrament of geography' always has this quality of validity and dispensability. It invites and ministers to faith but it will also sift how that faith relates itself to the locale of its convictions. That 'sifting' might be illustrated by the familiar notion of *barakah*, or acquirable 'virtue' latent in holy places, people and shrines. The idea is prominent in folklorist and popular Islam and in many superstitions. The 'mothers of Salem', for example, in the Gospel narrative, 'brought their children to Jesus that He might touch them' (Mark 10:13, Luke 18:15). The disciples seem to have felt that this naïveté was no part of 'the kingdom of heaven', or was distracting. But the mothers, and many others *in situ*, had the instinctive conviction that there was 'benison' to be had and that 'touching' was vital to receiving it. Unlike the disciples, Jesus met them on the ground of their own simplicity, while not approving it (cf. Matthew 9:20–22, 'thy faith ... saved thee').

In the crudest way, this theme of 'blessing by proximity' and 'access by contact' could arguably be the rationale of pilgrimage, depending on how the place is perceived as the locale of what is sought, of how what is found is conceived to avail from the place. Certainly in various forms and theories, *barakah* is understood to accrue from pilgrimage, thanks to the journey that contrives the association and the sojourn that prolongs the 'touching'. To seek, by this analogy, what Christian pilgrimage to 'the holy land' is, and is not, requires some prior study of the Judaic theme of 'the place of the Name'.

II

The Biblical juncture of 'place' and 'Name' is clearly a pivotal theme, the 'Name' being, of course, no mere label but where the reality, we may even say the identity, of God is known for its truth via some event – and therefore some place (since all events are physically and historically 'situated') – where it is believed to be intrinsically given, by God, into human knowledge, where the divine, we might say, was dependably credentialized. Such an event-in-place for the Judaic tradition was certainly the Exodus. When, in his experience at the burning bush, Moses understands himself commissioned to lead his people out of Egypt, he knows how timidly incredulous they will be.[2] He visualises them saying to him about this summoning Lord: 'What is His Name?' and adds his own question: 'What shall I say to them?'

Then comes that enigmatic 'playing on the verb "to be"', and so the Name 'Yahweh': 'I am who I am', which, in context, should surely read 'I will be there as there whom I will be.' A riddle like 'I am that I am' would never motivate a slave people. The point, surely, is that only in exodus can the God of exodus be known. The 'guarantee' about the risk, which is what querying 'the Name' is seeking, is not to be had in advance. Trust must proceed[3] and only in the going will 'the Name' be proven. 'Experience will decide' its content. Only in and through exodus will the God who presides over it be known for 'who He is'.

The historic Exodus was, thus, for Jewry the first 'place of the Name'. Their Lord *had been there*, as whom there He had been. The knowing assured them of being 'His people' and the event had sanctioned their 'chosen peoplehood'. 'All our fathers passed through the sea' and Passover ritualized in abiding memory the event-cum-sacrament of their identity as Jewry, 'the tribes of Israel'.

Exodus, however, was prospective to entry. 'He brought them out that He might bring them in.' Through the wilderness, beyond Moses to Joshua, they held themselves destined for a territory and a territory destined uniquely for themselves (albeit pre-occupied and needing to be conquered). Their ultimate access to it and appropriation of it changed 'the place of the Name' from history to geography, from a journey to a tenancy. The *barakah* of the first had been meant to inaugurate the *barakah* of the second, with both as tokens of the divine 'election'.

It is evident that, within the land once fully possessed, there were several local shrines and foci of worship, like Bethel and Shiloh and 'seats of the tabernacle', that symbol of divine Presence during nomadism. However, with David's acquisition of Jerusalem (which Joshua never possessed) and the aura of the Davidic/Solomonic monarchy and the Temple building, Jerusalem became the focal point both of worship and of the land. Hence the repeated plea of Solomon at the inauguration of the Temple: 'When we pray towards this place of which Thou hast said, My Name shall be there, then hearken' (I Kings 8:29, 30, 35). Subsequently the 'place and Name' theme runs through the language of psalmody and prophethood. Isaiah 60:13, 'The place of my feet ... the place of my sanctuary' and Psalm 26:8, 'the place where thy honour dwells' are typical. Or, as Rabbi Abraham Heschel used to love to say: 'Yahweh has an address on earth.'

III

The flag of the modern state of Israel has two equilateral triangles set across each other to yield a six-pointed star. It may be read as telling the material truth of a tri-unison of people, place and past which embodies the triple theme of the spirit, namely how Yahweh bestowed the land on the people, that in the land they might glorify the Lord. The Temples, David's and Herod's alike, as it were consummated the holiness of the whole territory. Indeed the latter was for the Temple's sake as the apex of its hallowing, the theme song of its destiny.

It is at once evident, however, that this triunity of place, folk and story is a universal shape of human life. Witness the constant interplay of names of places and people (Finns and Finland, Caribs and the Caribbean, Nepal and the Nepalese), with habitats and tribes identifying each other. For all nations have ancestors, land and history. Who we are, where we dwell and whence we came are universal denominators of humanity. All cherish histories, live by generational sequence and know where they belong territorially. Hence, on every count, the pain of exile, of old Mother Joad crying, in forced migration: 'How shall we know it's us without our past?'[4] Ezekiel's 'in thy blood thou shalt live' (16:6) is true of all birthing, parenting and genealogy.

It was the intensity Judaic tradition gave to these common denominators that made their sense of 'chosen peoplehood' so insistent 'from generation to generation'.[5] But it must be clear from any doctrine of divine creation that God – if not Yahweh – has only 'chosen peoples', in that habitats sustain all, memories belong to all and ancestors prepossess all. Anthropological studies have familiarized us with the number of land/people amalgams which are believed divinely donated and ordained.[6] Climates and terrains vary endlessly and vitally condition their peoples. Wordsworth would never have written *The Prelude* in the Sahara. 'Providence' has its mysteries but the Biblical (and Qur'anic) doctrine of creation argues a given destiny for all habitats and habitands. The Noahid 'covenant' of 'possess and multiply, dwell and manage' is indifferently a human charter. Emotionally it can have something of an equal tenacity of attachment. The point was well made by Kipling:

> God gave all men earth to love,
> But since man's heart is small,
> Ordained that each one spot should prove
> Beloved over all, that as He watched creation's birth
> So we, in God-like mood,
> Might of our love create our earth
> And see that it is good.[7]

It would clearly be a travesty of any faith in divine creation to think of unilateral 'covenant' attaching to earth tenancy, folk awareness and historic memory.

That logic is contradicted by the urge, in some quarters of Biblical exegesis, to argue that the Bible really begins at Genesis 12 with the call of Abraham and that for this 'history' creation was merely setting the stage. The exceptionality that ensues in 'redemptive history', via Abraham, Jacob, Joseph, Moses and their sequential story, can only well belong with, and in, the inclusive reality of 'all nations of one blood' housed and environed in a universally 'gifted earth'. Certainly modern space awareness and planetary globalism, if not Biblical sanity, have required us to know it so.

It follows that '*a* holy land' is a sounder usage than '*the* holy land'. For unless all lands are hallowed none could be. The exceptionality will arise from history and tenancy, not from locale itself, if it is to arise at all. Nature-wise it will be fair to sing:

> Where'er we seek Thee, Thou art found
> And every place is hallowed ground.

That it *did* arise from history and tenancy – with these read as a pre-ordained destiny – was the Jewish truth of 'the land of Israel'. Hence that threefold awareness of who, where and whence, of tribe, terrain and time–story which, albeit humanly in common, reached in Israel a distinctive and 'peculiar' reality, whereby Jewry constituted 'an elect people' where Yahweh was 'known' as nowhere else (Psalm:16.1). They saw themselves, because of where they dwelt, as 'a people dwelling alone' (Numbers 23:9) though surrounded, interpenetrated and affected by 'other nations' on whom their apartheid reacted both ways. They were, through their whole history, we must say, an ethnicized, territorialized people with their own mother language. Even in the tragedy of exile the burden of their special category persisted, if not in the irony of foreign sojourn, then in the yearning for repatriation. The command to them, 'You shall have no other gods but Me' was somehow assured to them by the pledge: 'I will have no other people but you.' The land was to be exclusively theirs and they were to be exclusively the land's. Its *barakah* would enshrine their worship, authenticate their history and enwomb their generations. History knows no more tenacious, no more tremendous land–people equation than 'this Israel of Israel'.[8]

IV

The point, in this context of a study of Christian pilgrimage, of a summary review of Hebraic land awareness is simply to say that in the New Testament each dimension is radically neutralized. For good or ill, the Church emerged there as de-ethnicized, deterritorialized and capable of being multilingual. It neither needed nor possessed a sacred space, nor a sacred *ethnos*, nor a sacred tongue – or, rather, it received these in the meaning of faith in the Christ-event, so that its great locative was 'in Christ',[9] their folk heritage and their 'citizenship'.

Thus Jerusalem became a focal point of missionary diaspora. By the apostolic understanding of the ministry and the passion of Jesus there came 'the Christ of faith'. That Christhood was perceived as having an inherent worldwideness as its logic and its nature. From the sort of Messiah that 'Jesus as the Christ' had been, only the world of sundry races, many tongues and scattered lands could properly contain it. This view of its perceived Christ antecedents has often been disputed by those who have preferred to conclude that there was only properly a 'Jesus of history', a maverick rabbi, an itinerant charismatic like Hanina Ben Dosa, who should never have been read in any other (inflated) terms. The whole issue is too massive to call for detailed attention here.[10] We are proceeding on the de facto apostolic sequence to Jesus in which alone the Church lived and from which its Scriptures derived. The issue is no realm for guaranteed proof/disproof. It would not then be a matter of faith. But despite all Geza Vermes-style disavowal of the Church's 'Christ-event',[11] faith's theme is eminently trustworthy as appropriate to faith's proper quality.[12]

The sequence from Jesus to Christ to apostolicity to the world might be captured in T.S. Eliot's 'Time future contained in time past' and 'home is where one starts from'. 'The words' (and the deeds *qua* Jesus) 'sufficed to compel the recognition they preceded.'[13] That recognition, it is urgent to note, was an interior Jewish decision. 'Gentile' participation in the openness that followed was consequent on, not contributory to, the crucial verdict about their due inclusion in a new 'people of God'. The story is not one of 'Gentile' conspiracy to invade and corrupt a Jewish perquisite and violate its exclusivity but rather of a logic, perceived by Jews themselves, that 'Messiah according to Jesus' had an inclusive, multi-ethnic quality. No 'Gentiles' attended the Council in Jerusalem of Acts 15 to influence its decision on the issue of circumcision.

The thrust in it, however, stemmed from the way Jesus, in their perception, had been 'the Christ', namely in the crucified terms of the love that suffers. And 'the love that suffers' is the only power from which redemption results. If the Cross was enacted as, and by, 'the sin of the world', then 'the sin of the world' had been *there* forgiven, veritably in the words and wounds of Jesus suffering in those love terms, as 'the cup his Father willed'.

Any other pattern of Messiahship – Zealot, Essene, 'holy land purity' – would have related only to Jewry and a national liberation from Rome, or a notional regime of some 'Teacher of righteousness'. There were also many aspects of Jesus' ministry which suggested, if they did adumbrate, this worldwideness, notably the unrestricting of 'restrictive greeting' in Matthew 5:47–8, with 45, and the 'a certain man' phrasing of so many parables.[14] Though, as he told the woman near Sidon, there were limits to the locale and human reach of his ministry, the logic of its sequel was told as inherently universal.[15]

A sense, therefore, of being 'in Christ', whether 'at Philippi' or 'at Corinth' – the epistolary style of Paul to his churches – made physical access to Galilee or Judea or Jerusalem in no way imperative. By the same token the Christ-drama there needed to be documented, the more so as the immediate apostolic generation of 'eye-seers' was passing by the lapse of time and the expanding spread of the churches planting the faith far from its local origins.

Hence the coming into being of the New Testament writings. Their very shape, as Letters and Gospels, corroborates the case we have made. Without the diaspora they would not have been needed, nor could they have been penned. If we liken the Christ-event to the stem of a tuning-fork, then its two parallel prongs (by which the note is struck) are, inseparably, the community and the text. The former both produced and received the latter. Since the one were many, and the many one, they needed the unifying care of apostolic guidance. Being newly discipled, they needed education in their own meaning.

And since 'Gentile' inclusion was so strenuous a development, so loaded an innovation on the Jewish side, doubtful Jewry needed reassurance, via prophetic citation, no less than 'Gentile' folk needed education. The Letters of Paul and Peter and 'to the Hebrews' were plainly deeply solicitous of Jewish feeling and for Judaic case making, so potentially embittering among Jewry was the revolution Christian Jewry had made.

All this is evident enough in the very fabric of the New Testament as literature and, because the world of the Letters was this way, that world gave being to the Gospels as texts for memory and for corporate self-possession as, in Jesus the Christ, the new 'people of God' inclusive of Jew and 'Gentile' alike. The Gospel texts, which modern disputers have, for the most part, to invoke even in doubting them, only emerged from the dispersed reception of their central figure as 'the Jesus of faith'. It is important to realize that, in line with 'time future contained in time past' earlier noted, they tell the story within the experience of its fruition. The evangelists write 'gospels' not treatises, but they are writing committedly and mingle their experience with their faith narration. This is most markedly so with the Fourth Gospel, where the narrative is suffused with the theology by which it has been read and for which it is believed to have been meant. Thus we have Jesus speaking, from within the actuality of ministry, as being already 'the Christ of faith', as in 'I and my Father are one' or 'I came to save the world'. We should not think to say here, mistakenly, with C.S. Lewis: 'We have three conclusions, either the speaker was insane or a megalomaniac, or he was God.' Those are never intelligible options. Such would not be the divinity of Incarnation. They tell us that Jesus in the divine status by which faith came to identify him proleptically is present in the very life immediacy in which the narrative belonged, the narrative from which the evangelist learned it had been so.

John tells of a Jesus who, in his Christhood, has become the new 'temple of the body'. Matthew, in his different way, presents Jesus as 'the new Moses' 'on the mount' giving the new law. All the evangelists have their editorial mind, as in both narrative and theological liability for the presentation. For our purposes, the fact is that a textual, 'here we find him' Jesus the Christ is where faith always sufficiently 'visits' to seek and find him 'whom our souls love'. In being 'literaturized',[16] Jesus is delocalized. 'These are they which testify of me' for, the 'me' he was apart, they would not exist.

This literary way of repairing to origins was soon seconded, in the early Church, by the sense of the sacrament, where, in the language and the imagery of Luke 24:13–32, 'he was known to them in the breaking of the bread'. It seems right to think of that telescoped chapter at the end of Luke's Gospel (where the 'one day' of Easter morning stretches to the mount of ascension) as comprising the growing self-awareness of the spreading Church. It was itself a much-travelled community[17] well pictured in the journeying pair, Cleopas and one nameless disciple, types of a community slowly identifying their 'Christ in all the Scriptures' in the necessary task of justifying their open faith to dubious Jews, but also companying with Christ in the developing sacrament of 'bread and wine'. What might still stay unpersuading in the text was made intimately theirs in 'holy supper' – the broken bread in the wounded hands. This would be the rite which made Jesus deeply present irrespective of the space (and time) that sundered them from the Jerusalem from which their story had also travelled. Thus any Christian 'theology of pilgrimage' has to be consistent with the re-enacting in any and every local scene of 'the night in which he was betrayed'.

Given 'faith's story in faith's interpretation' (a fair formula to describe the New Testament document) it seems clear that 'the place of the Name' has fully passed from the sense it had in respect of its first meaning for Jewry in a 'holy land' via a private history. 'The place of the Name' has deepened and widened (or, rather, 'personified') into 'our Lord Jesus Christ'. Yahweh, 'his God and Father', had been there in him, as who there He had been. The Exodus formula, answering Moses' question about how he (and his people) could be assured about their divine liberator had been taken up, and taken into, the Christ-event. Jesus, in word and deed, was, for the Church, 'the place of the divine Name', the history in which God was dependably known for who He was – and is.

'Christ our passover,' Paul wrote to the Corinthians (I 5:7), making the first story a metaphor (*mutatis mutandis*) for the redemption in Christ crucified. According to Luke there was a hint of the same theme when Jesus spoke of 'the exodus' he would 'accomplish in Jerusalem' (9:31). 'The Word' had been 'made flesh, dwelling among us' and so, as in a time span place, the divine Name had its living legibility in 'the Christ of God'. He was the index to the divine nature only in that from the divine nature he had come to be the one he was.

V

It might seem to follow from all the foregoing that the geography of this Christ would have no necessary place in the faith or devotion of Christians. The living reality, so to say, had 'de-requisitioned' it. By the ever present Holy Spirit, through the new peoplehood, and via the now given Scriptures and the perpetual sacrament, the unforgettable Lord was present to his Church in terms that required no travel. 'The place of the Name', being now so essentially understood, was by the same token ubiquitous, cognized in worship anywhere and everywhere.

However, all these considerations, by their very sufficiency, still left not only intact but eminently desirable the sight and feel and memory of the land of origins. Necessary or mandatory? No! But proper and likely? Yes. Jerusalem might well have been late to come to patriarchal status in the Church, with Antioch and Alexandria prior, but no locale could ever displace the there-and-then-ness of the lakeside and the city where all had eventuated.

Moreover the forward thrust of the New Testament as we have it is all a 'westward-ho', 'from Jerusalem round to Illyricum' (Romans 15:19).[18] There is no scriptured eastward or southward to balance the apostolic expansion and it is well to listen in history, as far as we can, to the silences. Perhaps, as some conjecture, there was a partially differing Judean element in Christian origins of which, for very lack of evidence, we need to take account. Not that any such factor would consciously affect pilgrimage, but pilgrimage could certainly acknowledge that the vital centre of gravity was not to be identified with the locally visited one, nor the New Testament's meaning be confined to its narrative's outreach.

In any event, associationism is always instinctive in human memory and its emotions. Plaques go on buildings where the famous have lived. We lay flowers on the immediate site of the tragedy. 'Where' enters mysteriously into 'what' it was. So there was always an urge to go and see, a means of grace in 'treading where the feet had trod'. To be sure, some three decades into apostolicity Jerusalem was captured and the Temple destroyed. Some 70 years later, after the debacle of Bar Kokhba in 135 AD the city became the pagan Aelia Capitolina. Given the Jewish diaspora, there were those who read in its desolation a sort of nemesis, but after Constantine and the 'recovery' of the Holy Sepulchre the scene was better set for the travels of such as Egeria and for the evocative travelogues that such as she bequeathed for emulation.

The actual course of Christian pilgrimage to Jerusalem is handled elsewhere in this volume. The emphasis here is on the *barakah* still negotiable, in sober Christian terms, via actually walking in the way, realizing the olive grove Gethsemane or testing the acoustics of a hillside in Galilee, so making vivid the means whereby the throngs 'heard him gladly'.[19] Greenleaf Whittier was well so named, with his luxuriant lines about 'the calm of hills above' and 'Sabbath rest by Galilee', but there is no doubt of the charm of the Lake, or Peter's fish or recruits once drawn from 'mending nets'. Present-day tourism may have left some participants, as Ernest Hemingway had it elsewhere, 'like bunting on the water-front', but, given a due preparation of heart, the sacred geography will truly educate the faith.

In Matthew's account of the Passion the reader may well isolate two arresting words, 'him there' (27:36), telling how the Roman soldiers 'sitting down watched him there'. They were doubtless assuming a long duty stint, with the dimmest sense of 'who' was 'there' and why, 'the Christ' and 'crucified'. The two words unwittingly capture the whole mystery of Christianity concerning 'God in Christ', such a person in such a place: 'thorn-crowned divinity ... proven in the human wearing.'

All theology apart, 'him here' (historically but not exclusively) is the actuality awaiting pilgrim visitation. Those who have sought and known it so confirm its authenticity. Galilee and Jerusalem were indeed fulfilled far beyond their own perimeter, but returning within it is a precious soul experience where devotion informs itself, no less – and more vitally – than archaeology unearths and investigates for scholarship with truth.

VI

If, further, we would have the New Testament instruct us about pilgrimage to Jerusalem, its practical contribution must be the 'Gentile offering'. The concern of the Christian diaspora, from this angle, was for the material poverty of Jerusalem people, a practical compassion, not a pious wistfulness. It was the first model of 'Christian aid' and it seems to have been a spontaneous gesture among the churches which at first Paul treated matter-of-factly but which later seems to have seized on his imagination. In I Corinthians 16:1 'concerning the collection', he speaks of 'sending it' by hand of those he will nominate. In II Corinthians 8 and 9 he takes up the initiative himself. To deliver it personally he resolves to go to Jerusalem. It is noteworthy that the great evangelist risked his liberty not in preaching but in being ecumenical. The journey to Jerusalem in fact brought him into Caesar's custody as, thus far, mere preaching had not done.

Pilgrimage that seeks to 'tap' *barakah* for the soul must know to bring the *barakah* of a caring compassion. The 'poor saints' (only materially such – the adjective is not 'pitiable') at Jerusalem matter more than holy walls and sacred sites. Few passages in the Bible are more tragically ironic than Psalm 122, 'a city compact in itself' where 'those who love prosper' seeing that 'peace is within thy walls'. How, then, can Christian pilgrimage to Jerusalem today be a soul journey of devotion, if not also a ministering service (cf. Romans 15:25 and 31) answering the current tragedy? Or, maybe, the latter is the only present validity in the former. There can hardly be a valid pilgrimage that stays oblivious of the steady Judaization of Palestine or of the tragedy of local Christianity, the bane on the land of its birth.

For there is no doubt that all – and Israel in the all – is in radical straits. 'They shall grieve who love thee.' For there is 'no peace within thy walls', and there is 'no seat of judgement, even the seat of the house of David'. Rather, it has to be said, with the old prophet Isaiah: 'Woe unto them that join house to house and field to field until there be no room, that they may be left alone in the midst of the earth' (5:8). Encroaching settlements give no promise of feasible co-occupancy, yet a Palestinian population remains irreducibly situate, experiencing what more and more spells irreconcilability. Is Zionism itself spreading the 'tents of Kedar'?[20]

Perhaps the modern pilgrim to Jerusalem can best comprehend – before it can ever be brought – what an active compassion must realize, by returning to the words of Eleazar the leader of the Zealots on Masada, just before their corporate suicide. They had retreated to a last bastion, still just inside 'promised land' borders (a vital consideration), and one that seemed impregnable. However, the Roman ramp, and adverse winds, and raging fire, proved their game was up. Ought they (according to Josephus' account) Eleazar asked: 'to have conjectured at the purpose of God much sooner'? That, he concluded 'had been proper to us'.[21] Should they ever have allowed their self-assurance – or their arrogance – to lead them into a tragic impasse in which they had left themselves no redeeming way back?[22]

It is not suggested that this is a right analogy for 'Israel today', sustained, as it is, by a massive sense of sublime achievement and in no way reducible, except in that its redoubtable actuality has inflicted a people tragedy which could have been foreseen, and its guilt not incurred, if it had realistically anticipated 'the purpose of God much sooner'. For it is evident enough that Israel, with all its resources of self-fulfilling vitality and *savoir-faire*, has been monumentally 'suffered for', in the cumulative immolation of another people.

To be sure, the sequence and the sequel have been, in part, the product of decisions and factors to which that other people were party. 'Are we to be blamed for winning?' is an Israeli question which only seems not to make its answer obvious. But, involved in the issue as Palestinians have been, that truth in no way mitigates the current status of Israeli oppression and 'costliness' in Palestinian terms. This means that Zionism has darkly defeated its own best ambition by the very form in which it brought it, namely aggressive statehood requiring monopolized territory. The tragedy is that the 'final solution' to make good Jewish 'unwantedness' in a 'Gentile' world of unrelievable hostility has invoked a local unwantedness that has a thoroughly legitimate quality in its plea for justice. Thus what Zionism has done to Zion has only darkly renewed a bitter anti-ness that is far from being merely vindictive or unethical. Has Zionism, therefore, betrayed Judaism – or at least the supreme ethicism of its own greatest prophetic mentors? Yet, by Herzl's logic, statehood was the only option the 'Gentile' world, with its frequent pogroms or its bland and subtle assimilations, had left to Jewry. Overwhelmingly, though long post-Herzl, the Holocaust seemed to have confirmed his logic. Thus the Shoah added its horrendous sanction to the incontrovertibility of the State of Israel, without in any way lightening its costliness as known to age-long Palestine in injustice and dispersion. Rather, there could be a sinister dimension of age-long victims unthinkingly reversing the roles.[23]

Could the tragic current situation have been foreseen and by foresight precluded by better 'conjecturing the purpose of God sooner'? There has always been divided mind in the counsels of Zionism. There was a time when even 'the holy land' was itself dispensable so long as some territory availed. That folly was quickly abandoned, yet still there were dreamers who thought that bifederalism could succeed and two 'states' politically possess the same small piece of earth. Or there was a kind of willing innocence that somehow let the de jure dream of Zion hold in oblivion of the de facto reality of (what the Balfour Declaration grudgingly conceded) an 'existing population'.

Others, though, were more realist and forthright. Vladimir Jabotinsky, for example, did not write his novel *Samson* without echoes of 'the Philistines be upon thee'. He, with Max Nordau, knew that peoples with lands do not readily forgo them when they understand that others intend to dispossess them. Our very Zionist ideology, he insisted, must make us 'invaders' even as Joshua was. We will need a similar end to all compunction. We need not be finally unreconciled or unreconciling, but can only be either in the clear wake of unambiguous victory. We must first crush and only so concede a parallel 'existence on our sufferance' after they have understood how adamant and invincible we have proved to be.

That policy is broadly now in the saddle with Jabotinski's lineal heirs in the Likud Party. The scheme of things was first known as 'the iron wall',[24] or, better, 'the iron fist', since the 'wall' language meant the superior presence-in-power. Happily, Israeli policy since Partition has had more lenient protagonists and even genuine 'peace-makers' in terms willing to accommodate recognized legitimacy in the other nationalism. But, thanks to divided counsels and to the steady pragmatism of the likes of Ben Gurion and Golda Meir, the stresses of international politics and the dominance of the USA, the effective legitimation and actualizing of Palestinian statehood have been far to seek and long to await.

It would now seem that Israel is unable to make the kind of peace settlement which would remotely satisfy the Palestinians without inducing civil war within itself. So strong and so insistent are the emotions that would not tolerate the costs, both ideological and material. No government can well concert a policy that would threaten its very inner survival. Nor can a fragmented Palestinian authority contemplate the terms Israel might ever brace itself to offer, without surrendering itself to anarchy or chaos. Such seems to be the desperate current impasse and such, too, the real explanation of the collapse of 'Camp David' late in 2000, when Yasser Arafat is alleged to have bungled a 'perfect last chance' which, anyway, an Israeli election was within days of rescinding and which made no progress towards even token 'refugee return', reparations for seized properties and the status of Jerusalem.

The Jerusalem pilgrim may well be defeated in anything approaching comprehension but the effort must be made, or 'holy places' become idols of the mind and snares of the heart as long as their inhuman unholiness is held invisible. Greek tragedy believed itself as only happening to great heroes and in order to be truly tragic had to offer no end solution, comprising only the fatal elements of its own grandeur. Jewish Zionism has in truth, a heroic quality. It has not yet found the heroism that can, even yet, 'conjecture at the purpose of God' and set that better purpose on its wiser way.

Whatever is, or can be, vicarious in the human scene and in the human condition, pilgrimage says there are centuries and territories that in heart we co-inhabit. If we visit because we belong, we must passionately belong with what we visit.

Notes

1   Such as pre-journey advice will now often anticipate with cautionary recommendations.

2   They were, in fact, awed slaves to whom pharaonic power seemed as massive as the pyramids. Moreover, Egypt is a country from which people did not readily emigrate, by land, for its great vital river traverses forbidding desert either way.

3   Only the event lived would/could 'prove' the God in reckoning. One might compare Isaiah 7:9 in another context: 'If you will not trust you will not be entrusted.' Such are the ways of faith.

4   In John Steinbeck's *The Grapes of Wrath*, the dispossessed Joad family is trekking west in search of house and job and has to jettison cherished things the overladen truck cannot take.

5   The vital importance of the generational sequence makes this among the most recurrent phrases in the Hebrew *Tanakh*. It is significant that it is nowhere found in the New Testament.

6   One example is Jomo Kenyatta's aptly named *Facing Mount Kenya, The Tribal Life of the Gikuyu* (New York, 1950), written with both the expert anthropological insights learned from Malinowski and the intimate knowledge from birth and rearing. The mount territory is received as the gift of gods to those 'sponsored' people.

7   Rudyard Kipling, *Definitive Edition of His Verse* (London, 1943), p.216, 'Sussex'.

8   Hence the adoption of 'Israel' as the much debated, much queried, designation of the new state in 1948. 'The Jewish State', though ambiguously correct, would not have captured its whole significance as a land–people equation.

9   The term that comes to be frequent in Paul's Letters, always distinguished from 'at' in respect of where addressees live. With 'Hebrews' exceptional, for reasons of its ritual case-making, no Letters go to 'peoples', or 'nations' as such.

10   Some effort was made in my *The Education of Christian Faith* (Brighton, 2000), pp.3–81, to enlarge on this reading of 'things Christic – and Christian' in the context of the old 'Jesus of history never the Christ of faith' view, of late championed by, for example, Geza Vermes. (See note 11.)

11   His most recent publication is *The Changing Faces of Jesus* (Oxford, 2000), in line with his earlier *Jesus the Jew* (London, 1973) and *The Religion of Jesus the Jew* (London, 1993).

12   The will to believe is in no way groundless or a wilful 'forcing of the truth', but it has a responsive part to play, given the credentials that invite it – and gently await it. Thus there is a clear resemblance between faith and love where only what is trusted can vindicate entrustedness. (See note 13.)

13   T.S. Eliot, *The Four Quartets*, 'Burnt Norton', line 44, and 'Little Gidding', lines 101–2.

14   *Teleios* in Matthew 5:48, meaning 'inclusive' – the Lord sending his rain on the just and on 'the unjust'. Greeting restricted to fellow-Jews was common practice. One does not have to ask whether, in the parables, the certain man was Jew, 'Gentile', Greek or other: the point transcends these differentials. And what of 'Where-ever this Gospel is preached throughout the whole world' (Matthew 26:13)? Cf. also Jesus' remarks about the Temple and 'the court of the nations' and much more.

15   There is always the exegete's problem of handling passages that run counter to the desired overall view, but it is bizarre to argue – of indigestible pieces – that they are late insertions. Cf., for example, Geza Vermes, wanting an exclusifying Jesus: 'In order to legitimise the growing presence of non-Jews in the church, fictitious sayings were inserted into the Synoptics in which Jesus himself envisages, even orders, the universal promulgation' (*The Changing Faces*, 157).

16   The word is clumsy but 'literalizing' will not serve. The point is to distinguish between 'the New Testament' as a piece of writing, a text, and the New Testament as the drama of the Christ, the reality that came to be 'enscriptured' the way it was.

17   Note the intriguing directive in 3 John 6 about guests received: 'You shall speed them on their journey worthily of God', that is, with care for their further well-being onward. (No evading hospitable tasks, no sponging.)

18   It is a strange paradox that a faith intending the world has a definitive document that is wholly in one direction and ignores the then-known world outside the Mediterranean basin. Apostolic ministries elsewhere – Thomas/India, Mark/Egypt, Thaddeus/?Armenia – have no scriptural role. The loss can only be made good by a creative theology now.

19   Intelligent leaders know how to scatter their groups on the slopes, read from 'the Sermon' and invite hearers around the natural amphitheatre to raise a hand in token that they are hearing, so demonstrating how great crowds had been open-air audiences.

20   Cf. the psalmist's lament that he has 'to dwell in Mesech and among the tents of Kedar', those incorrigible descendants of Ishmael who will repudiate all peaceableness (Psalm 120:5).

21   See Flavius Josephus, 'The Jewish War', in Yigael Yadin, *Masada*, 232.

22   The gesture of mass suicide looks heroic, but did not the Sages of Yavneh and their synagogues have to work out a nobler way still of living to serve Yahweh as beyond all defeat with Rome? Nor was Rome intolerant of Jewry: it only required a political quiescence, a posture the Zealots had no will to bring. Why, one wonders, did Josephus bring this note of self-scrutiny into Eleazar's mind? How many 'if onlys' there are in history!

23   The temptation to victimize others in becoming 'victors' was ever present in handling of the *Intifadas* by Israeli forces and identified and reproached by Israeli conscience itself. See Cragg, *Palestine*, 89–107, and the citation from the novelist Amos Oz, 89.

24   See the exhaustive study in Shlaim, *The Iron Wall*. Another 'host nation', a Palestine instead of a 'Poland', was no part of the Zionist 'dream', though initially a Palestine would have been ready to be one, as earlier pioneers in non-political *Hibbet Zion* had discovered. Political Zionism intended to end host-nation status forever. Thus Jewish statehood was implicit from the start.

Bibliography

Cragg, K., *Palestine: The Prize and Price of Zion* (London: Cassell, 1997).

——, *The Education of Christian Faith* (Brighton: Sussex Academic Press, 2000).

Eliot, T.S., *The Four Quartets* (London: Faber and Faber, 1944).

Kipling, R., *Definitive Edition of His Verse* (London: Macmillan, 1943).

Shlaim, A., *The Iron Wall: Israel and the Arab World* (London: Macmillan, 2000).

Vermes, G., *Jesus the Jew: A Historian's Reading of the Gospels* (London: Collins, 1973).

——, *The Religion of Jesus the Jew* (London: SCM, 1993).

——, *The Changing Faces of Jesus* (Oxford: OUP, 2000).

Yadin, Y., *Masada* (London: Weidenfeld and Nicolson, 1966).

I
BIBLICAL PERSPECTIVES
ON PILGRIMAGE

CHAPTER 2

Pilgrimage and 'Place': an Old Testament View

Gordon McConville

Pilgrimage and 'Place' in the Old Testament

The idea of pilgrimage is rooted in the Old Testament, and Old Testament pilgrimage is rooted in the land of Israel. When Israelites went on pilgrimage three times a year to their central sanctuary (which was for most of Old Testament history Jerusalem) they were celebrating their occupation of the whole promised land. Behind every journey from the remote places of Judah, Ephraim or Naphtali lay the memory of an occupation of land, narrated in the Books of Exodus to Joshua, with partings of sea and river, fall of Jericho and dispossession of an existing population. The journey to land itself reads at times like a pilgrimage: 'Let my people go,' says Yahweh through Moses to Pharaoh, 'so that they may celebrate a festival to me in the wilderness' (Exod.5:1 NRSV). 'Festival' here is *ḥag*, 'pilgrimage-feast', just like the three annual pilgrimage-feasts required in Exod.23:14–18; Deut.16:1–17; Lev.23 (Passover-Unleavened Bread, Feast of Weeks, Feast of Tabernacles). Similarly, one of Joshua's first acts on entering the land is to keep the Passover, as a sign that the time of wilderness and manna was at an end and the time of land and cultivation had come (Josh.5:10–12). The journey to the land of Canaan can be portrayed as a progression of Yahweh from Sinai (the place of the 'feast' referred to in Exod.5:1) to Mt Zion, from the place of Yahweh's appearing once in the wilderness, to the place of his settled dwelling in the heart of the land he has given to Israel (Ps.68:18 [Eng.17]).

Pilgrimage, therefore, expresses a strong attachment to place. It is based on Israel's memory of its deliverance from slavery in Egypt, its formation as the covenant people of Yahweh at Mt Sinai, Yahweh's gift of land to them by the dispossession of others, and his dwelling among them in the central sanctuary. Pilgrimage Psalms, as they evoke the worshippers' regular journeys to the holy place, recall and celebrate the original, decisive journey to land (Ps.68:8–11 [Eng.7–10]; 81:2–11 [Eng.1–10]). In doing so, they openly rejoice in Yahweh's victory over other peoples (Ps.68:22–4 [Eng.21–3]) and proclaim the superiority of Mt Zion (Jerusalem and its Temple) over other holy mountains (Ps.68:16–17 [Eng.15–16]).

It is clear immediately from this brief introduction that pilgrimage in the Old Testament is part and parcel of the particularity of Old Testament religion (election of Israel, conquest of Canaanites, rejection of non-Yahwistic religion). As we seek a Biblical theology of pilgrimage we are faced with the fact that it is the Old Testament which gives us our basic texts and concepts, yet also poses difficult questions about particularity. These are the issues that we need to negotiate. It may be that the very particularity of the origins of pilgrimage will prove to have positive consequences for interpretation. But there are fences to jump before we can see what those are.

Pilgrimage in the Context of Christian Theology

For all the reasons just outlined, Israel's pilgrimage presents problems to Christian theology. The point has been well made by Kenneth Cragg in the present volume. The Church needed no sacred land, people or language: 'its great locative was "in Christ".' Similarly Oliver O'Donovan, in an essay on a theology of 'place', says this:

> it was the elective purpose of God to move out from Jerusalem, the traditional focus of election, into every part of the world, without tying the universal church to a pilgrimage, either on foot or in spirit, to the local origins of the message of God's good favour.[1]

It follows that we shall not find a mandate for pilgrimage in Christian theology.

However, both Cragg and O'Donovan move beyond their caveats to forms of recovery. Cragg identifies two factors: the proper desire for 'the sight and feel and memory of the land of origins' and a consideration, from human experience in general, that 'the triunity of place, folk and story is a universal shape of human life'. The hallowing of Israel (*a* holy land) becomes a ground of the hallowing of other places. O'Donovan reflects that 'the divine word ... communicates itself in the particular'. He goes on:

> the 'transitory promises' of particular election, upon which Old Testament faith founded, are not abolished by Christian faith into pure universality, but their exclusivity is taken up; they are, as it were, replicated. They become the matrix for the forms in which God universally meets mankind.[2]

These qualifications bring the idea of pilgrimage back into the frame of Christian theology, no longer as mandate, but as a possible avenue for self-understanding and spirituality. The tribes' seeking of Jerusalem becomes, not a stage, no longer relevant, in the unfolding salvation history, but a paradigm of life before God, an inescapable speaking of one particularity to a host of others, which is a truer representation of inclusion than abstract notions of universality.

With this encouragement, we turn again to the Old Testament's theology of pilgrimage. In doing so we will see some lines that the discussion so far has not brought to light, which will show that the Old Testament's particularity was keenly aware of broader horizons.

The Old Testament Re-conceives the 'Journey'

The Old Testament qualifies its own picture of pilgrimage as exclusive attachment to people, history and land in four ways: the internalizing of the 'journey', the reinterpretation of 'holy space', an extension of holiness and the inclusion of the nations in the pilgrimage to Zion. These qualifications could be seen as steps on the way to the abolition of the idea of pilgrimage. However, they may also be a means to its recovery in ways that we shall consider below. We now look more closely at each of these qualifications.

The Internalizing of the Journey

There are certain well known Old Testament expressions of an inward religion, that is placed in direct contrast to one that misreads the significance of religious practice. Psalms 40 and 50, with their critiques of sacrificial practice, exemplify the point. So does King Solomon's prayer, in the very act of dedicating the temple, when he insists that Yahweh is by no means limited to that location, and when, in the place of *sacrifice*, he lays heavy emphasis on *prayers* made elsewhere (I Kings 8:27–30).

We can take this point further by showing that there are important correspondences in the poetry of pilgrimage between the spatial and temporal journey and the inner, spiritual, life. The worshipper who would 'ascend the hill of the LORD' must do so with 'clean hands and a pure heart' (Ps.24:3–4). Those who make the journey, according to Ps.81, are also required to '*walk* in my ways', 81:14[13]; the verb, *hlk*, literally means 'walk, go', but its capacity for transfer to the sphere of the moral life, which finds its way in one direction to the Jewish idea of *halakah*, is already evident here.

A closer look at Psalm 84 will bring out the point more clearly. The Psalmist evokes the journey to Zion vividly. The rigours of the road (v.7[6]) are contrasted with the happiness of those who are already in the temple, the sparrow and swallow which all unknowingly make homes there for their young (v.4[3]), and those who 'live' in the temple – priests or musicians, perhaps, or just worshippers who are fortunate enough to be able to spend extended time there (v.5[4]). The physical features of the temple are prominent: 'dwelling-place', 'courts', 'altars', 'house' (vv.2–5[1–4]). The Psalmist's delight in the temple, remembered from past experience, is clear from the beginning in his deep longing, which consumes his whole being (vv.2–3[1–2]). The name of Zion appears only at v.8[7], withheld till this point as the arrival itself was withheld during the long journey, and coming now as an expression of joy and relief as the longed for destination comes into sight.

Yet the other side of this coin is the turning of the physical particularities of journey, arrival and place into an inward, human experience. First, the pairing of vv.5–6 [4–5] shows a progression from those who 'dwell' in the temple, to the 'one [*'adam*] whose strength is in you, and in whose *heart* are *highways*'. The latter line both generalizes and internalizes. The word used for the worshipper is *'adam*, 'human being', familiar from the creation narratives. His happiness no longer consists in being in the temple, but in that his 'strength is in you [God]'. And the 'highways' that are 'in his heart' are expressly not 'the highways to Zion' (in spite of NRSV), but stand unqualified, the absence of 'to Zion' allowing the weight to fall on the inner paths.

The internalizing continues in vv.7–8[6–7], where the pilgrimage itself is pictured. The 'valley of Baca' (v.7[6]) may be the name of a place along the way, but the word resembles the word for weeping. As this dry place is watered by the early rain, so it is also, apparently, by the pilgrims' weeping. Thus it becomes a place of 'blessings'. NRSV and NIV have 'pools' instead of 'blessings', a reading obtained by changing one vowel pointing in the Hebrew word (*berekot* instead of *berakot*). The poet, however, plays on the similarity between the two words. Throughout the verse physical actualities are brought into correspondence with concepts in the affective realm. On the image of a walk in a dry valley watered by early rain is superimposed weeping and blessing. 'They go from strength to strength' could connote either a gathering crowd along the way, or strengthening itself.

The physical reality comes back into clear focus in v.8b[7b] and continues to v.11[10]. But the Psalm closes on the note of inwardness, the 'walking' (*hlk*) now a 'walking uprightly', in the language of the ethical life, as in Ps.81:14[13]. And blessing, finally, is bestowed on the ' *'adam* who trusts in you'.

The Reinterpretation of Holy Space

In addition to the particularity of Israel's story that undergirds its pilgrimages, the structure of Old Testament worship presupposes a strong notion of holy space. The temple preserves in its architecture the division of reality into profane and holy realms, a pattern replicated throughout the ancient world, in which places of worship are, literally, 'houses' of the god. 'Holiness' has a geography; there is a 'holy sphere'. The language of holiness (frequent in Exodus and Leviticus), with its gradations ('most holy', 'holy of holies'), together with that of cleanness and uncleanness, corresponds to this concept of a differentiated reality in the material world. This geography imposes itself upon worship. The gradual approach symbolizes increasing degrees of holiness, culminating in the intimate presence of the deity in the most holy place. The pilgrimage is ultimately a movement from profane to holy space. Psalm 24 appears to be a liturgy for the final approach to the sanctuary itself, possibly at the end of a pilgrimage.

However, here too the Old Testament itself brings qualification. The Old Testament texts are unanimous in their witness that the God of Israel might not be imaged. In its world, this is radical theology, a bulwark against any crassly material conception of the divine presence. In what way, then, is Yahweh thought to be 'present' in the place of Israel's worship?

Exodus 25:22 is the pinnacle statement on the topic in the 'priestly' parts of the Old Testament (sometimes thought to be opposed to the deuteronomic). Here is the nearest thing to a depiction of the presence in the 'most holy place'. But it is sublimely reticent about the manner of it. Does Yahweh *dwell* there, or does he rather come and *meet* his people?

The *dwelling* symbolism, that is, the concept that God sits enthroned, permanently, in the inner sanctum, is suggested by the imagery of the cherubim and the ark. In ancient Near Eastern iconography cherubim thrones are attested, in which a receptacle under the throne serves as a footstool. There are Old Testament texts which reflect these conceptions rather directly. In Psalm 132:7 the ark is called Yahweh's 'footstool' (though there is an extension, *pars pro toto*, to Jerusalem). And Hezekiah, praying for deliverance from the siege of Sennacherib, addresses Yahweh as 'enthroned on the cherubim' (II Kgs19:15 = Isa.37:16; cf. Ps.80:2[1]; 99:1; I Chron.13:6). The verb is literally 'sitting', but this often implies sitting on a throne, and does so in these contexts; in Psalm 99:1 it follows 'Yahweh is king'. Exodus 25:22, however, avoids these direct appropriations of the ANE concepts. The verb *yashab*, 'sit', is absent, as is a reference to the ark (which is thus not depicted as footstool; it is, as in Deut. 10:5, a receptacle containing the commandments, Exod.25:16). The 'geographical' relationship between Yahweh and the cherubim is not expressly stated. And the mode of presence is conveyed by the verb 'I will meet you' (LXX translates 'know', either a scribal misreading, or a theological hesitation). This 'meeting' is as in the concept of 'tent of meeting', an idea that corresponds to the journey of Israel through the wilderness in which Yahweh comes to them from time to time and place to place.

Exodus 25:22, therefore, subtly holds together the distinct metaphors of permanent dwelling (*yashab*) and coming to meet. I do not think it necessary to trace an elaborate pre-history of these ideas (*pace* G. von Rad[3]). But the tension maintained is plainly deliberate.

In the same connection may be mentioned the Old Testament's hesitation about the *vision* of God. What did people expect to see at the end of the road? A vision like Isaiah's (Isa.6)? But then was not that precisely a vision? The textual tradition of the Old Testament betrays a theological hesitation on this very point. Did the worshippers go to *see* God, or to be *seen* by him? By a deft rearrangement of the vowels (which are in any case not original to the text), and without touching the consonants, this significant theological change can be made (Deut.16:16, cf. Ps.84:8[7]). The ambivalence itself is evidence that there is nothing simplistic here.

The very concept of the tabernacle in Exodus, within which the most holy place, with its cherubim and ark, is situated, is itself highly significant theologically, as a means of expressing the nature of the divine presence. The tabernacle used to be regarded in critical scholarship as an idealized retrojection of the Jerusalem temple.[4] It is more likely, however, that it provides a counterbalance to the static symbolism of the temple, expressing rather Yahweh's mobility (cf. 2 Sam.7:5–7), which is in turn a symbol of his freedom, and even his lordship in the world. It is no accident that the Old Testament story is one of movement; Yahweh took Israel from Egypt, 'found' her in the wilderness (Deut.32:10), led her into land, went with her into exile where he remains enthroned (Ezek.1), and can restore her to land as and when he wills. This story puts Zion in perspective. In the broadest Old Testament context, it is no more than a place where Yahweh dwells for the time being, and which even attracts suspicion of having connotations of presence that are not truly Israelite.

An Extension of Holiness

In sections of the Old Testament holiness is extended from a narrow location in the central sanctuary and its personnel to a more general location in Israel. Deuteronomy's distinctive concept of holiness illustrates this, with important implications for pilgrimage. Its laws concerning worship frequently repeat the command to go to 'the place that the LORD your God will choose to put his name and make his habitation there' (Deut.12:5), bringing sacrifices and offerings (12:6), and celebrating the three annual feasts (16:1–17). Its requirement to make pilgrimage is more deeply embedded in the structure of its law code than is the case in any of the other Pentateuchal books. This interest in the 'chosen place' is almost always interpreted as a centralization of worship in Jerusalem, promoting the claims of the temple in the context of a royal–cultic synthesis, as in the Zion theology. However, in my view the reverse is happening. The theology of special holy places is actually relaxed in Deuteronomy, along with the special claims of the clergy. It is Israelites who are 'sons of Yahweh', not the king (14:1); they are 'chosen' (again, not the king); holiness belongs to them, not to the priestly elite (7:6); and the physical locus of holiness is the land, not the place of worship narrowly conceived. It is this *extension* of holiness, not a suspicion of it, that explains Deuteronomy's relative lack of interest in the personnel, actions and places of the 'holiness sphere' that is so elaborately described in Exodus–Leviticus. The law of

Passover-Unleavened Bread in particular (16:1–8) enshrines this doctrine, with a carefully worked out balance between the actions at the 'chosen place' and the effective keeping of the feast throughout the land of Israel.[5]

And the function of the gatherings of the people to worship is specially enlightening in this book. Deuteronomy 16:13–15, the law for the Feast of Tabernacles, typifies its understanding of the people before God, with its elements of memory (implied), grateful worship, assembly, rejoicing and inclusiveness (slaves, widows, orphans, resident aliens; that is, the marginalized). Here is the essence of Deuteronomy's theology of pilgrimage. It is precisely pilgrimage, for the vision offered follows from the opening: 'You shall keep the Feast (*ḥag*) of Tabernacles seven days'; and the invitation is repeated with a verbal form (*taḥog*, 'you shall [pilgrimage-]feast') in v.15. But there is so much more here than a call to make a journey. The law is a vehicle for Deuteronomy's portrayal of the people in its truest nature – a unity created by its common experience of the salvation of Yahweh, resisting all divisions created by inequality or oppression, giving back to God as he has given to them and, in all this, rejoicing. Here is holiness theology turned into nothing less than a vision of the kingdom of God.

Deuteronomy is not alone in reinterpreting the underlying idea of holy space in the Old Testament. Ezekiel's vision of the restored holy land tends in the same direction. The depiction of the tribal divisions of the land, and of Jerusalem in relation to them, in Ezek.48 is highly schematized, and the name of the city itself is telling, namely *Yahweh shammah*, 'the LORD is there', a play on *Yerushalayim* that focuses the meaning of true Jerusalem. Here too holy space as such is dissolved in the expression of deeper meaning. Ezekiel's visionary temple in its schematic territory seems to come full circle from the tabernacle in refusing to restrict Yahweh's presence to a single spot.

Finally, the idea of Zion is reinterpreted in the Book of Isaiah. The vision of it is part of 'the new heavens and new earth' which Yahweh is about to create (Isa.65:17). Jerusalem will be 'a joy' and its people 'a delight' (65:18) and the portrayal of the 'holy mountain' takes on paradisal lineaments (65:25). Metaphors suggesting transcendence are also used in Isa.60:17–20. These visions do not abandon hopes for the Jerusalem of history and geography; nevertheless, the language in the texts opens the concept of Zion to deeper interpretations released from such restrictions.

Pilgrimage and the Inclusion of the Nations: a Universalizing Tendency

The universalizing of salvation in the Old Testament is well enough known. The promise to Abraham, that in him 'all the families of the earth would be blessed' (Gen.12:3) finds echoes in the Books of Isaiah, Jonah and several Psalms. The features of Old Testament theology that we have noticed already play a part in establishing this direction. As soon as the object of Yahweh's saving action is seen to be the creation of a 'righteous' people, and 'holiness' has an ethical dimension, the symbolism of one chosen people gathered round a particular holy space is undermined. The ethicizing and spiritualizing of fundamental ideas such as 'holiness', 'election' and 'the people of God' has a momentum that leads all the way to the inclusion of the nations. The trend is also driven by the Old Testament's theology of *creation* (recall 'happy is *'adam* who trusts in you', Ps.84:13[12]). Reading the Old Testament *back* from Zion and Sinai, we encounter Abraham who came from 'Beyond the River' (Josh.24:2), Yahweh known by the name of El Elyon, who was worshipped by Canaanites in Jerusalem, and Adam and Eve, who lived in a garden. The Old Testament leads back (and forward, cf. Isa.65:25) to Paradise, that is, a whole world living in the presence of God.

The universalizing of salvation may be seen in certain Psalms. In Ps.67:2[1], the 'Aaronic blessing', bestowed first on Israel in the wilderness (Num.6:24–6,) is now applied to the nations ('may God make his face shine upon us'). In v.5[4], the nations rejoice, not just Israel in its feasting (as in Deut.16:14–15). God judges the nations, that is, to bring them justice (not just in Israel). Furthermore he *guides* them (a concept drawn from the leading of Israel from exodus to land). And the nations praise Yahweh (v.6[5]), another prerogative of Israel made universal. After this it seems clear that the *'eres* in vv.7–8[6–7] is the whole earth, and not just the 'land', that has received Yahweh's blessing, in yet another extension of the Deuteronomic promises of land (cf. Deut.8:7–10). (The term can do duty for both, and the ambiguity often invites reflection on particular and universal.)

This universalizing of salvation now surfaces in pilgrimage contexts. Certain texts put the particularistic Zion theology directly in question. For example, in Ps.65:2–3[1–2] we find 'praise is due to you *in Zion* ... to you *all flesh* shall come' (cf. Isa.40:5), with a remarkable extension of the pilgrimage idea to humanity in general. The line of thought continues in v.6[5] with 'you are the hope of *all the ends of the earth* and of the farthest seas'. Finally we read, 'you make *the gateways of the morning and the evening* shout for joy' (v.9[8]), in a sweeping reference to the whole world. The creation language used in this inclusive Psalm (7–9[6–8], 10–14[9–13]) echoes that which was found in the more traditional Zion Psalm, Ps.72.

Psalm 87 is the most unusual Zion Psalm, because of its vivid picture of non-Israelite nations coming to Jerusalem. It opens conventionally (vv.1–3) with 'the LORD loves the gates of Zion'. But suddenly a new thing is encountered, in v.4, when Rahab (Egypt) and Babylon are counted among 'those who know me'. And finally (v.6) Yahweh writes the names of foreigners 'as he registers the peoples' (literally 'in the writing of the peoples'), in an expressly universalizing application of the concept of a 'book of the living' (Ps.69:29[28]).

The unusual character of the Psalm makes it difficult to understand exactly what is being said. The basic imagery is undoubtedly one of a pilgrimage to

Zion. But are these genuine foreigners coming to Zion, or Jewish people returning from Diaspora for one of the three annual festivals?[6] In my view the terms of vv.4 and 6 are best understood as a recording of the names of other nations as if they were 'born' in Zion.[7] It is impossible to identify a specific event here, or even any one of the three annual feasts. The portrayal may be entirely visionary. (There are adumbrations, perhaps, of Pentecost in Acts 2.) The pilgrimage-feast, therefore, becomes a metaphor for the salvation of the nations on the same terms as Israel.

This interpretation can be supported by a similar vision in the Book of Isaiah. This book is well known for its portrayal of the universal scope of Yahweh's salvation, especially in chs40–55 (for example in the two Servant Songs which see him as a 'light to the nations', 42:6; 49:6). But two key texts for the theme in the book fall outside that section. The first stands near the beginning, in Isa.2:2–4, in which all the nations go up to Zion to learn the Torah of Yahweh. The passage has some typical Zion features: Mt Zion itself is regarded as supreme among the mountains (Pss.48:3[2]; 76:5[4]). It is the 'house of the God of Jacob', and Yahweh is regarded as having authority over the nations (cf. Ps.46:7–12[6–11]). But the developments of the Zion theology are more striking. The Isaiah passage is apparently a conscious reversal of Ps.2, with echoes of Ps.122.

Whereas in Ps.2 Yahweh and his 'anointed' (that is, the Davidic king) are at war with the nations which attack Zion, now nations come willingly to it. Most remarkably, the language is exactly that of pilgrimage: 'many nations will *go* (*hlk*) and say, come (*hlk*), let us go up (*'lh*)'; cf. Ps.122:1, 'let us go [*hlk*]', v.4, 'there the tribes go up' (*'lh*). And they will learn from Yahweh's *torah*, which goes out from it. Yahweh's 'judging' is on a world scale (again cf. Ps.122:5, 'the thrones are set for judgment'). And the result is peace, no longer just the peace of Jerusalem, but peace between the nations.

The second key universalizing pilgrimage text comes in what is often known as the mini-apocalypse (Isa.24–7). In the middle of this section there is a contrast between two cities, one that is overcome in judgment (25:2) and one that is vindicated (26:1). The texts are tantalizingly reticent about the cities' identities. Is the condemned city Babylon, or could it be Jerusalem? It is the character of the cities that is paramount. The idea of the city has become symbolic, standing for organized society, whether righteous or unrighteous. Of the vindicated city it is said: 'Open the gates, so that the righteous nation that keeps faith may enter in.' Who is the 'righteous nation'? It is simply that, neither more nor less. If it is Israel it is an Israel that has fulfilled its mandate to be God's righteous people. But it might equally be any people that can wear the mantle.

The point is confirmed by the image in 25:6–10, sometimes called the 'messianic banquet'. The underlying concept is that of pilgrimage-feast, a feast 'on this mountain' (that is, Zion), 'for all peoples' (v.6). The vision is eschatological ('he will swallow up death for ever', v.7). Here is a culmination of the pilgrimage theme in the Old Testament, pointing beyond every present-tense particularity, to a union of all peoples in the presence of God. In this vision Mt Zion has become a metaphor for the presence of God, and the pilgrimage-feast a metaphor for the salvation of all the world.

A Recovery of Pilgrimage?

Our study of Old Testament texts concerning pilgrimage has shown that the idea undergoes transformations. These transformations take it in the direction of the universalizing of salvation, and separation from the geographical location of Jerusalem. As we have already noted, Christian theology also insists on both of these developments.[8] Christians do not make *ḥag* to Jerusalem (as Muslims do to Mecca). There is no one holy place; God does not 'live' in Jerusalem, or view the world from a vantage-point there. The place of Jerusalem even in the story of the Old Testament was never final or definitive. There is no 'merit' in making a long, dangerous journey there. Even the idea of a 'Holy Land' is dubious.

We have seen, however, that some Christian theologians at any rate seek to recover a significance for pilgrimage even though accepting that theology makes it redundant. Our remaining question is whether the study offered here can contribute to the recovery of a theology of pilgrimage in a Christian context. I think it can, with only this caveat, that no single answer to the question can be compelled by the evidence considered (which follows from the fact that we are not actually required to make pilgrimage in the Old Testament sense).

I have sympathy with Kenneth Cragg's belief that there is a proper interest in Christianity's place of origin. Jerusalem, in experience, still makes an impact on the believer, as a place which uniquely and dramatically focuses that which Christians have in common. It also focuses the claims of Christ in the world, because of the (equally dramatic) presence of Judaism and Islam. There is, no doubt, a reality in the strong sense in certain places that 'God has been here'. There is a symbolic power in a Good Friday walk in procession from the Mount of Olives into Jerusalem that is quite unlike anything else, and that touches deep chords of identity and belonging.

But can the pilgrimage pattern be more firmly grounded theologically? To answer this I propose to follow the other line suggested by both Cragg and O'Donovan, that the combination of locality and memory in pilgrimage corresponds to something that lies deep in human experience and spirituality. O'Donovan has turned to unexpected advantage the argument of the Letter to the Hebrews in this regard. If the promises to the Israelite patriarchs were (mere) shadows of the eschatological reality, then they must have been intrinsically powerful and thus deserving of attention.[9] He discovers in Josh.13–19, not a dry cataloguing of the boundaries between the tribes, but a deep love of the land that is described there in detail, made the more poignant because, in the form in which the Book of Joshua comes to us (embedded in the exilic corpus of Joshua–Kings, or the Deuteronomistic History), it is preserved in the knowledge and experience of the loss of that land.[10]

O'Donovan relates this Israelite attachment to its 'place' to the particularities of place and memory in which we all live, and in which we understand and practise the Christian faith. It is in this context that he claims that the exclusivity of the ancient promises is replicated in the forms in which God meets human beings (see note 2). His argument is directed to a theology of place as such. Is there a pointer in it for a theology of pilgrimage? The following observations may be made.

People in pilgrimage express their ultimate loyalty to God, giving a way of relativizing all other claims. Here we may perhaps construe pilgrimage rather broadly. For example, events of public united prayers in Ireland can put in right perspective the different allegiances that people otherwise have, politically and even religiously. In fact Old Testament pilgrimage gives a paradigm of this, for the territory between Dan and Beersheba encompassed diversity; Israel north and south achieved unity only briefly, and then by the force of its most outstanding personality, David. The unity portrayed in Deuteronomy's picture of worship is precisely a convergence of diversities, people finding that they are 'brothers and sisters' as they gather before the God of Israel. This unifying force of pilgrimage (as of Christian teaching generally) is no light thing. Sometimes our felt differences from others are strongest in respect of people nearest to us. Love of neighbour is tougher than an abstract love of 'everybody'.[11]

Even so, pilgrimage is bound to express particularity, perhaps even highlight it. Christians are not reduced to a lowest common denominator of identity. That fundamental point is made abundantly clear by a visit to Jerusalem (or indeed to Rome or Athens or Kerala). They remain Irish Christians, Welsh Christians, South Indian Christians (and even these broad-brush designations conceal further diversities). The diversity is one of the glories of Christianity, which not even Pentecost abolished. Pilgrimage may offer a way both of expressing our own particular Christian identity and of respecting that of others. The universality of Christianity should not be confused with other kinds of universalizing motives (such as the monocultural globalization that regards minority identities as disposable).[12]

Finally, the expression of and respect for particularities need not preclude the challenge to them that may be involved in convergence. Particularities can sometimes be definitions of the self or the group in opposition to the other, indeed the neighbour. Pilgrimage (again broadly understood) may involve a rethinking of identity. Christian identity has at times been thought to entail other kinds of commitment (usually political). But this belief may be shaken if I find myself sharing worship and witness with another whose Christian belief has led him to the opposite commitment. Pilgrimage could mean bringing the transforming power of the Gospel to bear, in local contexts, on what it may mean to be Irish, Welsh, European, Indian or Chinese.

Notes

1   O'Donovan, 'Loss', 53.

2   Ibid., 56.

3   von Rad, 'The Tent and the Ark'.

4   The idea of the tabernacle as a projection of the Solomonic temple into the wilderness age goes back to J. Wellhausen, *Prolegomena to the History of Israel*. Cf. M. Haran, *Temples and Temple Service in Ancient Israel*, 189–204. Haran's version of this thesis is complex, as he thinks the tabernacle is based on memories of the shrine at Shiloh, but the memories of this were transferred to the Jerusalem temple. The tabernacle tradition is essentially, for him, a 'temple legend' (204).

5   For an elaboration of this view, see my 'Deuteronomy's Unification'.

6   See the discussion in Tate, *Psalms 51–100*, 387.

7   Here against Goulder, for example (*Psalms*, 179).

8   I do not claim that the survey offered has been comprehensive, or that I have described a unilinear progression in Old Testament ideas. In the history of Old Testament religion there are counter-tendencies that re-emphasize exclusivist interpretations of Israel. Some of these have even been found in the Book of Isaiah, though Isaiah emerges here as a key book in the transformations I identify. My argument only needs to show that the foundational concepts about pilgrimage have in them the capacity to be opened up in the ways described, and that this happened in certain important developments.

9   O'Donovan, 'Loss', 49–50.

10   Ibid., 52.

11   O'Donovan points out that the parable of the Good Samaritan challenges a neighbourly love precisely for those with whom we find ourselves in close proximity, though we may perceive them as utterly different ('Loss', 54).

12   Dewi Hughes has shown the dangers of such confusion in his *Castrating Culture*; cf. O'Donovan, 'Loss', 39–48.

References

Goulder, M.D., *The Psalms of the Sons of Korah* (Sheffield: JSOT Press, 1982).

Haran, M., *Temples and Temple Service in Ancient Israel* (Oxford: Clarendon, 1978).

Hughes, D., *Castrating Culture: a Christian Perspective on Ethnic Identity from the Margins* (Carlisle: Paternoster, 2001).

McConville, J.G., 'Deuteronomy's Unification of Passover and Massot: A Response to Bernard M. Levinson', *JBL*, 119 (2000), 47–58.

O'Donovan, O., 'The Loss of a Sense of Place', *Irish Theological Quarterly*, 55 (1989), 39–58.

von Rad, G., 'The Tent and the Ark', *The Problem of the Hexateuch and Other Essays* (London: SCM Press, 1984) (first published London: Oliver and Boyd, 1966), pp. 103–24.

Tate, M.E., *Psalms 51–100* (Dallas: Word Books, 1990).

CHAPTER 3

Pilgrimage and the New Testament

Andrew T. Lincoln

The year 2000 saw the convergence of two myths, that of the millennium as sacred time and that of Israel as sacred space. The power of the convergence could be seen in the increased uptake of tours to the so-called 'Holy Land' until the outbreak of further serious conflict towards the end of that year. The Roman Catholic Church declared the year 2000 the Great Year of Jubilee, the year of grace, and, because of the importance of the Holy Land, the Pope made Jerusalem, along with Rome, one of the two geographical reference points of this jubilee. Christians from around the world were, accordingly, encouraged to make pilgrimages to Jerusalem to discover their roots and find spiritual renewal.[1] A variety of other Christian groups and tour companies also heavily promoted the occasion. Interestingly, all this activity had its parallels in responses to the year 1000 when there were also increased numbers of people going on pilgrimage to the Holy Land and to other closer shrines. In the year 2000, however, those who did not want to make the actual journey could make it virtually, courtesy of Virtual Pilgrimage to the Holy Land at *www.Jesus2000.com*, depositing a prayer or blessing in a holy site over the Internet.

To move from recent and current enthusiasms about pilgrimage to the writings of the New Testament is to go on a journey to alien territory. Not only, of course, did New Testament writers have no expectation that history as they knew it would continue until our year 2000 but they also had a quite different perspective on journeying to Israel and Jerusalem as sacred places. This chapter will contend that, for Christians, the encounters made in alien territory should not be treated as interesting experiences to be slotted somehow into what they consider to be the rather different needs and less rigorous views on such matters of the present day. Rather, they should allow for the journey to be a transformative one, in which what is encountered calls some of their own assumptions into question and becomes determinative for their continued theologizing, not least in rethinking the perceived needs of their own time and place.

Within the limits of this chapter the attempt will have to be made to establish these contentions through an overview of three major New Testament theological perspectives that have implications for pilgrimage, those of Paul, Hebrews and John's Gospel. There will, therefore, be no attempt to reconstruct from behind the texts of the Gospels the probable or possible pilgrimages of the historical Jesus to Jerusalem and how far he is likely to have shared or differed from the attitudes surrounding such events and their significance among 1st-century Jews.[2] Although inevitably the topics overlap, the chapter attempts to focus specifically on pilgrimage rather than simply the place of the land or Jerusalem or the Temple in the New Testament.[3] One final preliminary observation is needed. Important as a backdrop to this treatment of pilgrimage is the strand of expectation within Second Temple Judaism that has come to be designated as the 'eschatological pilgrimage of the Gentiles'.[4] Accompanying the reversal of Israel's fortunes in the end-times, signalled by the glorification of Jerusalem or Zion, would be not only the return of scattered exiles but also the inclusion of Gentiles. Sometimes these Gentiles are depicted as bringing back the exiles or serving Israel and sometimes they are depicted as full participants in the end-time blessings, joining in the worship of God, and part of the inclusion of the Gentiles motif is often the notion of a pilgrimage to Zion. The most significant passages for the latter include Isaiah 2:2–4 and its parallel in Micah 4:1–4; Isaiah 25:6–10a; 56:6–8; 60:1–22; 66:18–23; Zechariah 8:20–23; 14:1–21; Tobit 13:8–17; 14:5–7; Sibylline Oracles 3:702–31,772–5. In these passages and in others when God acts to restore Zion, the Gentiles will also forsake their idolatry and come to worship God, sharing in the glory of Israel's end-time salvation.

Paul

We shall pass over the implications for pilgrimage of the striking assertions by Paul that the temple of God is now in Corinth (cf. ICor. 3:16,17; IICor.6:16) or other locations in which the Church is found because the presence of God is there in the Spirit in the midst of the believing community (cf. also Eph.2:20–22). Instead primary attention will be paid to some of his explicit references to Jerusalem in Galatians and Romans. Most important is the contrast of two Jerusalems in Paul's discussion in Gal.4:21–5:1, and the background of the inclusion of the nations in Jewish end-time expectations is what links that discussion to the theme of pilgrimage. In this passage Paul returns to his argument about the way in which one becomes a true descendant of Abraham and employs his own interpretation of the law against Jewish Christian teachers who claim that the Galatian Christians need to observe the law and particularly its requirement of circumcision in order to be full heirs of Abraham. Those who wish to be under the law ought to hear what that law says, Paul claims in 4:21.[5] He has in mind a particular verse from the Pentateuch (Gen.21:10) that he will cite in 4:30: 'But what does the scripture say? "Drive out the slave and her child; for the child of the slave will not share the inheritance with the child of the free woman."' The function of the citation in the Galatian context is a call for decisive resistance on the part of the Galatian believers in regard to those whom Paul sees as advocating the slavery of adherence to the law.

Before he employs this explicit citation as his punchline, however, Paul prepares the way with an allegorical and counter-conventional reading of the Genesis narrative from which the citation is taken. In the course of it he reminds his Galatian converts that Abraham had two sons and that their lines of descent were very different. One son came by a slave, the other by a free woman. Now, as then, he argues, there are also two sorts of descendants of Abraham, those born according to the flesh and those born according to the Spirit. In order to relate the two situations more specifically, Paul makes an unusual interpretive move. Hagar and Sarah, he says, represent two covenants. In a comparison that would have been shocking and insulting to loyal Jews, Hagar, bearing children for slavery, is said to represent Mount Sinai and, although Mount Sinai is in Arabia and outside the land of promise, Hagar is then also seen as corresponding to the present Jerusalem because both are held to be in slavery with their children. So, in the context of this polemic against Jewish Christian teachers who were confusing his converts, Paul views the present earthly Jerusalem not as the holy city that is the focus of God's presence on earth but as the epitome of the Jewish Christianity, and behind it the Judaism, that in its allegiance to the law creates bondage.[6]

In face of contentions that he was in fact dependent on the mother Church in Jerusalem and should fall back into line with its practices,[7] Paul's complex application of Scripture is directed instead to the claim that it is not the present Jerusalem but the Jerusalem above who is 'our mother' (Gal.4:26). He means his readers to assume that in his allegory Sarah corresponds to the Abrahamic covenant that finds its fulfilment in Christ and so can simply give the last part of this comparison: 'But the other woman corresponds to the Jerusalem above; she is free, and she is our mother.'

Paul also assumes his readers will be familiar with the notion of a Jerusalem above. As his supporting citation from Isa.54:1 in Gal.4:27 indicates, the notion has its roots in Old Testament prophecy with its hopes for a new eschatological Jerusalem. Yet Isa.54 and the texts that depict a glorified Jerusalem and its temple as the centre of the world to which all nations will make pilgrimage in the last days, though idealizing the future city, remain very much in continuity with Israel's national hopes for the earthly Jerusalem. The vision of the new Jerusalem that most transcends the bounds of the earthly is that contained in Isa.65:17–25, where Jerusalem is created as part of the new heavens and new earth and the depiction of its glory is mixed with motifs of paradise. The development of ideas about this eschatological Jerusalem found in the apocalypses of 2 Baruch and 4 Ezra comes closest to what we see here in Galatians, though it is difficult to tell how early the traditions incorporated in these writings from just after the time of Paul originated. In 4 Ezra, the new Jerusalem will appear from heaven and will be revealed along with paradise (7:26; 13:35). Meanwhile it is already visible to the seer (8:52; 10:25–7,38–59). In 2 Baruch also Jerusalem is to be restored and transformed in the age to come

(6:9; 32:2–4), while at the same time it is seen as, along with paradise, already prepared and preserved in the presence of God (4:2–6). For Paul too the Jerusalem to come already exists in heaven. This is part of his realized eschatology in which believers already share ahead of time in the benefits of the age to come. The Jerusalem above stands for the salvation and freedom of the age to come that can be experienced now by faith. In 4 Ezra and 2 Baruch, the existence of the heavenly city serves to guarantee the destiny of the earthly city, but for Paul it is no longer the case that the inheritance promised to the descendants of Abraham is the land of Canaan with its centre in an earthly Jerusalem. The inheritance now comes to those who are descendants of Abraham by faith and has its focus where the risen and exalted Christ now is – in the heavenly Jerusalem.

As his citation of Isa.54:1 shows, Paul is taking what had traditionally been applied to the earthly Jerusalem and claiming it for the heavenly. He sees the Isaianic prophecy as being fulfilled in what God has begun to accomplish through Christ among the Galatian Christians and therefore as most appropriately applied, not to the present Jerusalem with its reliance on natural descent, but to the participants in the eschatological reality whom he describes as those 'born according to the Spirit' (Gal.4:29). The symbol for that presently existing eschatological reality is, then, the Jerusalem above that can be depicted as the mother of, and the source of life for, the true people of God, consisting of both Jews and Gentiles.

Two implications for the notion of pilgrimage can be spelled out. First, no earthly city such as Jerusalem (or, for that matter, Antioch or Rome) is the sacred centre of the Christian movement to which those in Paul's churches owe allegiance or need to make pilgrimage. Rather than looking to an earthly centre for their religion, believers are to look to the Jerusalem above, since Christ their Lord is now in heaven, and they are to live out in the midst of the conflict in Galatia the freedom of the new age symbolized by the heavenly city. Second, as we have seen, in becoming part of God's people through Christ and the Spirit, Gentile Christians have already participated in the fulfilment of the pilgrimage of the nations to Jerusalem. Despite the radical discontinuity with Jewish expectations about Jerusalem, there is also a basic continuity. The Scriptural and other Jewish texts saw the salvation of the end-times with its pilgrimage of the Gentiles in terms of a 'centripetal' movement in which all the nations would be gathered or make their journey to a renewed and glorified Jerusalem. For Paul, as his mission to the Gentiles took him away from Jerusalem and out across the empire in a 'centrifugal' movement, those Gentiles who are children of promise do nevertheless participate in a 'centripetal' movement, because they come to a Jerusalem glorified by the presence of God in Christ but one that, because of Christ's exaltation, is not on earth but has become the focal point of the heavenly dimension.

We can survey much more briefly Paul's more eirenic letter to the Romans, written on the eve of an impending critical visit to Jerusalem, that fills out but does not alter this basic perspective.[8] As regards the earthly Jerusalem, his impending visit is of great significance for Paul, not because he holds it to be a pilgrimage to a sacred site or because he believes it will usher in the end of history, as some have argued, but because it will signal the end of his mission in the eastern part of the empire and enable him to turn westward to Rome and, beyond Rome, to Spain. He wants it also to be a sign of the successful completion of this half of his mission to the Gentiles, and that success will be evidenced if the collection from Paul's Gentile churches for the Jerusalem church and its needy Jewish Christians is accepted. This would then constitute a symbol of the unity of the churches in the east, of the solidarity between the Jerusalem church and the churches of the Gentile mission. Paul recognizes a temporal priority of the Jerusalem church in the experience of the Gospel's blessings, and therefore sees Gentile churches who have come to share in these spiritual benefits as owing the poor among the Jerusalem believers a material debt (cf. Rom.15:25–7). He does not, however, equate such a priority with a hierarchical authority for this church or treat its location in Jerusalem as sacred. Christ the Lord in the Jerusalem above remains the authoritative centre to which all churches are to look both in the present and for the future consummation of God's purposes.

As Paul envisages the place of ethnic Israel in the climax of salvation in 11:25–7 and talks of all Israel being saved, he cites the Scriptures to indicate that this will occur through the coming of Christ: 'as it is written, "Out of Zion will come the Deliverer; he will banish ungodliness from Jacob."' In doing so, Paul follows neither the wording of the MT of Isa.59:20 that had originally talked of the Deliverer or Redeemer coming *to* Zion nor that of the LXX that read *on behalf of* Zion. Since elsewhere Paul talks consistently of Christ coming from heaven at the end of history (cf., for example, IThess. 1:10; 4:16; Phil.3:20), it is usually held that he has made the change to conform to this perspective, so that Christ is conceived of as coming from the heavenly Zion to include all Israel in the salvation of the end-time.[9] To anticipate later reflection, one cannot help thinking that, from Paul's perspective in Galatians and Romans, what Christians outside Palestine today were doing to support Jewish and Palestinian Christians in Israel would be far more important than whether they were able to participate in trips to supposed sacred sites. Indeed, from that perspective, the whole notion of Gentiles making a pilgrimage to Jerusalem to encounter Israel's God has become superfluous, because it has been fulfilled in the reality of what takes place when Gentiles encounter Israel's God in the Gospel about Jesus Christ.[10]

Hebrews

Both IPeter (cf. 1:1; 2:11) and Hebrews (cf. 11:13) use the term *parepidēmos*, 'sojourner', of those who live in faith. But it is Hebrews that connects this with the notion of a journey to a city to come and that has been particularly influential in the development of the metaphor of Christian existence as a pilgrimage, not least through John Bunyan's *Pilgrim's Progress*.[11] Key elements of the phenomenology of a religious pilgrimage – separation from one place, transition or journey to a sacred place with difficulties, trials and the threat of failure en route, and incorporation rites on arrival at the goal – have all been taken up and transformed in Hebrews' view of Christian existence.[12] This homily in written form with an epistolary conclusion was in all probability addressed to Jewish Christians tempted to go back on their Christian confession in the face of persecution and has as a major purpose encouraging them to persevere. Early on in Heb.3:7–4:13 the readers' situation is likened to the generation in the wilderness with its liminal position on the verge of the promised land, as they are exhorted not to fail to attain the rest that God has promised for them. The starting point for the writer's understanding of rest is its use in the psalm he cites – 'As in my anger I swore, "They will not enter my rest"' (Ps.95:11) – where its primary reference is to the resting place of the land of Canaan. The resting place in the land, linked with Zion as God's own resting place in the land in Old Testament interpretation (cf., for example, Ps.132:7, 8, 13, 14; IChron.23:25; IIChron.6:41), is interpreted by Hebrews in connection with God's sabbath rest as described in Gen.2:2 and becomes the symbol for the salvation of the end-times that has been prepared from the beginning.[13] There is a continuity with the experience of the wilderness generation but also discontinuity. For Christian believers there is an 'already' as well as a 'not yet' in their experience of this rest. They are already in the process of entering the heavenly resting place (cf. Heb.4:3, 10) that is prepared in the presence of God but can at the same time be exhorted to make every effort to enter it, that is, to appropriate what is already theirs, and not to forfeit it through hardness of heart or disobedence (3:12; 4:1, 11).

The temporal and spatial, horizontal and vertical aspects of Hebrews' eschatology and their shaping of the pilgrimage motif become more explicit in the final three chapters of the epistle. In Heb.11:8–16 it is Abraham, Isaac and Jacob, depicted as heroes of faith, who are described as 'foreigners and sojourners on the earth' (11:13). Abraham in particular is said to have 'looked forward to the city that has foundations, whose architect and builder is God' (11:10), while all three are portrayed as 'seeking a homeland' (11:14) and desiring 'a better country, that is, a heavenly one' (11:16). As in the case of the heavenly resting place, God is the one who has prepared the appropriate city for them (11:16). So the city is both future and at the same time already prepared by God and therefore existent in heaven. Just as in Jewish apocalyptic writings the already existent and prepared heavenly realities are an assurance and guarantee of the salvation of the end-times, so here in Hebrews this pattern serves a similar function. Christian believers are encouraged to persevere on their pilgrimage, emulating the faith of the patriarchs that entailed 'the assurance of things hoped for, the conviction of things not seen' (11:1).

But again Christian pilgrims both share the situation of the heroes and heroines of faith of Hebrews 11 and yet are also in a significantly different position, since they live in the time after God has spoken God's final and decisive word in Christ (Heb.1:1,2). That word now takes the form of an oath that guarantees God's promises about the future, and the oath is embodied in Christ who, as the exalted high priest, has entered into the heavenly holy of holies (cf. 6:17–20; 7:20–22). The high priest's entry into the Holy of Holies was the climax of the national fast of Yom Kippur, since the high priest made his entry on behalf of all the people. Now Christ has done this once for all, and believers are to consider their lives anchored to Christ in the permanent heavenly dimension into which he has gone ahead as a forerunner on their behalf (6:20). This image of Christ is linked with that of the pioneer (cf. 2:10; 12:2) who has blazed the trail ahead for his followers. This makes all the difference for their pilgrimage. That pilgrimage can now be seen to entail not only a movement forward but also a movement upward, as they enjoy already the salvation of the world to come through 'the new and living way' opened up by their high priest as forerunner (cf. 10:20).

This enables the writer to make his striking claim in 12:22: 'But you have come to Mount Zion and to the city of the living God, the heavenly Jerusalem.' One of the pilgrimage motifs of the Old Testament is the movement of the people of God from Mount Sinai through the wilderness to Zion, the mountain that Yahweh had chosen for the divine dwelling place (cf. Ps.68). And in prophetic visions of the end-time, as has been noted, it is at the place of God's self-revelation, Zion, that God's people, Israel, gather. Now Hebrews is telling its readers that they are already part of the great covenant assembly of the last days. Like Paul in Galatians, this writer also links the fulfilment of the covenant with Mount Zion and the heavenly Jerusalem in a contrast with Mount Sinai (cf. Heb.12:18–24). In their pilgrimage the readers have left behind Mount Sinai, described in terms that emphasize its earthly, tangible and transitory features, and have drawn near to the, at present, heavenly and invisible but permanent reality represented by the Jerusalem above, the city of the living God. The verb employed here, *proserchomai*, is regularly used in the LXX for cultic worship and is the same term found in Heb.4:16 and 10:22, where it is employed to exhort the readers to draw near to God's throne of grace in full assurance.

So there is a realized aspect to believers' pilgrimage in Hebrews and it is found in the context of worship. The benefits of the salvation of the world to come and the city to come are already present in heaven, and in worship

believers have access to them and can enjoy them. The earthly assembly at
Sinai had been enrolled (cf. Num.1–4), those born in Zion are said by the
Psalmist to be registered by the Lord (cf. Ps.87:5, 6), and now in Hebrews the
members of the new covenant community have their names on the assembly
roll of the citizens of the heavenly Zion. The goal of pilgrimage for Jewish
Christians is no longer the earthly Jerusalem but the heavenly Jerusalem to
which they already have access. Despite the celebration of their anticipatory
arrival at Mount Zion, they are reminded in Heb.12:25–9 that they have not
yet finally arrived. There will be a final cosmic shake-up, but in that end-time
judgment, because of their link with the exalted Christ, believers know
themselves to be citizens of the permanent heavenly realm, recipients of the
kingdom that cannot be shaken and that will replace the old order.

The readers' anticipation of the goal of pilgrimage in their worship not only
means that they can face the future with thanksgiving rather than fear but also
shapes their present activity and decision making. The latter point emerges in
Heb.13:9–16. The assertion that 'here we have no lasting city, but we seek the
city to come' (13:14) occurs in a context that again contrasts Jewish and
Christian systems of worship. This time the writer makes use of the cultic
background of Lev.16:27, 28 that legislates the practice of carrying the bodies
of sacrificial animals (their flesh, skin and dung) outside the camp and burning
them. The person who did this had to wash his clothes and bathe his body
before being permitted back into the camp, because to be involved in this
activity was to become defiled or unclean. The writer sees an analogy in the
fulfilment of the sacrificial system in Christ's death that took place 'outside the
gate', that is, outside Jerusalem. His point is that in both cases the sacrificial
victim is associated with the notion of 'outside'. But whereas under the
Levitical system outside was unsanctified, Christ's death that actually took
place outside, on unsanctified territory, is precisely what sanctifies (cf. Heb.
13:12: 'in order to sanctify the people through his own blood'). In this way it
subverts the whole system of clean and unclean, holy and profane, sacred and
secular.

The Jewish Christian readers are exhorted to live out the implications of this
insight: 'let us go out to Jesus outside the camp, and bear the abuse he endured'
(13:13). They have to be willing to move beyond the Jewish religious system to
what in their mind might still appear to be unholy and unsanctified territory, a
move that would invite further shame and persecution. But it is a move that
their perspective on pilgrimage should help them to make. Knowing that the
present order, including its religious systems and values and including
Jerusalem, is not lasting and that they are on the way to the permanent city
to come, to which they already have access, should enable them to take the
risks and costs involved in identifying with Christ outside that system. In this
way the pilgrimage of the Christian community through this world to the world
to come can be seen to entail not only a forward and an upward movement but

also, as a key feature of both routes, an outward movement – out from the earthly Jerusalem and what it represented into what appears to be the unsanctified territory of this world in solidarity with the way through this world of the crucified and exalted leader of its pilgrimage. On such a view of pilgrimage, as M.E. Isaacs puts it, 'given Hebrews' starting point – that Jesus is now in heaven (1:1–3) – and the analogies its author chooses to explain the route by which he came to arrive at this destination – as the pioneer who gains entry into the promised land and the High Priest who enters the Holy of Holies on the Day of Atonement – it follows that all earthly sacred space is relativized'.[14]

John

This relativization of sacred space is, if anything, even more pronounced in the Fourth Gospel, which epitomizes W.D. Davies' dictum that 'for the holiness of place, Christianity has ... substituted the holiness of the Person; it has Christified holy space'.[15] John depicts Jesus as embodying in his own person the significance invested by the Jewish people in the Jerusalem temple and the festival pilgrimages that had that temple as their goal. There are four journeys of Jesus to Jerusalem in John, with each one being described in greater detail and with the fourth and final journey including the climactic events of the Passion.[16] The first journey (John 2:13–3:21) is for the festival of Passover, significantly designated as 'the passover of the Jews', a label that is also attached to other festivals and already suggests a distance between believing readers and Jewish pilgrimage festivals.[17] When Jesus reaches the goal of the pilgrimage, the temple, John leaves readers in no doubt about how they are to understand the relationship between Jesus and the temple and in his interpretation takes up one of the key passages from the eschatological pilgrimage tradition. In the vision of Zechariah 12–14, in the end-times Yahweh will come to Zion as king, bringing glory and reigning over all the earth, and Yahweh's name will be one (cf. 12:7–9; 14:1–5, 9). There will be victory over the nations, and 'then all who survive of the nations that have come against Jerusalem shall go up year after year to worship the King, the Lord of hosts, and to keep the festival of booths [or Tabernacles]' (14:6). What is more, 'on that day ... the cooking pots in the house of the Lord shall be as holy as the bowls in front of the altar; and every cooking pot in Jerusalem and Judah shall be sacred to the Lord of hosts, so that all who sacrifice may come and use them to boil the flesh of the sacrifice. And there shall no longer be traders in the house of the Lord of hosts on that day' (14:20, 21). There will be no need for the trading associated with the sacrificial system, because in the renewed Jerusalem and Judah all aspects of life – every cooking utensil and even the bells of the horses – will have become sacred.

Zech. 14.16, 20-21

Now in John 2:13–22 Jesus' action temporarily brings to a halt the whole point of other people's pilgrimage. If they were to complete their pilgrimage and to offer sacrifices, they needed the supply and inspection of sacrificial animals, they needed to be able to change their money into coinage acceptable by the temple. But Jesus smashes up this whole arrangement and commands, 'Take these things out of here! Stop making my Father's house a house of trade!' (2:16). Jesus' prophetic action and his explanation with its allusion to Zech.14:21 signals the end of the present Temple order and of the sort of pilgrimage he has disrupted. What he goes on to say in justification for this sacrilegious outrage is 'Destroy this temple, and in three days I will raise it up' (2:19). In order that the readers may not be caught along with Jesus' audience as victims of this metaphor, the narrator intervenes in 2:21, 22 to supply its correct interpretation. The temple is Jesus' body and what readers need to understand is that God's presence, previously focused in the Jerusalem temple, is now to be found in the crucified and risen body of Christ. Jesus himself constitutes the new temple of the eschatological order.

2nd Journey
3rd Journey

Zech. 14.7-8

Jesus' second pilgrimage in John 5:1 is to an unnamed festival, and the narrative does not explicitly exploit this setting. It is with the third pilgrimage for the festival of Tabernacles and then Jesus' extended stay through Hanukkah (7:1–10:39) that this motif is taken further. The two principal symbols in the celebration of Tabernacles were water, with a daily ceremony involving drawing water from the pool of Siloam and a prayer for the gift of rain on the final day, and light, with four great lamps set up to illuminate the court of women and enable dancing through the night. Earlier Zechariah's vision of Jerusalem at the end had taken up the water and light symbolism with living waters flowing from Jerusalem in a time of continuous light (cf. Zech. 14:7, 8). Now Jesus claims to be the source of living water, with rivers of living water flowing from his belly (7:37–9) and to be the light of the world (8:12; 9:5).

4th Journey

Hanukkah, or the Feast of Dedication, celebrated the reconsecration of the temple altar in 164BCE after its desecration by the priests of Antiochus Epiphanes, but now in 10:36 Jesus is said to be the one whom the Father has consecrated and sent into the world. The narrative builds suspense over whether Jesus will attend what turns out to be his final Passover pilgrimage (11:55–7). As the events of the Passion unfold, there are reminders of its Passover setting and timing (cf. 18:28, 39; 19:14, 31, 42). In this Gospel, Jesus is crucified at the same time that the Passover lambs were slaughtered. His bodily sacrifice is compared to that of a Passover lamb, as the evangelist employs the citation from Exod.12:46, 'none of his bones shall be broken' (cf. 19:36), and in this way the earlier testimony of John the Baptist is recalled: 'Here is the lamb of God who takes away the sin of the world' (1:29, 36).

Jesus' death entails no abandonment of the notion that the Shekinah, the glory of the divine presence, is to be found no longer in the Temple but in him. Quite the reverse. The glory, which is now to be seen in the Logos, who became flesh and tabernacled among us (1:14), and which was manifested throughout his mission, has its own climactic hour and, in a radical redefinition of all human notions of glory, is supremely demonstrated in Jesus' Roman-style execution that is at the same time the means of his being lifted up and exalted.

Perhaps the passage that best encapsulates John's perspective on pilgrimage to sacred places is the well-known exchange that provides the climax of Jesus' dialogue with the Samaritan woman in 4:21–6. The woman's recognition of Jesus as a prophet prompts her to change the topic of conversation to worship: 'our ancestors worshipped on this mountain [Gerizim, whose temple had been destroyed earlier in 128BCE], but you say that the place where people must worship is Jerusalem.' In Jesus' reply he sides clearly with the Jewish tradition: 'You worship what you do not know; we worship what we know; for salvation is from the Jews.' One would therefore expect him to agree with the second part of the woman's statement and say, 'Yes, you need to make your pilgrimage to Jerusalem to worship.'

Instead, the statement we have cited is prefaced and followed by two very surprising assertions that announce an eschatological change that affects both the previously erroneous Samaritan view and the previously correct Jewish view. First is the prediction, 'the hour is coming when you will worship the Father neither on this mountain nor in Jerusalem' (4:21), and then comes the announcement of its present realization, 'the hour is coming, and is now here, when the true worshippers will worship the Father in spirit and in truth' (4:23a). The arrival of that hour is further signalled when in response to the woman's statement of her knowledge that Messiah is coming, Jesus' claim incorporates but transcends that title as he employs the formula of divine self-revelation, 'I Am [is] the one who is speaking to you' (4:26). It is in and through Jesus that God is now revealing Godself and seeking worshippers. In line with the earlier promise to Nathanael that he 'will see heaven opened and the angels of God ascending and descending upon the Son of Man' that takes up the language used in Jacob's vision in Gen.28:12 and views Jesus, the Son of Man, as the new Bethel or house of God (1:51), and in line with the earlier notion of Jesus' crucified and risen body as the temple, it is in Jesus that the divine presence is now to be located. If God has an address on earth, it is no longer in Jerusalem but in the incarnate Logos. The place of the Name – here 'I Am' (cf. 4:26) – is now an embodied location, the person of Jesus. The Spirit will be sent in Jesus' name as his fully authorized representative (14:26; 16:17) and the truth, that God is known in him and that he is one with God, is disclosed in Jesus' person and mission, so that it is Jesus who now makes possible the worship of the Father in Spirit and in truth. It could not be clearer that 'for John's Gospel worship in the time of eschatological fulfilment has as its focus the relationship to a person rather than a place. The goal of pilgrimage, temple worship, has been transformed Christologically. Jesus is the true place of worship and so to go on pilgrimage is to come to Jesus.[18]

[handwritten margin note: God's "address" is now the incarnate Logos.]

So What About Christian Pilgrimages?

The three representative writers examined point unquestionably in the same direction. Indeed, there are no New Testament documents that encourage Christians to hold as normative for themselves the notion of pilgrimage to Jerusalem or to any other particular place that is to be regarded as sacred.[19] But to explicate the New Testament is not necessarily the same as to do theology. Is there some way to hold to its perspective and still to allow for our basic human attachments to place and our basic religious attachments to sacred place? Can we still say that in some way Jerusalem and the supposed sites of Jesus' career are sacred and should therefore be the goal of pilgrimages? In my view, a faithful Christian theology will want to show that it is in continuity with the witness of the New Testament, a witness that does not undermine the importance of places but that does clearly subvert the notion of particular sacred spaces. Perhaps then taking this witness seriously will mean not allowing some formulations of present-day Christian spirituality with their enthusiasm for literal pilgrimages to go unchallenged. So, to choose at random one assertion, among many possible candidates, that needs to be countered, a feature in the *Church Times* contained the following extraordinary claim: 'The land of the Bible is unique and it surely should be the aim and objective of every Christian to make this unforgettable pilgrimage.' [20] Leaving aside this claim's view of every Christian as affluent enough to meet its mandate, there seems no way such a mandate could be justified theologically.

true (affluency issue)

But in case it is thought to be too easy to fire shots at unguarded propaganda for pilgrimages, interaction with a more heavyweight theological sparring partner is called for. One of N.T. Wright's recent books is entitled *The Way of the Lord: Christian Pilgrimage Today* and contains material designed originally 'to prepare a party of pilgrims for a ten-day trip to the Holy Land'.[21] Wright is, of course, too good a New Testament scholar not to be aware of the perspective set out here and he is sensitive to the authority of Scripture for Christian theology, so how does he justify continued talk of pilgrimage to the Holy Land and other holy places? He wants to give actual pilgrimages theological significance while making clear that this is only a secondary significance.[22] So, for example, in his preface he contrasts 'a geographical pilgrimage' with 'the pilgrimage that really counts' and in conclusion reminds us that whether or not we have 'the chance to go on an actual pilgrimage ... all of us are summoned to go on this inside-out pilgrimage, following in the way of the Lord'.[23] But does not the inside-out pilgrimage that really counts not merely relegate literal pilgrimages to a lesser status but actually undermine their raison d'être? Wright is loath to draw this conclusion, because it smacks too much of the sort of dualism and opposition to ritual associated with versions of evangelicalism that once formed part of his thinking ('I no more contemplated going on pilgrimage than I would have considered kissing the

Wright seeks to avoid a dualistic spiritualizing + opposition to ritual.

Pope's ring'[24]). Initially, then, he distances himself from the use made of some of the texts from John and Paul we have noted, because he now associates this use with evangelical Marcionism. These texts, he tells us, were taken to mean 'that all sense of continuity with the Old Testament's geographical focus, with the idea of pilgrimage to a holy city, was done away with; as with other aspects of some English evangelicalism, there was always the danger of Marcionism slipping in by the back door'.[25] After speaking of his increased 'recognition of the sacramental quality of God's whole created world' and of finding the unexpected presence of God in particular places and buildings, Wright relates a particular religious experience that occurred on his first visit to the Church of the Holy Sepulchre, after which he realized that he 'had become a pilgrim'.[26]

It is at this point that Wright returns to the troublesome texts. He does still agree with his former view based on those texts that 'there is no such thing in the New Testament as a Holy Land'[27] and later he will phrase this in characteristically effective fashion: 'With Calvary and Easter, the Holy Land has become the holy person, Jesus himself, who goes ahead of us into all the world, to the places of pain and despair, and summons us to follow him and work for reconciliation and hope.'[28] Strangely, however, this belief makes no difference to the way in which <u>he will continue throughout the book to talk about pilgrimage to *the Holy Land*</u>! At the same time, Wright draws on the conviction that had failed to inform his previous views, namely, that the whole world has become holy and is under the lordship of the crucified and risen Jesus, a lordship that will become fully realized in the redemption of the whole cosmos. Yet then, rather unexpectedly, at the end of the same paragraph that sets out this unexceptional New Testament theology, he asserts, as if on the basis of it, that followers of the risen Christ 'are invited both to contemplate the place where he was [and by this Wright means pilgrimages to the sites] and to recognize that there is more to following him than geography'.[29]

Where the first part of this invitation comes from, we are not told, but, as he goes on to explain, <u>Wright holds that such Christian pilgrimages take place in the space and time between the life of Jesus and God's restoration of the whole creation.</u> He claims it is '<u>a characteristically Pauline position of now-and-not-yet</u>'.[30] <u>But this is not a compelling claim.</u> His position in fact simply reverses the emphasis of the 'already' and 'not yet' dialectic not only of Paul but also of Hebrews and John. For them, as we have seen, it is what has already happened in Christ that has transformed the notion of literal pilgrimage to Jerusalem. The period of 'not yet' until the consummation of Christ's lordship over the cosmos does not for them reintroduce what had been transformed but provides the opportunity to live out ahead of time in all places the new reality guaranteed by Christ's present rule in the heavenly realm. The only way in which pilgrimage functions as part of the 'already' and 'not yet' tension is as a metaphor for the whole, as Hebrews leaves its readers in no doubt. When, in the epilogue to his book, Wright deals with the view held by many Christians that the return by Jews to Palestine in modern times can be seen as part of yet unfulfilled prophecy, he is adamant that this is tantamount to denying the significance the New Testament attributes to what God has already done in Christ's life, death and resurrection in fulfilment of Old Testament expectation.[31] One cannot help but think that the same hermeneutic ought also to apply in the case of his own attempt to reintroduce literal pilgrimages to Jerusalem despite what the New Testament writers say about the fulfilment of such a notion for both Jews and Gentiles in what God has already done in Christ.

Does Wright contradict himself?

Let us be clear what the issue is here. It is not whether there can be spiritual benefit in going to particular sites in Israel. It is not whether God can and does meet people in profound ways at particular places. It would be foolish in the extreme to imply otherwise. The issue is whether there is any theological justification on the basis of the New Testament for calling for pilgrimage to such locations because they are deemed to be sacred. We can clarify the issue further by considering the three positive points Wright makes in support of pilgrimage.

The main issue.

First, 'Pilgrimage to holy places has a valuable role within the Church's teaching ministry'.[32] Countless tourists to Israel and participants in study visits would attest to fresh appreciation of aspects of biblical stories, but this by no means requires the use of the notion of pilgrimage to holy places. Second, 'Pilgrimage to holy places is a stimulus and an invitation to prayer'.[33] So are a great variety of experiences, and again a visit to the Sea of Galilee or to Canterbury Cathedral does not need to be held to be a pilgrimage to a sacred place in order to serve as such a stimulus or invitation. Later Wright will make use of the distinction between tourism and pilgrimage, employed by many other writers on pilgrimage, in which the latter entails going to Jerusalem to meet God and being prepared to change in the encounter.[34] But, in many ways, this undercuts the case for literal pilgrimage from a New Testament theological perspective. One cannot imagine as part of New Testament paraenesis the advice that, in order to meet God and experience spiritual transformation, the addressees need to contemplate a trip to Jerusalem. Third, 'Pilgrimage to holy places, though neither necessary nor sufficient for Christian living, can be for many a time of real growth and depth in discipleship'.[35] This heavily qualified claim then links discipleship to what is said about Abraham's pilgrimage of faith in Hebrews. Any journey, whether to alleged sites in Israel or to Rome or to Santiago, can serve such a function in one's life of discipleship or Christian pilgrimage seen as a metaphor. No attempted Christian theology of particular holy places is needed to hold this. But Wright follows his reference to Hebrews' metaphorical use of pilgrimage by saying, 'there is every reason to regard the act of pilgrimage in itself as a metaphor, or even a sacrament, for and of the pilgrim's progress through the present life to the life that is to come'.[36]

One can appreciate the thought, yet this is a potentially confusing notion of metaphor. For Christians the metaphor of pilgrimage already exists to depict the eschatological reality inaugurated by Christ and by which they live. It is, by definition, parasitic on an original literal notion of journey to a sacred place. They do not need to re-enact its literal referent so that that can then somehow become the metaphor of a metaphor. Would it not be more appropriate to say that any journey undertaken for spiritual benefit or growth in discipleship can be a means of fuller appreciation of the realities expressed in the pilgrimage metaphor by which we live?

Some Concluding Reflections

Once it is acknowledged that journeys to particular places, though by no means mandatory, can play a valuable role in Christian discipleship, it may seem pedantic to query whether these should be thought of as pilgrimages. The contention of this chapter is that such a query can be a reminder of the definitive Christology of the New Testament and its radical implications and is not simply a linguistic quibble. It is to ask that experience, however deeply felt, be normed by theology and not simply given theological justification after the fact. Cragg's moving and insightful chapter in this book, despite its clear perception of the New Testament perspective, in the end justifies Christian assertions of virtue latent in particular holy places by allowing experience to trump theological considerations. He writes, 'All theology apart, "him here" (historically but not exclusively) is the actuality awaiting pilgrim visitation and those who have sought and known it so confirm its authenticity' (see p. 9). Given the loose usage of the term 'pilgrimage' and the confusion it generates, perhaps Christians, on the basis of the New Testament witness, would be clearer in their thinking if they were clearer in their language and, when talking about their Christian experiences, reserved the term 'pilgrimage' for use as a metaphor for Christian existence as a whole. After all, as has been stressed, the New Testament views the literal sense of pilgrimage as a journey to a sacred place as fulfilled through what has taken place in the life, death and resurrection of Christ, so that pilgrimage now becomes a metaphor for the journey of Christian living that has as its already anticipated goal the heavenly Jerusalem that stands for the life of the age to come. In continuity with this perspective, Christians could then be clear that journeys to Jerusalem, Canterbury, Oberammergau or Rome are not literal pilgrimages but can, and often do, play some significant part in the pilgrimage that is Christian existence. Visits to Israel would then not be pilgrimages to the Holy Land, but study visits, sightseeing tours, projects to promote solidarity with Christians in Palestine/Israel. If one has good reason to do these things, then they are enterprises to be undertaken prayerfully and are part of one's overall spiritual pilgrimage.

[handwritten margin note: a need for clear language... "pilgrimage" as metaphor for Christian existence as a whole only?]

It is significant that early Christians appear to have managed to retain this perspective until the 4th century, when, under the influence of Constantine, the notion of worship at particular sacred sites became linked with visits to Jerusalem.[37] The first recorded special visit to Jerusalem is that of Melito of Sardis (c.170CE) whose motive was simply the scholarly one of confirming aspects of the Gospel accounts for himself, and Jerome later expressed the view that a visit to Jerusalem would enable Christians to understand Scripture better. These were what we might call study visits. But later, for Constantine, it became important to excavate particular sites and build on them (the Church of the Holy Sepulchre being the prime example) so that these could become special places for worship. It is also not without significance that this move immediately led to a power struggle between Christians and those who lived there and who were believed to have deliberately let the sites deteriorate or become concealed. From the first this reintroduction of notions of particular sacred spaces into Christian thinking was a deeply ambivalent move, combining both sincere, if misplaced, desires about Christian worship and desires for power over land and over others that were in sharp contrast to the message of the Christian Gospel.

But does a New Testament perspective lead to the sort of dualism that Wright and others correctly wish to abandon, a dualism that regards the places in God's dealings with Israel as unimportant and denigrates earthly places in favour of a spiritual, heavenly realm? The answer is in the negative in regard to past, present and future. In regard to the future, the consistent vision of the New Testament writings, expressed in a variety of ways, is that the present emphasis on heaven as the sphere from which Christ rules is not an end in itself but serves as the guarantee of the future goal of the reuniting of heaven and earth in a renewed cosmos.[38] In the meanwhile, in the present, an appreciation of the Christological transformation of sacred space is meant to make all the difference to the way believers live in their particular places. Knowing that their allegiance is to the heavenly rather than the earthly Jerusalem is precisely what should enable the recipients of Galatians to participate appropriately in the progress of the Pauline Gospel in Galatia. This is part of a consistent picture for the Pauline letters, in which believers are both 'in Corinth' and 'in Christ Jesus' (cf. ICor.1:2), with the latter as determinative for the shape that their life takes in the former, and in which belonging to the heavenly commonwealth for Philippian Christians (cf. Phil.3:20) by no means takes away from the importance of Philippi as the specific location where they live out this allegiance in appropriate fashion (cf. Phil.1:27). Similarly, the perspective of Hebrews with its view of its recipients' relationship to the city that is to come, already realized in their access to Christ in the heavenly Zion, provides the necessary guidance for the way to face both the threat of Roman persecution and the attractions of a return to their previous allegiance to Judaism in the concrete setting of their own city, traditionally held to be Rome.

The portrayal of Jesus as the fulfilment of the significance of Jewish pilgrimages and the true locus of worship in John's Gospel both arises out of and speaks to the needs of those very much concerned about place, the social and religious place of those expelled from their local synagogue within the broader context of a Judaism struggling to come to terms with issues of place in the wake of the destruction of Jerusalem and its Temple.[39] Pilgrimage as a metaphor for Christian existence does not mean the abandonment of our particular place or cultural space but provides the resources for reorientation within the places and spaces we inhabit.

As regards the past, what is important about places is the memories attached to them by particular traditions. For early Christians, as they retained the Jewish Scriptures and treated as authoritative their own foundational stories preserved in the canonical Gospels and Acts, the memory that the God of Israel had acted for salvation not only at particular times but also in specific places remained central. But the memory of what the God of Israel had done in Jesus and through his followers in particular locations was preserved by treating these not as sacred spaces but rather as 'storied places'.[40] On their pilgrimage of Christian existence believers continued to tell each other the foundational stories with their embedded memories of places such as Nazareth, Galilee, Jerusalem, Damascus, Antioch, Ephesus and Rome. It is the significance of the place in the story that counts for Christian belief. A robust doctrine of incarnation certainly entails that there were actual and particular settings for Jesus' mission and Passion, but the significance of the incarnation and of what happened in those settings is not altered one iota by attempting to locate, reconstruct or visit such sites. Profound as may be the experience of sitting looking across the lake of Galilee, it simply is not a prerequisite for the memories of the stilling of the storm preserved in Mark 4:35–41 and its parallels to have their intended effect. For the benefits for faith of what happened at alleged sites, Christians, whether they have been to Israel or not, remain dependent on the interpreted memories of the Gospel narratives. Access to the reality of the person of Jesus in particular locations is found now through the canonical stories, through liturgy and sacraments.

So, for a variety of reasons, this exploration of the topic of pilgrimage in the New Testament leads to advocating a reappropriation rather than an accommodation of its perspective. What may be needed in the face of current enthusiasms for literal pilgrimages to Jerusalem and elsewhere is an acknowledgment of the spiritual yearnings these reflect and the benefits they may confer, yet, at the same time, a reminder of the New Testament's theological framework, which can help to reconfigure the construal of such experiences, and a redirecting of attention to the central realities the New Testament writers believed God had already accomplished in Christ.

For those who want to encounter the living God in a fresh way, that God is seeking just such worshippers and is available for such an encounter wherever they are, because access to the divine presence has now been given through Christ and in the Spirit. For those who want to rediscover the roots of their faith, what is important is to find their own stories in the Biblical stories, allowing the former to be shaped by the latter, and to realize that it is through faith, baptism and Eucharist that they are related to the particular story of the Jew who lived, died and rose again in 1st-century Palestine. To rediscover one's Christian roots is primarily to rediscover what it means to participate in Christ's death and resurrection. Scott's chapter provides helpful and penetrating reflection on the Eucharistic dimensions of a theology of place. Its premise, however, is that the notion of pilgrimage to Jerusalem is theologically valid but needs to be given a more appropriate theological construal. Its closest approach to actual justification of pilgrimage to Jerusalem is in terms of a liturgical closeness to Jerusalem, claiming that in the Eucharist Jerusalem or Golgotha is invoked.

But if it is true that Golgotha is invoked in the Eucharist, not only is this a deeply ambiguous invocation, since it recalls Jerusalem not so much as the place to which Jesus belonged but as the place from which he was rejected and excluded, but also, of course, such an invocation by no means entails visiting the site. Just as Christians do not need to go back in time in order to be able to say they died and were raised with Christ but do so in the dramatic sacrament of baptism, so they do not need to traverse space to be able to invoke Golgotha adequately but do so in the dramatic sacrament of the Eucharist itself. They are connected to both the events and the places of the climax of Jesus' career through participation 'in Christ'.

Finally, for those who want to gain a transformed perspective on everyday life and places, that is precisely what is offered by Christian pilgrimage as a metaphor by which to live. Its symbol of the 'heavenly Jerusalem' speaks of the reality of the salvation and its values that has been accomplished through the crucified and exalted Lord and that is now to be worked out in liberation, joyful worship and solidarity with others in the real places of this world, including, of course, Jerusalem, with their ambiguities, conflicts and pains. Its symbol of the 'city to come' speaks of the sustaining hope of the full realization of what God has purposed in Christ for a transformed cosmos.

Notes

1   See, for example, the declaration of the General Secretariat for the Great Jubilee of the Year 2000, Jerusalem.

2   For one possible reconstruction of the historical Jesus that attempts to take seriously his activity in the Temple as a result of his pilgrimage to Jerusalem and his sayings that reflect the view that this coming to Jerusalem was also in some way an enactment of Yahweh's expected return to Zion, see Wright, *Jesus*, 413–28, 490–510, 612–53, and the similar sketch in Walker, *Holy City*, 269–89. On the pilgrimage festivals in Judaism, see Sanders, *Judaism*, 112–16, 125–43.

3   On these topics, see especially Davies, *Gospel*, and Walker, *Holy City*.
4   See especially the exposition of this expectation in Jeremias, *Promise*, 55–62.
5   See the fuller treatment of this passage in Lincoln, *Paradise*, 9–32; cf. also Walker, *Holy City*, 127–32.
6   For a recent justification of this interpretation, see Martyn, *Galatians*, especially 457–66, and Martyn, *Theological Issues*, 25–36. As Martyn, *Theological Issues*, 205, allows, Judaism may well stand somewhere in the background, because Paul does hold the conviction that the law leads to enslavement, but it is the teaching of the rival missionaries rather than Judaism as a whole that is the focus of his polemic in this passage.
7   Hence the type of argument Paul mounts in Gal.1 and 2 with its emphasis on his independence from Jerusalem and yet the Jerusalem church leaders' essential agreement with his stance.
8   Cf. also Walker, *Holy City*, 136, 144–51 and, on Israel and the nations, especially 139–40, 144n111, *contra* Donaldson, *Paul*, 187–97. In espousing the view that it is the model of proselyte conversion that provides the key to Paul's thinking, Donaldson asserts that he no longer believes that the eschatological pilgrimage notion is reflected in Paul at all and relates that his study of Romans 11, with its treatment of Israel's rejection of the Gospel, led him to abandon his previous view. But, if one keeps in mind that there is an 'already' and a 'not yet' in Paul's perspective on Israel, there is nothing in that passage that is incompatible with Paul stressing elsewhere what God has already done for Israel through Christ. Donaldson does not treat Gal.4:21–31 in his book, nor does he tell us how he understands the reference to Zion in Rom.11:27. It seems more likely that, if one considered Donaldson's historical quest for which notion from Paul's background motivated his Gentile mission to be a separate issue, one would find both Jewish models reflected in Paul's writings. Indeed, Galatians 3 and 4 provide a prime example, where the Zion tradition reflected in the heavenly Jerusalem reference is incorporated into the argument about Abraham's descendants and its taking up of proselyte issues.
9   Cf., for example, Dunn, *Romans*, 692–3; Moo, *Romans*, 728, *contra* Walker, *Holy City*, 140–43, who somewhat tentatively opts for the interpretation that Paul understands this part of the Isaiah prophecy to have already been fulfilled in the first coming of Christ and the Gospel's going out from Jerusalem.
10   Though Luke–Acts does not contain the notion of a heavenly Jerusalem, in its perspective on the earthly Jerusalem and its relation to the Gentile mission it confirms the Pauline notion that the eschatological pilgrimage of the nations is already taking place in the conversion of Gentiles. This is made explicit in James' use of LXX Amos 9:11–13 in Acts 15:16, 17. The Hebrew text of Amos will not bear any sense of an eschatological pilgrimage of the Gentiles, but the LXX does. Despite the fact that Luke's account itself indicates that mission to the Gentiles entailed movement away from Jerusalem and occurred in part as the result of the rejection of the Gospel and persecution of Jewish Christians by other Jews (cf. 8:1–4; 11:19–21), the Gentiles who come to faith are seen in James' citation of Scripture at the Council in terms of those who come to seek the Lord in the restored temple. The restored temple is evidently to be found in those Jewish Christians who have experienced 'the times of refreshing from the presence of the Lord' (Acts 3:20) that have taken place with the outpouring of the Spirit at Pentecost. On this passage, see Walker, *Holy City*, 96–7.
11   Two books on Hebrews pick up on this motif in their titles; cf. Jewett, *Pilgrims*, and Käsemann, *Wandering People*. Cf. also Johnsson, 'Pilgrimage Motif'. For Bunyan's dependence on Hebrews, see Stranahan, 'Bunyan'. For a fuller treatment of the related issues of land, Jerusalem and temple in Hebrews, see Walker, *Holy City*, 201–34.
12   Cf. Johnsson, 'Pilgrimage Motif', 244–7.
13   For fuller exposition of Hebrews' notion of rest, see Lincoln, 'Sabbath', especially 205–14.
14   Isaacs, 'Hebrews', 149.
15   Davies, *Gospel*, 368. For a fuller treatment of the related issues in John, see again Walker, *Holy City*, 161–200.

16 On the journey motif in John, see Segovia, 'Journey(s)'.

17 On festivals in John, see Yee, *Jewish Feasts*.

18 On the basis of his study of John, Walker, *Holy City*, 191 makes the strong assertion that 'Any Christian attempt to invest the places associated with Jesus in Palestine with a new spiritual significance should be ruled out – Jesus himself was the only true "holy place".'

19 Paul hastening to be in Jerusalem to celebrate Pentecost (Acts 20:16) is part of Luke's picture of Paul as no apostate who broke with the law but a good Pharisaic Jew who remained scrupulously faithful to his heritage. The charges against which Paul has to be defended are related by James in 21:21. It is significant that the notion of a pilgrimage to Jerusalem makes little sense in the immediate context as the reason for not stopping at Ephesus, since Paul then stops at Miletus anyway in order to have the Ephesian elders come to him! Other aspects of this portrait are equally suspect historically. The accounts of Paul cutting his hair because of a vow at Cenchreae (18:18) or of Paul actively cooperating to allay suspicions that he has undermined Jewish law by purifying himself and paying the expenses of four men in Jerusalem who had a vow (21:24–6) lack correspondence with what we know of Jewish practice and are difficult to square with the Paul of the epistles. None of them are presented by Luke as examples that are normative for the Christians of his own day but as part of his legitimation of the Christian movement in terms of its continuity with Judaism. At best, he has taken what was an occasional tactic on Paul's part (cf. I Cor.9:20) and made it a major characteristic of the apostle.

20 Weston, 'Live'.

21 Wright, *Way*, ix.

22 To be fair, he does state that he is not proposing to offer 'a full theology of contemporary pilgrimage'; cf. Wright, *Way*, 9.

23 Ibid., ix, x, 118.

24 Ibid., 4.

25 Ibid., 3.

26 Ibid., 4–7.

27 Ibid., 7.

28 Ibid., 117.

29 Ibid., 8.

30 Ibid., 8.

31 Ibid., 124–7.

32 Ibid., 9–10.

33 Ibid., 10.

34 Ibid., 63–4.

35 Ibid., 10.

36 Ibid., 11.

37 On this, see also Walker, *Holy City*, 320–23 and his earlier studies cited there.

38 So, for example, in Rev.21:1–22:7, the heavenly Jerusalem comes down from heaven to be the focal point of the new heaven and new earth.

39 For the former aspect, cf. John 9:22; 12:42; 16:2. For the possibility of the latter aspect as part of the background of John's Gospel, cf. especially the thesis of Motyer, *Your Father*.

40 To take up an expression employed by Brueggemann, (*Land*, 185).

Bibliography

Brueggemann, W., *The Land* (London: SPCK, 1978).

Davies, W.D., *The Gospel and the Land* (Berkeley: University of California Press, 1974).

Donaldson, T.L., *Paul and the Gentiles* (Minneapolis: Fortress, 1997).

Dunn, J.D.G., *Romans* (Dallas: Word, 1988).

Isaacs, M.E., 'Hebrews', in J. Barclay and J. Sweet (eds), *Early Christian Thought in Its Jewish Context* (Cambridge: CUP, 1996).

Jeremias, J., *Jesus' Promise to the Nations* (London: SCM, 1958).

Jewett, R., *Letter to Pilgrims* (New York: Pilgrim Press, 1981).

Johnsson, W.G., 'The Pilgrimage Motif in the Book of Hebrews', *JBL*, 97 (1978), 239–51.

Käsemann, E., *The Wandering People of God*, English trans. (Minneapolis: Augsburg, 1984).

Lincoln, A.T., *Paradise Now and Not Yet* (Cambridge: CUP, 1981).

——, 'Sabbath, Rest and Eschatology in the New Testament', in D.A. Carson (ed.), *From Sabbath to Lord's Day* (Exeter: Paternoster, 1982), especially pp. 205–14.

Martyn, J.L., *Galatians* (New York: Doubleday, 1997).

——, *Theological Issues in the Letters of Paul* (Nashville: Abingdon, 1997).

Moo, D., *The Epistle to the Romans* (Grand Rapids: Eerdmans, 1996).

Motyer, S., *Your Father the Devil?* (Carlisle: Paternoster, 1997).

Sanders, E.P., *Judaism: Practice and Belief 63 BCE–66 CE* (London: SCM, 1992).

Segovia, F.F., 'The Journey(s) of the Word of God: A Reading of the Plot of the Fourth Gospel', *Semeia*, 53 (1991), 23–54.

Stranahan, B.P., 'Bunyan and the Epistle to the Hebrews', *Studies in Philology*, 79 (1982), 279–96.

Walker, P.W.L., *Jesus and the Holy City. New Testament Perspectives on Jerusalem* (Grand Rapids: Eerdmans, 1996).

Weston, J., 'Live the Holy Land dream', *Church Times*, 29 October 1999.

Wright, N.T., *Jesus and the Victory of God* (London: SPCK, 1996).

——, *The Way of the Lord: Christian Pilgrimage Today* (London: SPCK, 1999).

Yee, G.A., *Jewish Feasts and the Gospel of John* (Wilmington, DE: Michael Glazier, 1989).

CHAPTER 4

Paul and Pilgrimage

Steve Motyer

Was Paul a 'Pilgrim'?

In Acts 20:16, Luke presents us with a picture of Paul not taking the opportunity to revisit Ephesus, which he had left the previous year and where doubtless he had many friends, because 'he was eager to be in Jerusalem, if possible, on the day of Pentecost'. *Why was he so eager?* To sharpen the question in terms of the interest of this book, we could ask, 'Was he a pilgrim, hurrying for the same kind of reasons that always make pilgrims hurry – impelled by a combined sense of the sacred *moment* (Pentecost) occurring in the sacred *place* (Jerusalem, the temple)?'[1]

Luke himself offers us few clues. Did he want us to believe that Paul genuinely wanted to celebrate Pentecost in Jerusalem?[2] Or that he was rushing to seize a priceless evangelistic opportunity, hoping at last to see his testimony bear fruit in the city of his youth?[3] Or is it simply a matter of the impulsion of the Spirit and Paul's obedience to the Spirit's leading, so that the reference to Pentecost is just a matter of *date*: Paul wants to be in Jerusalem early in the year because he hopes to travel west again, as far as Rome, before the travelling season ends (see Acts 19:21)? In fact, Luke seems uninterested in whether Paul arrived in time for Pentecost or not. He does not tell us.[4]

We must widen the picture, and ask whether evidence from Paul's letters can help us. But, rather than ask generally about Paul's attitude to Jewish festivals, we will focus on his view of Jerusalem as the *centre* at which the three annual pilgrim festivals took place. The 'standard' view at the moment, very ably represented in this volume by Andrew Lincoln, holds that, for Paul, the earthly Jerusalem had ceased to have any 'spiritual' significance, because 'sacred space' has been redefined around the *person* of Christ. I shall suggest that, while this is true, this view needs to be nuanced in order to take full account of Paul's situation as apostle to the Gentiles in the 'interim' period while God restrains his judgment on Israel.

More of this anon! Let us first enquire about a feature of Paul's ministry about which Luke is strangely silent, namely the collection for the 'poor saints in Jerusalem' (Rom.15:26). The evidence of the letters suggests that, on the Acts 20 journey to Jerusalem, Paul was accompanied by the representatives of the contributing churches (IICor.8:23, cf. Acts 20:4) and was bearing the money that he had laboriously collected from the churches in Achaia, Macedonia and possibly also Asia and Galatia,[5] over a period of some years. James Dunn (1996, p.269) finds the reason for his haste in this: 'there could have been no more appropriate time than the feast of Pentecost to offer the firstfruits of the Gentile mission in Jerusalem (the collection) and to acknowledge to Jerusalem the debt which Gentile experience of the Spirit owed (Rom.15:16, 27).' Pentecost, we remind ourselves, was the festival of the first-fruits, an image applied potently to the collection by others besides Dunn,[6] though not by Paul.

Is Dunn right to use sacrificial terminology in this way? 'Pilgrimage' would certainly be an appropriate word to use, if the collection is in some sense an 'offering', like the first-fruits. Paul uses sacrificial language of his ministry in Romans 15:16, where he calls it his 'priestly service' rendered 'so that the offering of the Gentiles might be acceptable'. The 'offering' here is not the collection, but when he mentions the collection later in the same passage he uses the same word in asking the Romans to pray that his 'ministry to Jerusalem' might be 'acceptable' to the church there (15:31).[7] Here 'Jerusalem' may, of course, be a metonym for 'the Jerusalem church', but, even if so, Paul has chosen to use an expression redolent with pilgrim motivation.

Paul's favourite word for describing the collection, 'fellowship' (Greek κοινωνια),[8] does not have sacrificial connotations, and in his long passage on the collection (IICorinthians 8–9) he makes no prominent use of sacrificial language. However he calls it 'the ministry of this priestly service' in II Corinthians 9:12, and uses the cognate verb 'to render priestly service' (Greek λειτουργειν) of the collection in Romans 15:27. Luke concurs, in his single oblique reference to the collection in Acts 24:17, where Paul says 'After some years I came to bring alms to my nation and to offer sacrifices'. The giving of alms and the offering of sacrifices are the twin signals of devoted worship, and both would be zealously undertaken by pilgrims from the Diaspora to the major festivals in Jerusalem. Paul fits the model.

Paul was doubtless thinking of this offering metaphorically: the presentation of the first-fruits of the Gospel from among the Gentiles, for the good of the poor in Jerusalem. But we can fill out the picture a little, with the help of Johannes Munck. He has won general acceptance for his view that Paul's collection visit to Jerusalem was a conscious fulfilment of the prophecies of the pilgrimage of the nations to Zion.[9] Munck emphasized that the group accompanying Paul was bigger than necessary just to transport the collection. They were meant to represent the nations, converted in fulfilment of prophecy. This is the 'magnification' of his ministry by which Paul seeks to 'save some' of his fellow-Jews (Rom.11:13–14). Paul seized every opportunity to display the glory of God in the face of Christ, and expected his company of saved Gentiles to cause a stir.[10]

It seems not inappropriate, therefore, to conclude with Dunn that Paul saw the collection as an 'offering', to be presented not just to the church in Jerusalem, but *in* Jerusalem, and in some sense *to* Jerusalem, with the aim of 'provoking Israel to jealousy' (cf. Rom.11:14). But this raises a vital question for us. Is there a *theology of Jerusalem* implicit in this that might found a theology of pilgrimage for us today? We need to ask exactly why *Jerusalem* was the vital place for Paul to deliver this 'offering', and whether the reasons that impelled him could or should still apply to Christian 'pilgrims' today.

Jerusalem in Paul's Theology

F.F. Bruce argues for straight continuity between Old and New Testaments in this respect. The special covenant role of Jerusalem, he argues, has devolved onto the church there, so that 'the geographical Jerusalem is for Paul the metropolis on earth of the new Israel in the sense that the people of God there constitute the mother-church of all believers'.[11] So, yes, indeed, the collection visit is the fulfilment of the prophetic expectation of the ingathering of the Gentiles to Jerusalem;[12] and when Paul describes 'the present Jerusalem' as 'in slavery with her children' (Gal.4:25), he is attacking not the city but the Jewish religion. His relationship with the Jerusalem church and its leadership was tense and difficult, particularly because he disagreed with the ruling of the Acts 15 Council;[13] yet Paul knew that he could not dissociate himself from them, for 'Jerusalem filled an important role in Paul's eschatological thinking. Not only was the Gentile mission to be, in the purpose of God, the precursor of Israel's salvation; Jerusalem was to be the place from which this crowning phase of the salvation of mankind would be displayed'. Paul was looking forward to the appearance of the Deliverer out of Zion (Rom.11:26), and so 'not only did the Gospel first go out into all the world from Jerusalem; Jerusalem ... would be the scene of its glorious consummation'.[14]

It is not difficult to supply background for this in prophetic texts from the Old Testament and intertestamental period, which emphasize the central role of Jerusalem in God's plan for the world. The vision of the exalted Zion to which the nations stream in Isaiah 2:2–4 (cf. Mic.4:2–4) is translated into descriptions of Jerusalem as 'in the centre of the nations' (Ezek.5:5) and as 'the navel of the earth' (Ezek.38:12). The theology behind such descriptions is vividly alive in (for example) Jub.31:11–20; Pss.Sol.17:30–31; Sib.Or.3:702–31, 5:414–33; IEnoch26:1–27:5; IIApoc.Bar.71–3. According to this view, Paul's conversion made little difference to this theology. He continued to believe that Jerusalem is the covenant 'home page' from which God operates his plan for the world, even though the Gospel has gone out to all flesh, and Jews and Gentiles are now equal within the people of God.

If true, this would have very significant implications for Christians today. Faithfulness to this Paul would mean regarding Gentile Christian pilgrimage to Jerusalem as a specific and unique kind of self-offering, or self-presentation before God, in fulfilment of the Scriptural expectation of the 'pilgrimage of the

nations', and in anticipation of the glorious consummation which will be
centred in Jerusalem and from there embrace the whole world. Christians could
regard the example of Paul, hurrying to Jerusalem for Pentecost, as one for
direct emulation today, even if they might also believe that time has robbed the
Jerusalem church of its role as a functioning 'mother-church' of world
Christianity.

But this view has been strongly criticized. W.D. Davies[15] leads the charge,
followed more recently by Tom Wright,[16] Peter Walker[17] and by Andrew
Lincoln in this volume. Davies argued that Paul's view of Jerusalem cannot be
separated from his view of the law, the land, the temple and (underlying them
all) the covenant with Israel, and that in each case Christ replaces the particular
with the universal. As Davies puts it,

> The logic of Paul's understanding of Abraham and his personalization of
> the fulfilment of the promise 'in Christ' demanded the deterritorializing of
> the promise. Salvation was not now bound to the Jewish people centred in
> the land and living according to the Law: it was 'located' not in a place but
> in persons in whom grace and faith had their writ ... In the Christological
> logic of Paul, the land, like the Law, particular and provisional, had
> become irrelevant.[18]

Davies argues that Paul did not carry through this logic with consistency.
There is some evidence that his thought developed between the earlier and
later letters, he suggests, so that gradually his 'apocalyptic geography' became
less focused on Jerusalem, and more simply on Christ as the living Lord,
though Romans 11:26 is a blip within this development, for here Paul clearly
expects, Davies argues, that the Parousia will take place in Jerusalem, and
salvation for Israel will issue from that event. But this is out of line with the
main thrust of his theology, in which 'he had in principle broken with the
land'.[19]

But Wright and Walker do not accept that Romans 11:26 is a blip,
inconsistent with Paul's fundamental thinking. They both argue that 'the
Deliverer will come from Zion', quoted from Isaiah 59:20, is referred by Paul
not to the Parousia, but to the *first* coming of Christ.[20] Thus, in line with his
application of other Isaiah texts to himself,[21] Paul is able to find his Gentile
mission prophesied in Isaiah, and in particular to find in Isaiah 59:20 a verse
which neatly coordinates the mission to the Gentiles ('the Deliverer will come
from Zion') with the salvation of Israel ('I will turn ungodliness from Jacob') in
just the way he wants to assert the connection between them.

Granted this re-reading of Romans 11:26, which has much to commend it,[22]
it is possible for Wright and Walker to read Paul consistently in line with the
fundamental 'logic' discerned by Davies. Christ replaces the Torah: he is its
'end' (Rom.10:4), and the one in whom all God's promises receive their 'yes'
(IICor.1:20). Christ becomes the location of the glory of God (IICor.4:6, etc.),

the 'seed' in whom the Abrahamic promises find their fulfilment (Gal.3:15–18); and so 'in Christ' Gentiles become the seed of Abraham (Gal.3:29), inheriting the promised blessing, which is the gift of the Spirit (Gal.3:14). Consequently the church, indwelt by the Spirit, is now the temple: Wright emphasizes the 'immense change' that has taken place in Paul's thinking, that he could apply the image of 'temple' to the church, and indeed to individual Christians, within 25 years of the crucifixion, and while the Jerusalem Temple was still standing (ICor.3:16, 6:19). This simply underlines that 'the earthly Jerusalem was no longer of any spiritual significance' for Paul.[23]

Wright and Walker, like Lincoln, both develop this perspective out of a consideration of the single text where Paul clearly expresses a judgment about Jerusalem (Gal.4:21–31).[24] They build upon an influential article by C.K. Barrett,[25] which argues that Paul is here engaging with and reversing the viewpoint of his opponents, the Judaisers: whereas they were putting pressure on the Gentile Galatians to submit to the authority of Jerusalem and to commit themselves to obeying the law, Paul insists that the champions of the law, and of Jerusalem, are *not* the legitimate children of Abraham. The heirs of Abraham, through Isaac, are those who *resist* adherence to 'the present Jerusalem' because they belong already to 'the Jerusalem above'. This is radical thinking, indeed.

Walker also surveys Paul's quotations of 'Zion' passages, and shows how 'in all these instances Paul was taking verses which originally had spoken of a specific work of God in and for Jerusalem and was applying them to God's work in the gospel'.[26] Paul clearly believed that the blessings promised to 'Zion' were being poured out *now*, through his ministry among the Gentiles. He even takes the famous 'new covenant' passage in Jeremiah 31:31–4 – which was of course a prophecy of the spiritual restoration of *Israel* – and claims its fulfilment through the transformation of the *Gentile Corinthians* (IICor.3:3). Walker argues that Jerusalem was significant for Paul just as the starting-point of the Gospel (Rom.9:33, 15:19); but it had lost any significance for the future. His Gentile converts needed to acknowledge their debt to 'Zion', but as a city Jerusalem held no special significance for them. The collection, therefore, was simply a way of making indebtedness concrete in an 'ecumenical' gesture aimed at securing the practical unity of Jewish and Gentile churches.[27]

There are thus powerful arguments securing this overall view of Paul and his attitude towards Jerusalem. We may add that Paul nowhere tells his Gentile churches to pray for Israel, nowhere encourages a mass pilgrimage to Zion for one of the festivals, nowhere tells them that, as the 'seed' of Abraham in Christ, they are stake-holders in the Land – and of course tells them that they are 'not under law, but under grace' (Rom.6:15).

Lincoln suggests that this view of Paul does not yield any *theology* of pilgrimage for today. Because earthly 'sacred space' no longer exists for

Christians, our journey of faith is *into Christ*; and while that journey might take us past many helpful locations to encourage and inform us, we are not *required* to visit any of them, because 'our citizenship is in heaven' (Phil.3:20). As an overall perspective, this is undoubtedly right. And yet we are still left with the puzzle of Paul's journey to Jerusalem, and the sacrificial language he uses of it. Asked 'to remember the poor' (Gal.2:10), why did he focus on the poor of Jerusalem (as opposed to the poor of Judea, or Samaria, or Antioch) and devote so much effort to raising the collection? If part of the 'agenda' of the collection was to reinforce the unity of Jews and Gentiles in the church, why did he achieve this through a collection for *Jerusalem* rather than through something more widespread, focused on the actual distribution of Jews in the Diaspora?

Jerusalem as Paul's *conscious starting-point* seems clear from his remarkable statement in Romans 15:19 that he had 'fulfilled' the Gospel of Christ from Jerusalem as far as Illyricum. He actually began his missionary journeys, of course, from Antioch in Syria, and so this reference to Jerusalem is theological rather than autobiographical. The gospel started from Jerusalem, even though Paul did not. But is Jerusalem really only a starting-point?

At this point we turn to a much-neglected text highly relevant to our theme, and ask what impact it has on our discussion if we rescue it from neglect and let it play a full role in shaping our understanding of Paul's eschatology. The remarkable thing about this text is that it clearly assigns an eschatological role to Jerusalem, and if we take it seriously we will have to allow that the earthly Jerusalem had not lost all significance for Paul.

The Man of Lawlessness and the Temple

The text is IIThessalonians 2:3–12, where Paul predicts the appearance of 'the man of lawlessness' in 'the temple of God', where he will perform signs and wonders to deceive people. The appearance of this figure is currently 'restrained' by something which Paul describes using both a neuter and a masculine participle (2:6–7). But this 'lawless one' will then be swept away by the Lord Jesus at his Parousia, 'by the Spirit of his mouth' (2:8). Here alone in Paul (if Romans 11:26 is not referred to the Parousia), the Parousia takes place in Jerusalem, as the climax of a series of end-time events.

The reasons for the neglect of this passage are threefold: (a) the Pauline authorship of IIThessalonians has been widely doubted, (b) the reference to the temple has been widely interpreted as symbolic, or (c) this passage has been taken to represent an early, highly apocalyptic phase in Paul's eschatological thinking, which happily he left behind in his later letters. We must briefly counteract each of these reasons for not allowing this passage to exert an impact on our understanding of Paul's eschatology.

Authorship

The strongest arguments against Pauline authorship have always been that the eschatology of IIThessalonians is incompatible with that of IThessalonians, and more widely that the relationship between the two letters makes common authorship impossible.[28] However neither of these arguments is particularly strong. In both letters Paul is reminding his readers of elements of teaching given to them in person, and in both cases he chooses elements which relate to particular needs: in IThessalonians, to the problem of death prior to the Parousia; in IIThessalonians, to the rumour that 'the day of the Lord has [already] come' (2:2). The fact that he describes the Parousia as coming 'like a thief in the night' in IThessalonians 5:2 is not incompatible with the description of events that must take place first (the coming of the man of lawlessness and so on),[29] for, as several scholars now note, both passages show clear evidence of dependence upon the synoptic apocalypse, where these ideas occur together; and, as Larry Kreitzer comments, 'such diversity of detail and schematization is typical' of apocalyptic texts.[30]

The close relationship between the two letters does not in itself require pseudonymity: merely that IIThessalonians was written quite soon after IThessalonians, in response to the rumour mentioned in 2:1–2. On the positive side, it is surely *unlikely* (we can say no more) that a pseudonymous letter could credibly contain such a direct attack on pseudonymous letters (2:2); and *likely* that a pseudonymous author (a) would have ensured that the vital sentence in 2:3–4 did not contain a serious grammatical ellipse, leaving out the main clause, (b) would have made the identity of 'the Restrainer' (person or thing) more obvious, and (c) would have made the vital statement in 2:7b less syntactically odd. These oddities are really only comprehensible if Paul had already explained what he meant ('you know what is restraining him', 2:6), and so did not need to spell it out.

All in all there seems to be at least a fighting chance that IIThessalonians is Pauline. A canonical approach to the interpretation of Paul will in any case wish to take IIThessalonians seriously, as part of the anatomy of the canonical Paul, and to ask how he looks with this text drawn into the picture.

The Temple Reference (2:4)

Scholars who dispute Pauline authorship have tended to interpret the reference as literal,[31] while vice versa those who assert Pauline authorship are inclined to read it symbolically, sometimes with extraordinary glosses. The reason for this becomes explicit with Marshall, who comments that 'if we accept the Pauline authorship of the passage, we are faced by the fact that the prophecy was not fulfilled', so 'other possibilities than a literal reference to the pre-AD70 temple must be investigated'.[32] Marshall therefore argues that Paul is writing 'metaphorically and typologically ... to express the opposition of evil to God ... the reality and menace of the power of evil which attempts to deny the reality and power of God'.[33]

But surely we have here a literal reference to the Jerusalem temple. The verb 'to sit', expressing occupation rather than assault (2:4), makes it very difficult to understand the 'temple' as either the church or the heavenly temple; and the background allusions both to Antiochus Epiphanes in Daniel 11:36 and to the synoptic apocalypse (of which more anon) make it certain, I suggest, that Paul has the Jerusalem temple in mind.

We must recognize, however, the fascinating problem that this causes. Wanamaker expresses it sharply: 'The passage can no longer be understood as valid, since the Temple was destroyed in AD70 without the manifestation of the person of lawlessness or the return of Christ occurring.'[34] But how should we handle this, theologically and hermeneutically? We will consider this below.

Development in Paul's Thinking

If Paul's eschatology developed substantially during the writing of the letters, then it might be right to set this early view aside in favour of his later, less geographically focused view.[35] The problem with this is that the collection project spanned possibly seven or eight years of Paul's ministry, probably including the writing of I and II Thessalonians, and Paul shows no evidence of flagging in zeal for it, though his churches clearly did. Whatever 'Jerusalem theology' he had, it must have remained more or less constant throughout this period. Development is always a tricky proposal to sustain, in any area of Paul's theology, because of the occasional nature of the letters. It may be that Paul's expectation of personal experience of the Parousia faded as he grew older. But that should better be described as a change in outlook or perspective, than as a change in fundamental theology. Clearly his attitude to the collection remained constant, and so we may presume that his 'Jerusalem theology' did also.

Let us then adopt as a working hypothesis the view that there is in the Pauline corpus an unambiguous statement linking the Parousia to Jerusalem, in connection with the destruction of an eschatological figure of evil in the temple. What effect does this have on our overall understanding of Paul's attitude towards Jerusalem within his eschatology? And what effect might this have on our attitude towards Jerusalem today, thinking of it particularly as a focus of Christian pilgrimage?

To answer these questions we must first ask what exactly Paul was expecting, and why he believed this about Jerusalem's future. Here the allusive (elusive) nature of his language in IIThessalonians 2:5–7 is a particular problem for us (though not, presumably, for the Thessalonians). However, despair is not in order.[36] It is possible to reconstruct more fully what Paul had earlier taught in

Thessalonica, and his reasons for teaching it, by taking seriously what commentators have too much ignored, namely the way in which this teaching rests upon the synoptic apocalypse recorded in Mark 13 and Matthew 24. This dependence is well noted, for instance, by Beasley-Murray[37] and by Wenham,[38] but the theological significance of it for our understanding of Paul has yet to be fully explored, I believe. Wenham offers a detailed study in tradition-history, arguing that a close comparison of I and II Thessalonians with the synoptic material suggests that Paul knew the material well in substance, although the level of verbal allusion is not extensive.

What Paul was expecting, therefore, and what he taught the Thessalonians to expect, was *the fulfilment of Jesus' predictions about Jerusalem*: the destruction of the Temple, heralded by the appearance of 'the abomination of desolation', by the 'deception' of many, and by great suffering; and then the 'coming' of the Son of Man, whom Paul identifies with Jesus (IIThessalonians 2:8). He was clearly aware of the background to Jesus' teaching in Daniel, because his picture of the 'man of lawlessness' in IIThessalonians 2:4 draws on the same 'abomination of desolation' passage in Daniel 11:31–6. This is doubtless why he has conflated the many 'false messiahs and false prophets' in Mark 13:22 into a single figure performing signs to deceive (IIThess.2:9–10).

Beasley-Murray suggests that IThessalonians 4:15–17 is 'closer to the spirit of the [synoptic] discourse' than IIThessalonians 2.[39] But it seems more appropriate to suggest the reverse, because IIThessalonians retains (a) the focus on the Jerusalem temple, (b) the overall structure around the things that must happen first before the End comes, (c) the interest in 'testimony' and the preaching of the Gospel (Mark 13:9, cf. IIThess.1:10, 2:10, 3:1), (d) the 'deception' motif, associated with signs and wonders, and (e) the reworking of the Daniel 11 prophecy into a further eschatological expectation, beyond Antiochus Epiphanes.[40] These elements are all absent from IThessalonians.

Paul thus retains a focus on Jerusalem, because *that is what he hears from Jesus*. Therefore it is not sufficient simply to loosen Paul from Jerusalem and to say that it has lost all significance for him, or that it is only significant as the *starting-point* of the Gospel. Clearly, in some sense, it still sits on the horizon of his expectations. Stuhlmacher (1989) sees direct lines of continuity between Jesus and Paul in this respect: they both, he suggests, work within the 'Zion' tradition in which Jerusalem remains 'the end-time location of the realisation of God's promises of salvation, in line with Isaiah 54:10'.[41] Jesus saw himself as the messianic Son of Man, called not just to be worshipped and served as in Daniel 7:13, but first to give himself as a ransom for many (Mark 10:45), and then to come as the agent of the judgment on Israel and Jerusalem which he himself had pronounced (Matt.23:37–9, Mark 13:26) – but without abandoning the belief that 'Zion is ... the future centre of God's saved community of all believers'.[42]

Arguments will surround Stuhlmacher's reconstruction of Jesus' messianic self-consciousness. But this, I contend, is substantially how *Paul* received the Jesus-tradition as represented in the synoptic apocalypse. The coming of the Son of Man is to *Jerusalem* (Mark 13:26), and the elect are gathered to him there (Mark 13:27), so that the final drama of judgment and salvation takes place there.

Three questions are raised at this point, which will occupy us for the rest of this chapter. First, how can we fit IIThessalonians 2 into the rest of Paul? All his *other* references to the return of Christ – even in IThessalonians 4:15–17 – do not (apparently) tie it to Jerusalem, but give it *universal* significance and effect. Second, what effect does the *non-fulfilment* of Paul's expectation have on this theology? Jerusalem and the temple were certainly destroyed, by the Romans in 70AD, some five years after Paul's death; but the Parousia did not take place then as he envisaged. How would Paul have responded to this, had he lived a little longer? In what ways would his view of Jerusalem have been affected? Finally, what are the implications of all this for pilgrimage today?

We will think about each of these questions in turn.

Jerusalem in Paul's Eschatology

If the teaching now recorded in Mark 13, Matthew 24 and Luke 21 gave the framework to Paul's eschatology, then Jerusalem must have loomed large on his eschatological horizon. But is that what we really find in his writings? He makes no reference to Jerusalem in IThessalonians 4, even though he draws there also on the Gospel material. He pictures the Lord descending from heaven (4:16), but seems to imply that his 'presence' (Greek παρουσια, 4:15[43]) will somehow be for all. 'We who are left' (presumably wherever 'we' are) 'will be caught up into the air to meet the Lord' (4:17). However the word used for 'meeting' here connotes the delegation of city officials who meet a visiting dignitary outside the city, in order to accompany him back through the gates, as illustrated by Acts 28:15, where the same expression is used.[44] Does this imply that Paul envisages a *particular place* to which Jesus returns? If so, IIThessalonians 2 supplies the name of the place.

But did he really believe that 'we', together with all 'the dead in Christ', would somehow be gathered to join Christ in the air above Jerusalem, so as to be 'always with the Lord' *there*? Mark 13:27 envisages the 'gathering' of the elect to the Son of Man, and Paul uses the same Greek word in IIThessalonians 2:1. Such a 'gathering' has a clear Old Testament background, and Zion/Jerusalem is always the gathering-point, as we saw above when we touched on the 'pilgrimage of the nations' tradition.[45] But does it really make sense to gloss IThessalonians 4:16 with 'in Jerusalem'?

One solution to this conundrum is suggested by Stuhlmacher,[46] on the basis of the 'stages' outlined by Paul in ICorinthians 15:23–8. Stage One is Jesus' resurrection, which functions as 'firstfruits' to Stage Two, the resurrection of 'those who belong to Christ, at his Parousia' (15:23). But there is apparently then a Stage Three: 'then [comes] the End, when he hands over the Kingdom to God his Father' (15:24) and then 15:24–8 describes the elements involved in this 'handing-over', which includes the defeat of all enemies, including death. Stuhlmacher suggests that other elements should be included in this composite 'End', notably the salvation of all Israel (Rom.11:26) and the judgment of the *cosmos* and the fallen angels by the saints (ICorinthians 6:2–3). If the End is an extended process, for Paul, rather than a single event, presumably it would allow time for believers (dead and alive) to be gathered to the Returned Lord at Jerusalem.

Stuhlmacher does not emphasize the 'at Jerusalem' element of the picture, but then neither, it must be said, does Paul. But Stuhlmacher maintains that Paul drew upon a 'Zion' theology that qualifies the negative view of the earthly Jerusalem expressed in Galatians 4:25. The stone is laid 'in Zion' (Rom.9:33), and it is 'from Zion' that the Redeemer comes (Rom.11:26). In all this, he suggests, Paul was thinking within an eschatological–apocalyptic framework which we also meet in Revelation 21–2. So 'the Redeemer will come from the heavenly Jerusalem, which at the End of the days will descend upon Zion, raised to become the Mountain of God'.[47] Presumably, on this view, the returning Lord begins a *process* which leads to the full establishment of the Kingdom of Zion and the descent of the heavenly Jerusalem onto its earthly counterpart.

On the other hand, we must bear in mind the point made above about the 'Zion' texts which Paul quotes: namely, that he clearly envisages their fulfilment *now*, even through the success of his ministry among the *Gentiles*. He does not refer them on, to a future, more literal, fulfilment. And we must also bear in mind the extent to which he believed that the earthly Jerusalem *stands under judgment* for its rebellion against God: this is a much-neglected feature of the argument of Romans 9–11. The quotation of Psalm 69:23–4 in Romans 11:9–10, with its horrible climax, 'bend their backs for ever!', reminds us of the equally awful judgment Paul expresses in IThessalonians 2:16, that 'the wrath of God has come with final force' upon the Judean Jews who have so passionately opposed the Gospel.[48] Clearly, whatever he may (or may not) have believed about the *restoration* of Jerusalem/Zion, it was the *destruction* of the city under God's judgment (and in fulfilment of Jesus' prophecy) which he feared.

He may have been helped by the mental world-map which Scott discovers for Paul.[49] Scott seeks to discover the geographical shape of the term 'the nations' (or 'Gentiles': Greek 'ta ethne'), so important for Paul's sense of missionary call. He suggests that Paul worked with the standard Jewish geography based on the table of nations in Genesis 10, which saw the world as centred on Jerusalem and divided into three broad areas corresponding to the three sons of Noah: the African nations were descended from Ham, nations to the east from Shem, and Asia Minor and Europe from Japheth. At the apostolic conference reported in Galatians 2:9, Scott suggests (1995, pp.149–57), Paul accepted a commission to the Japhethite nations, to the west of Jerusalem, while Peter committed himself to the Shemite area where the Jewish population was great.

In this geography Jerusalem is set 'in the middle of the nations' (Ezek.5:5) and is 'the navel of the earth' (Ezek.38:12). We may therefore suggest that, for Paul, in principle *a return of the Lord to Jerusalem would be a universal return, impinging upon the whole world.* Geography and theology are interlocked. Paul thinks globally, within the worldview of Psalm 2: when the King sits on Zion's holy hill, the whole world is called to account.

Paul did not know when this would happen. We push him too far, I suggest, if we try to systematize his various statements into a strictly ordered chronology of end-time events, bringing Parousia, resurrection, judgment and re-creation into a timetable.[50] But Jesus' words must have burned in him, impelling him forward with a sense of indebtedness to the nations: 'Truly I tell you, this generation will not pass away until all these things take place ... first the gospel must be preached to all nations' (Mark 13:30, 10). He must have thought of himself as living in 'an odd interim period'[51] between the pronouncement and the execution of judgment, watching for signs of the appearance of 'the lawless one' in Jerusalem. The excitement and turmoil created by the emperor Gaius' threat to erect a statue of himself in the temple in 40AD may have created a *frisson* for Paul, if he already had this eschatology in place.[52] Wenham[53] further suggests that the rioting among the Jews in Rome in 49AD, resulting in their expulsion by Claudius, and the contemporaneous troubles in Jerusalem which led to the deaths and execution of thousands by the Roman governor Cumanus, would have confirmed Paul's view that 'wrath has finally come upon the Jews' (IThess.2:16).[54] We may thus concur with Walker's conclusion that 'If [Paul] had lived to witness AD70 and the end of the Temple, he would not have been surprised, for these events vindicated his theology'.[55]

So was Paul 'on pilgrimage' to Jerusalem in Acts 20:16? We are in a position now at least to speculate about his state of mind. He believes that Jerusalem will be the scene of the final eschatological showdown between the powers of evil (the 'abomination of desolation') and the returning Lord Jesus. He knows that Israel currently stands under judgment for her rejection of the Messiah. He longs to avert this judgment, even if the manifestation of the 'man of lawlessness' is inevitable. He is impelled, too, by a burning passion to 'preach the gospel to all nations' before the Son of Man comes. His own commission is to the Gentile Japhethite nations in the west, but he feels too a great responsibility for his own 'flesh'. So he travels to Jerusalem, in fulfilment of the prophetic vision of the eschatological pilgrimage of the nations to Zion, hoping thereby to bring about a great revival there, a 'turning to the Lord' (II Corinthians 3:16). This makes him a very unusual pilgrim, in current terms. His situation is so particular, that we might suggest – to anticipate our third question below – that we cannot use this 'pilgrimage' as a model for today.

For we stand, inevitably, *on the other side* of the great event on Paul's horizon. As Walker says, he would not have been surprised (though *deeply* saddened) by the destruction of the temple ten or eleven years after his 'collection' visit. But he would have been very surprised (and here we part company with Walker) that the Parousia and the judgment of the nations did not take place at the same time.[56] How can we cope with this, hermeneutically and theologically?

Debating with Paul About 70AD

This is tricky. We have to ask what Paul *would have* said, had he lived through the Jewish war (67–73AD) and realized that he would have to reinterpret Jesus' eschatological discourse, separating the coming of the Son of Man from the great tribulation. I make four suggestions about his reaction.

Yes to the 'Abomination' in 70AD

Would Paul think that his 'man of lawlessness' expectation had been fulfilled? I suggest that, like Josephus, he would have identified the corruptions in the temple by the zealots, prior to its fall, as 'the abomination of desolation'. This is a repeated theme of Josephus in books 4–6 of *The Jewish War*. He never uses the phrase 'the abomination of desolation' from Daniel, but uses plenty of other language that amounts to the same thing.[57] Although the events did not involve the appearance of a single 'lawless one', the whole event was so absolutely dreadful, the suffering and destruction so terrible, that surely he would have agreed that the Jerusalem church had acted rightly, in discerning the fulfilment of Jesus' prophecy in the early events of the war, and abandoning Jerusalem for Pella in obedience to Mark 13:14.

More Time for Preaching and Repentance

Paul's eschatology would provide him, I suggest, with a way of coping with the non-appearance of the Parousia. Clearly, he would conclude, the Gospel has not yet been preached to all the nations (Mark 13:10), and therefore the final End cannot yet be. God is allowing more time for the chosen vessels to be called, from Jews and Gentiles alike (Rom.9:24). How merciful of God to provide the world with more space for repentance and faith.

A response to the problem based on Mark 13:10 is more likely, I think, than one based on a radical re-reading of Mark 13:26, the saying about the 'coming' of the Son of Man. What would Paul think of the reading of Mark 13:26 associated now, especially, with R.T. France and N.T. Wright, which argues that the coming of the Son of Man (based on Daniel 7:13–14) is *to God*, to receive dominion, rather than *to earth*, and that Jesus expected this 'coming' to be fulfilled simply in the judgment on the temple which is the referent of the whole discourse?[58] The phrase 'by the appearance of his coming' (IIThess.2:8) makes it clear that Paul did not read Mark 13:26 as France and Wright suggest that Jesus intended it. He expected an appearing of the currently unseen Lord, a 'coming' equivalent to, and in response to, the 'coming' of the lawless one (IIThess.2:9). And one has to say that the use of 'see' in Mark 13:26 ('Then will they see the Son of Man') gives Paul the interpretative edge over France and Wright.

Rather, Mark 13:10 implicitly allows the 'coming of the Son of Man' (for Paul: 'the day of the Lord'[59]) to be separated from the judgment upon Jerusalem, although they are clearly linked in Mark 13 as it stands. It is interesting that the opening question in the Matthean version (Matthew 24:3) separates the two in a way which then shapes the reading of the whole discourse. (But presumably this was not part of the tradition as received by Paul.) So Paul would feel no pressure to continue to identify them by reinterpreting the Parousia to fit the events which had actually occurred. The preaching of the Gospel still has a *terminus ad quem*. So (I contend) even after the destruction of Jerusalem and of the temple, Paul would continue to believe in a Parousia of Christ for universal judgment and salvation.

The Parousia not at Jerusalem

But would Paul continue to believe that the Parousia of Christ would take place at Jerusalem? As we have seen, Paul's link between them is not strong, even before 70AD. To be a citizen of the heavenly Jerusalem does not *also* mean having a stake in the earthly city. Somehow, the Parousia is already universal for Paul: it will be possible for the Thessalonians *in Thessalonica* to 'strengthen your hearts and be blameless in holiness before our God and Father, at the Parousia of our Lord Jesus with all his holy ones' (IThessalonians 3:13). They do not have to be in Jerusalem for this, even though Paul is here using the language of Zechariah 14:5 which does locate the coming of the Lord in Jerusalem. The pressure within his theology for 'Church-as-temple' to displace Jerusalem is strong and, once judgment had fallen upon the holy city, that displacement would surely become total.

To some extent this depends upon bigger issues, especially whether Paul envisaged a continuing role for the Abrahamic covenant *alongside* Christ. Many have found this in the prediction of the salvation of 'all Israel' on the basis of God's love for 'the fathers' in Romans 11:26–8. But it is clear that, for Paul, the Abrahamic covenant continues in the form of the 'olive tree' (Rom.11:16–24), which consists of Jewish and Gentile 'branches' existing together and equally within one body. There is no *particular* covenant for Israel alongside this joint membership of Christ. And thus it 'fits' to say that all the other covenant distinctives, including the holy city and temple, are similarly subsumed into the 'new creation' which is 'in Christ' (IICor.5:17).

No Re-run of the 'Man of Lawlessness'

This follows on. If, following the judgment of the holy city, 'the temple of God' (IIThess.2:4) exists only in its Christological form, then it seems highly unlikely that Paul would endorse Irenaeus' reading of IIThessalonians 2, which seems to presuppose that the temple will be rebuilt in order to accommodate a literal fulfilment.[60] For the wrath 'to the uttermost' had already come upon Jerusalem (IThess.2:16): how could it be right for the temple to be rebuilt simply so that wrath could be poured out upon it again?

So (paradoxically) I suggest that Paul would eventually reach the position ascribed to him by Wright, Walker and Lincoln – but *after his death*, rather than before. After 70AD everything changed. The earthly Jerusalem has fallen under the predicted judgment. The temple now standing is the church of Jesus Christ, indwelt by the Spirit of God. The Jerusalem to which the Gentile world is summoned is the *heavenly city*, of which we are all citizens (Phil.3:20).

Pauline Pilgrimage Today?

It remains to ask what shape Paul might give to pilgrimage today. Lincoln argues that Pauline theology provides no ground on which pilgrimage can be *required* as a discipline, because 'sacred space' is no more, though it may be *helpful*. So it is open to us to ask how strongly Paul would urge that the 'helpfulness' of pilgrimage should be sought, and on what grounds.

We can ask: if he had lived through the Jewish war, would he have stayed away from the destroyed city? Surely not. But what would have motivated our Paul to travel to Jerusalem? I suggest that four interrelated desires would have led him there, and that these provide the basis for a 'theology of pilgrimage' for today.

The first is *a desire to express grief and sympathy* in the face of such loss and suffering. There is no vindictiveness in Paul's attitude to Israel, even though he expects the judgment of God. His heart would have been torn by the events of the Jewish war, had he lived to see them. The desire to *associate with the pain of others* can be a deeply *Christian* motivation for pilgrimage, as Wright movingly reveals.[61] Since Jerusalem sits at the heart of such conflict still, Christians can link the pain of present conflict with all the pain experienced by Jews through the centuries, including the agonies of the destruction in 70AD, and bear it all in prayer before Christ, especially since much of the pain has been inflicted by Christians. Pilgrimage sites are often centres of pain, either present or remembered, and indeed sites of new pain (Cambodia, Rwanda, Bosnia) can become new focuses of Christian prayer and care, for that very reason.

The second is *a desire to express fellowship with the Jewish Christians still in Judea* seeking to minister to their fellow-Jews. Doubtless this would have motivated Paul strongly. The chapter by Peter Scott in this volume sets this motivation at the heart of a theology of pilgrimage, focusing on the celebration of the Eucharist at the heart of that fellowship. Pilgrims must be much more than tourists, and it is fellowship with the living church in the place of pilgrimage which will mark the difference. Pilgrims will want to associate themselves with that church in its testimony there.

The third desire is *a desire to testify to the Gospel*. Undoubtedly, Paul would have felt that the Good News had powerful relevance for suffering Judaism, with its message that *the temple still stands*, formed now of the people of the Christ, indwelt by the Spirit. This element of 'confession' seems to me to be central to pilgrimage, to all destinations. Pilgrims confess their identification with the memories associated with the place, and thus confess their faith in the Christ manifested *there*. In so doing, they also confess their membership of the people of God who are *identified* by that place, in whatever way each place defines them.

The fourth desire is *a desire to pray for the nations*. Paul was moved by his desire to pray for the nations in the place where the house of prayer for all nations had once stood, where once the nations had been summoned to meet the living God, where the Christ had suffered for the sins of all, and the Holy Spirit had commissioned the church to go into all the world. I think that this, too, would have motivated Paul, as an aspect of the Christian confession appropriate to Jerusalem. And this too applies to all sites of Christian pilgrimage: each summons a particular kind of prayer, but at the heart of that prayer will be the longing that Christ should be glorified throughout the world, that pain should lead to glory, that his word should be believed and his kingdom come. Pilgrims journey to a particular place, therefore, in order definitely to leave again, called to be agents of the Gospel in the world, just as Paul travelled to Jerusalem, in order then to go to Rome.

Notes

1   We must of course agree with Andrew Lincoln that this is *Luke's* Paul, and that Luke consistently presents Paul as respectful towards Jewish observances (see Lincoln's chapter in this volume). But whereas Lincoln doubts the truth of this 'gloss' on Paul, the present chapter will suggest that Luke's picture is not inappropriate. The implications for 'Paul and pilgrimage' are significant, as we shall see.

2   So, for example, Johnson, *Acts*, 355; Larkin, *Acts*, 292f; Neil, *Acts*, 212.

3   So Calvin, *Acts*, 172: Paul was not hurrying 'because the sacredness of the day meant such a lot to him, but because strangers were in the habit of flocking to Jerusalem from all directions for the feast days'.

4   According to Barrett, *Acts*, 960, Stählin maintains that the great crowds present in Jerusalem in Acts 21 and 22 imply that Paul did indeed arrive in time for Pentecost.

5   For a detailed discussion of the participating churches, see Munck, *Paul*, 292–7.

6   So also Nickle, *Collection*, 138.

7   The notion of the 'acceptability' of the sacrifices is fundamental in Leviticus (for example, Lev.19:5–7, 22:19–25), although the term used by Paul does not appear in the LXX of Leviticus.

8   Used, for example, in Rom.15:26; IICor.8:4, 9:13.

9   Munck, *Paul*, 301–5. So also Whiteley, *Paul*, 86–8; Beker, *Paul*, 72 and 379 n.65; Ridderbos, *Paul*, 47 n.13; Dunn, *Theology*, 312, 709. The chapter by Gordon McConville in this volume examines this element of Old Testament expectation.

10 More contentious is Munck's view that Paul expected to precipitate the salvation of 'all Israel' (Rom.11:26) by his arrival in Jerusalem with these tokens of the wealth of the nations. W.D. Davies (*Gospel*, 201–3) and more recently Richard Bell (*Provoked*, 344–6) object to it on the ground that it makes nonsense of Paul's further plans to travel to Rome and then to Spain, after his visit to Jerusalem (Rom.15:23–4): how could he possibly expect the eschatological climax of Romans11:25–7 to occur during his visit to Jerusalem, *and* then to undertake a further extensive missionary journey? To be fair to him, Munck envisaged a massive increase in Gentile mission after the salvation of 'all Israel'. More serious is the objection that, if this was Paul's real agenda and expectation for his Jerusalem journey, it is inexplicable why he never 'comes clean' about it in any of the collection passages, most notably in IICorinthians 8–9 (so Nickle, *Collection*, 140–42).

11 Bruce, 'Jerusalem', 4.

12 Ibid., 23–4.

13 Ibid., 13–14.

14 Ibid., 25.

15 *The Gospel and the Land.*

16 'Jerusalem.'

17 *Jesus and the Holy City*, 113–60.

18 Davies, *Gospel*, 179.

19 Ibid., 220. Davies also lays some emphasis on Rom.9:26, where he argues that Paul's addition of 'there' to the LXX in his quotation of Hos.2:1 points to *Jerusalem* as 'the place' where sons of the living God will be named (pp.195–7). But the LXX text is in fact unclear: one major manuscript (Alexandrinus) has the same text as Paul; and in any case it is not at all clear that the words 'place' and 'there' have a 'plain geographic emphasis' (*Gospel*, 196), rather than (more likely) a metaphorical force.

20 Wright, 'Jerusalem', 66; Walker, *Jesus*, 140–41; *contra* Stuhlmacher, 'Stellung', 141, 154f.

21 Cf. Rom.10:15, 15:21.

22 See Motyer, *Israel*, 153–5; also Holwerda, *Jesus*, 171–5.

23 Wright, 'Jerusalem', 69–70.

24 Wright, 'Jerusalem', 68–9; Walker, *Jesus*, 127–32.

25 'The Allegory'.

26   Walker, *Jesus*, 139. The relevant passages are Rom.9:33 (Is.28:26), Rom.10:13 (Joel 2:32), Rom.10:15 (Isa.52:7), and Rom.11:26 (Is.59:20). We could also mention the quotation of Isa.55:10 in IICor.9:10, in connection with the collection for Jerusalem, but we note that it is *the Corinthians* who will enter into Zion's promised blessing through their participation in the collection, not the Jerusalem church.

27   Walker, *Jesus*, 145f, 151.

28   So, for example, Trilling, *Thessalonicher*, 21–6; Menken, *2 Thessalonians*, 25–43.

29   *Contra* Bailey, 'Who Wrote?', 136; Trilling, *Thessalonicher*, 22.

30   *Jesus and God*, 182.

31   So Trilling, *Thessalonicher*, 86; Menken, *2 Thessalonians*, 107; Townsend, 'II Thessalonians', 236.

32   *Thessalonians*, 191.

33   Ibid., 191–2.

34   *Epistles*, 248.

35   So Davies, op.cit.

36   *Contra* Witherington, *Jesus*, 162, who dismisses the passage from usefulness on this ground: 'the material is necessarily cryptic and no good purpose is served here by engaging in further speculation.'

37   *Jesus and the Future*, 232–4.

38   'Paul and the Synoptic Apocalypse', and *Paul: Follower*, 316–19.

39   Beasley-Murray, *Jesus and the Future*, 233.

40   It seems clear that Daniel 11:30–39 found initial fulfilment in Antiochus Epiphanes, the Syrian king who in 167BC abolished the sacrifices in the Jerusalem temple and attempted to enforce pagan worship there. But in Pss.Sol.17:11 the same language is later used of the Roman general Pompey who entered the Most Holy Place in the temple in 63BC, and then Jesus uses it again with reference to the coming desecration and destruction of the temple.

41   Stuhlmacher, 'Stellung', 155. See also Stulhmacher, 'Eschatology'.

42   Stuhlmacher, 'Stellung', 146.

43   This Greek word is usually translated 'coming', but is closer really to the English word 'presence'. It connotes the arrival and residence of a royal personage. The term 'Parousia' (a transliteration of the Greek) is often used, because no English word suitably covers both 'coming' and 'presence'.

44   So, for example, Marshall, *Thessalonians*, 131.

45   Cf. also Isa.66:19–20; Zech.2:6–12; Deut.30:4–5; Ezek.37:21–8.

46   'Eschatology'.

47   Stuhlmacher, 'Stellung', 155.

48   'With final force' is a paraphrase of the Greek 'eis telos'. NRSV and NIV both render this 'at last', as though Paul has been longing for it to happen. This gives the wrong impression. REB 'for good and all' is better, but sounds vindictive. Paul's point is that God's wrath comes to *final* expression against these rebellious children of Abraham.

49   *Paul and the Nations*.

50   I think Stuhlmacher oversystematizes Paul's eschatology. For instance, victory over the 'principalities and powers' is linked to 'stage 3' in ICor.15:24, but to the Parousia (stage 2) in Rom. 16:20, and to the resurrection (stage 1) in Eph.1:20–21.

51   Wright, 'Jerusalem in the New Testament', 65.

52   Bruce, *History*, 257, suggests that it was this event which prompted the circulation of Jesus' apocalyptic discourse in Christian circles, and that this would have been the referent, for its first readers, of 'the abomination of desolation'.

53   *Paul: Follower*, 300–1.

54   Wenham refers to Josephus, *Ant*.20:105–7; *War* 2:223–31: though wrongly gives the latter reference (*Paul*, 300 n.18) as *War* 11:223–31.

· 55   *Jesus and the Holy City*, 159.

56   Walker maintains (*Jesus*, 159) that Paul 'had separated these two events in his mind'. But he can only maintain this because he has marginalized IIThess.2 from consideration. He suggests (*Jesus*, 135 n.80 and 143 n.109) that Paul's reference to the temple is symbolic (but he does not say of *what*).

57   See the discussion and references given in Bruce, *History*, 382–3 and n.56.

58   France, *Jesus*, 227–39; Wright, *Jesus*, 360–67. Wright comments in passing that the eschatological outlook of IIThess.1–2 is 'profoundly similar' to that of Mark 13 and parallels (*Jesus*, 359 and n.146).

59   For an analysis and discussion of the relationship between the Parousia and 'the Day of the Lord' in Paul, see Kreitzer, *Jesus*, 93–129.

60   Irenaeus, *Adv. Haer.* 5:30:4: he gives as one of the marks of the Antichrist that he will reign for three years and six months, sitting in the temple in Jerusalem, 'and then the Lord will come from heaven in the clouds, sending this man and those who follow him into the lake of fire'. Cf. Marshall, *Thessalonians*, 191.

61   *The Way*.

References

Bailey, J.A., 'Who Wrote II Thessalonians?', *NTS*, 25 (1979), 131–45.

Barrett, C.K., 'The Allegory of Abraham, Sarah and Hagar in the Argument of Galatians', in J. Friedrich *et al.* (eds), *Rechtfertigung. Festschrift für Ernst Käsemann zum 70. Geburtstag* (Tübingen: JCB Mohr, 1976), pp.1–16

——, *The Acts of the Apostles* (Edinburgh: T&T Clark, 1988).

Beasley-Murray, G.R., *Jesus and the Future* (London: Macmillan, 1954).

Beker, J.C., *Paul the Apostle: The Triumph of God in Life and Thought* (Edinburgh: T&T Clark, 1980).

Bell, R.H., *Provoked to Jealousy. The Origin and Purpose of the Jealousy Motif in Romans 9–11*, WUNT 63 (Tübingen: JCB Mohr, 1994).

Bruce, F.F., 'Paul and Jerusalem', *TynBul*, 19 (1968), 3–25.

——, *New Testament History* (New York: Doubleday Anchor, 1972).

Calvin, J., *The Acts of the Apostles*, vol. 2 (Edinburgh: St Andrew Press, 1966).

Davies, W.D., *The Gospel and the Land. Early Christianity and Jewish Territorial Doctrine* (Berkeley: University of California Press, 1974).

Dunn, J.D.G., *The Acts of the Apostles* (London: Epworth Press, 1996).

——, *The Theology of Paul the Apostle* (Edinburgh: T&T Clark, 1998).

France, R.T., *Jesus and the Old Testament* (London: Tyndale Press, 1971).

Holwerda, D.E., *Jesus and Israel. One Covenant or Two?* (Leicester: Apollos, 1995).

Johnson, L.T., *The Acts of the Apostles*, Sacra Pagina 5 (Collegeville, Minnesota: Liturgical Press, 1992).

Kreitzer, L.J., *Jesus and God in Paul's Eschatology*, JSNT Supp. 19 (Sheffield: JSOT Press, 1987).

Larkin, W.J., *Acts*, IVP New Testament Commentary (Downers Grove: IVP, 1995).

Marshall, I.H., *1 & 2 Thessalonians*, New Century Bible (London: Marshalls, 1983).

Menken, M.J.J., *2 Thessalonians* (London: Routledge, 1994).

Motyer, S., *Israel in the Plan of God* (Leicester: IVP, 1989).

Munck, J., *Paul and the Salvation of Mankind* (London: SCM, 1959).

Neil, W., *The Acts of the Apostles*, New Century Bible (London: Marshalls, 1973).

Nickle, K.F., *The Collection. A Study in Paul's Strategy* (London: SCM, 1966).

Ridderbos, H., *Paul: An Outline of his Theology* (Grand Rapids: Eerdmans, 1975).

Scott, James, *Paul and the Nations: The Old Testament and Jewish background of Paul's mission to the nations with special reference to the destination of Galatians* (Tübingen: JCB Mohr, 1995).

Stuhlmacher, P., 'Die Stellung Jesu und des Paulus zu Jerusalem', *ZTK*, 86 (1989), 140–56.

——, 'Eschatology and Hope in Paul', *EQ*, 72 (4) (2000), 315–33.

Townsend, J.T., 'II Thessalonians 2:3–12', *SBLSP*, 19 (1980), 233–50.

Trilling, W. (1994), *Der Zweite Brief an die Thessalonicher*, *EKK* 14 (Neukirchen: Benziger/ Neukirchener Verlag, 1994).

Walker, P.W.L., *Jesus and the Holy City: New Testament Perspectives on Jerusalem* (Grand Rapids: Eerdmans, 1996).

Wanamaker, C.A., *The Epistles to the Thessalonians. A Commentary on the Greek Text*, NIGTC (Grand Rapids: Eerdmans; Carlisle: Paternoster, 1990).

Wenham, D., 'Paul and the Synoptic Apocalypse', in R.T. France and D. Wenham (eds), *Gospel Perspectives. Studies of History and Tradition in the Four Gospels II* (Sheffield: JSOT Press, 1981), pp.345–75.

——, *Paul: Follower of Jesus or Founder of Christianity?* (Grand Rapids: Eerdmans, 1995).

Whiteley, D.E.H., *The Theology of St Paul* (Oxford: Basil Blackwell, 1964).

Witherington, Ben, *Jesus, Paul and the End of the World: A Comparative Study in New Testament Eschatology* (Carlisle: Paternoster, 1992).

Wright, N.T., 'Jerusalem in the New Testament', in P.W.L. Walker (ed.), *Jerusalem Past and Present in the Purposes of God* (Cambridge: Tyndale House, 1992), 53–77.

——, *Jesus and the Victory of God* (London: SPCK, 1996).

——, *The Way of the Lord* (London: SPCK, 1999).

II
HISTORICAL PERSPECTIVES ON PILGRIMAGE

CHAPTER 5

Pilgrimage in the Early Church

Peter Walker

For anyone interested in understanding Christian pilgrimage, it is vital to investigate the practice and beliefs of Christians in the period of the Early Church. We have noted some of these issues within the pages of the New Testament, but what happened next? How did Christians in the first four centuries after Christ deal with this issue of an appropriate attitude towards the biblical sites associated with the life of Jesus? When did 'pilgrimage' begin and what did it mean for those involved? This chapter will provide a historical survey up to around 400AD and then evaluate this material for the task of constructing an appropriate Christian theology of pilgrimage for today.[1]

Throughout this volume at least three different questions are being discussed. They overlap in many ways, but they can also helpfully be distinguished. First, how do Christians view Jerusalem? Is there a peculiar status or sanctity that pertains to this city, the city at the centre of the Biblical narrative? If there is, then this will inevitably fuel the practice of pilgrimage today to this 'holy city'. Secondly, what about the places visited by Jesus himself? Is there something special about the scenes of the Incarnation, those places where, according to Christian orthodoxy, this planet was visited by the Divine Son? Are these 'holy places'? Finally, there is the question relating to other sites and objects of historic interest. How should Christians respond to places that have been significant in Christian faith and history?

We will examine each of these three separate questions in turn. How did the first Christians celebrate the history and geography of the Biblical story while maintaining the spiritual and universal dimensions of their faith? The answer will be found chiefly by noting their attitude to what we now know as the 'Holy Land', but which for them was the Roman province of 'Palestina'.

First, however, a brief reflection on the New Testament material relating to these three questions. As we have seen, the beginnings of some important answers are given to these questions, especially to the first one, relating to Jerusalem. As I have argued extensively elsewhere,[2] there is a conscious reflection by almost all the New Testament writers on the significance of Jerusalem. In their assessment the city is significantly re-evaluated in the light of the coming of Jesus. Confirmed by the momentous events of 70AD (when Jerusalem and its temple were destroyed by the Romans), the apostolic church was launched into the world without a doctrine of a 'holy city'. It functioned without a central geographical centre, and was hesitant as to whether Jerusalem would ever again play a significant role in God's purposes.

As for the other two questions, the New Testament is fairly silent. The New Testament writers are, of course, interested in the historicity of the Gospel events and affirm the enormous truth of the Incarnation. Yet there is no suggestion that the places associated with these events were held in especial regard. But this may be an argument from silence. On the one hand, the idea that New Testament believers were so 'heavenly-minded' (or focused on the return of Jesus) that they had no interest at all in earthly matters related to recent history should be dismissed as a caricature. On the other hand, there is little suggestion of any nascent cult of pilgrimage to the sites associated with Jesus and the apostles. Did Paul, when in Jerusalem, make a prayerful visit to Golgotha? Was Luke touched at a devotional level by being in Jerusalem and Caesarea (Acts 22–6)? We simply do not know.

Perhaps the best evidence we have for such a valuing of places comes in the traditions relating to the apostles' deaths. The burial places of Peter, Paul and John are treasured. The Jewish *Lives of the Prophets* reveals that there was a Jewish tradition of visiting the tombs of venerable ancients; the early Christians may have followed in this tradition. So, for example, according to our chief church historian, Eusebius of Caesarea (c.260–339), the bones of Polycarp (martyred in 156AD) were preserved by local Christians and thereafter gave rise to an annual service of remembrance.[3]

But in general the New Testament lays down some important principles concerning true worship which militate against too much focus on places for religious reasons. For example, Jesus castigates those who whitewash the prophets' tombs (Matt.23:27); in other words, there was no point in venerating historic sites associated with the prophets if you were not heeding the 'word of God' that those same prophets had spoken. Jesus also announces the imminent possibility of 'worship in spirit and in truth' (John 4:21–4). The book of Hebrews makes clear that access into God's presence is available to all without geographical stimuli or other types of intermediary (Heb. 4:14–16; 10:19–22; 12:22). Finally the Book of Acts emphasizes the centrifugal thrust of the Christian message, leaving Jerusalem behind as the Gospel goes out to the 'ends of the earth' (Acts 1:8).

This emphasis on the spiritual and universal nature of Christian worship, combined with a more negative view of Jerusalem, will be a hallmark of the Church's life in the first three centuries. New influences, however, in the fourth century, as we shall see, will lead to a dramatic shift in Christian practice.

Jerusalem in Early Christian Thought

As we move into the period after the first apostolic generation, it is hard to overestimate the significance of the Fall of Jerusalem in 70AD. This would have had an enormous impact on the early Church and its approach to Jerusalem. Jesus himself, correcting the disciples' comments on the physical magnificence of the temple, had expressly warned them that 'not one stone would be left upon another' (Mark 13:2). Sitting on the Mount of Olives he painted a graphic portrait of how the same panorama would look within a generation. Now that the Messiah had come, Jerusalem would never be the same again.

So when the Roman armies began to encircle the city in 67AD, the Christian community remembered Jesus' warning to 'flee to the mountains' (Mark 13:14) and escaped, almost certainly to a town in Trans-Jordan called Pella.[4] This act of apparent disloyalty to Jerusalem was deeply symbolic of the new, higher loyalty that these Jewish believers now possessed: Jesus, not Jerusalem, was the true centre of God's purposes.

Some of the believers who had fled, however, must have returned to the city, because Eusebius gives a continuous list of the leaders of this Jerusalem church in the years after 70AD.[5] But in 135AD history would repeat itself in the Second Jewish Revolt. Once again Roman forces attacked the city and this time they ensured it would not happen again.

The Emperor Hadrian razed the city, and replaced it with a small town modelled on the layout of a Roman camp and called by the pagan name of 'Aelia Capitolina'. 'Jerusalem' as such was no more. Moreover, all circumcised persons were forbidden from entering the city. From now on the names in Eusebius' list of the church's bishops are clearly Gentile and not Jewish. Once again the Jewish believers went into exile, this time never to return.

The message for Jerusalem seemed to be plain. These dramatic events vindicated the prophetic message of Jesus. They revealed that God's purposes had now moved into a new phase and that Jerusalem no longer had any enduring significance.

During the second century, however, there continue to be one or two Christian voices that believe that Jerusalem, even if no longer significant in the present age, will come back into prominence at the Return of Christ. This Christian 'millenarianism' is seen in the writings of both Justin and Irenaeus.[6] The Biblical texts which inspired this cluster of hopes seem primarily to have been those in Revelation 20, which spoke of Christ's reign 'for a thousand years' and the warfare around 'the city he loves' (vv.6, 9). Significantly this future hope for Jerusalem is not paralleled by a future hope for the ethnic people of Israel, or built on passages such as Romans 11. Nor did these millenarianist views cause these writers to give a privileged position in their worldview to their contemporary city of Aelia/Jerusalem.

These millennial views then die out in the third century, as the Church begins to interpret Revelation in what we would now call 'a-millennial' categories. In the Eastern Church there continued to be some unease about the canonicity of Revelation, fuelled perhaps by memory of the Montanist controversy back in the mid-second century. On that occasion Montanus and a couple of women living in Asia Minor, inspired by some fresh visions, had begun teaching that the 'New Jerusalem' portrayed in Revelation would be descending to their small village of Pepuza. The 'catholic' church reacted strongly against this, confirming their sense that the canon of the New Testament was now closed and that fresh prophecies with supposedly universal authority were not to be expected. If Christians wished to relate to the powerful Jerusalem motif of the scriptures, other means of doing so would have to be developed.

So the predominant Christian focus came to be on the 'heavenly Jerusalem'. Paul had spoken in Galatians 4:26 of the 'Jerusalem that is above' in strong contrast to his contemporary Jerusalem which he saw as in spiritual slavery; meanwhile the author of Hebrews had given his Jewish–Christian audience the goal of making pilgrimage to the 'heavenly Jerusalem' (Heb.12:22). These two texts became the key ones for Christian theologians such as Origen and Eusebius. Despite their both living in Caesarea Maritima (the capital on the coast of Palestine), both these major theologians strongly asserted that Christians were no longer especially concerned with the physical Jerusalem 'below'. Instead the believer's focus was to be on the 'Jerusalem above'.

This attitude can be seen throughout their writings, perhaps especially in Eusebius' commentary on the Psalms where he continuously cites these two New Testament texts to explain the true meaning of the many references in the Psalms to 'Zion' and 'Jerusalem'. 'Zion' now must be understood in the Christian era as a reference to 'the holy city of God, the heavenly one'.[7] Eusebius was seeking thereby to establish a distinctively Christian approach to these matters in contrast to Judaism. This was no academic matter, since they were in contact with local rabbis and there was a large Jewish population nearby in Galilee. Christians had to work out their own response to Jerusalem. In so doing, of course, they may have caricatured the Jewish approach – it was too simple to describe Christian worship as 'spiritual' as opposed to 'physical' – but it gave expression to a key New Testament insight as to the nature of New Covenant worship. Believers were to 'set their hearts on things above' (Col.3:1), to worship the exalted Christ, and not to be overly concerned with places, not even Jerusalem. The other key text was John 4:21–4: the important questions were no longer to do with places such as Jerusalem or Mt Gerizim, but rather with ensuring that there was 'true worship in spirit and in truth'.

Of course, there was no prohibition on Christians visiting Aelia/Jerusalem if they wished. We will see below that both Origen and Eusebius visited the city. But their writings suggest that they were not motivated by any desire to visit a place of elevated present importance. Rather, they visited the city in order to meet the local Christian community and also to pursue their historical enquiries. Thus the only time Eusebius talks about visitors to Jerusalem he says their purpose was to see the evidence of the city's *destruction* in 70AD.[8] In other words, what was significant was Jerusalem's past, not its present or future.

So until the coming of Constantine, the Christian Church is one that functions without a conscious geographical centre. Despite its origins within Jerusalem (which it could never forget, nor would it wish to do so), there was no sense that Jerusalem remained functionally at the centre of the Church. That centre was replaced by an understanding of Christ being present with his people throughout the world by his Spirit (contacted by faith, and made real in the Eucharist). When the organization of the Church began to require some nodal points or 'hub cities' during the second and third centuries, the Church instead chose to mirror the administrative structure of the Roman Empire; it centralized its life around the 'patriarchal' cities of Rome, Antioch and Alexandria. Jerusalem is significant by its absence. In terms of both politics and spirituality, no special place was given to Jerusalem.

The Change of the Eras

In the fourth century all this was set to change. After 324AD, Constantine had control of the whole of the Roman Empire, both east and west. Almost immediately the issue of what Christians should do with Jerusalem came onto the agenda. For Constantine, needing symbols to unite this new era, there was great attraction in bringing Jerusalem back onto the stage of imperial history, rescuing it from the oblivion to which his imperial predecessors had hoped to confine it. Jerusalem was 'waiting in the wings' unclaimed.

No doubt Christians too, quite apart from Constantine's political interest in the spiritual power of Jerusalem, were also pleased to express their interest in this historical jewel. Yet, after several centuries of playing down their spiritual investment in Jerusalem, it would need some careful manoeuvring to avoid the charge of inconsistency. The key figure in this process of rehabilitating Jerusalem within the Christian consciousness would be young Bishop Cyril of Jerusalem, appointed to serve from 348AD. During his long episcopate (he died in about 384AD) Jerusalem itself (in terms of church buildings and liturgical practice) would be vastly changed, but so too would the place of Jerusalem within the wider Christian world.

So Cyril is the first to promote the view that Jerusalem is without any qualification to be considered a Christian 'holy city'. We see this plainly from his *Catechetical Lectures*, delivered to baptismal candidates in the opening years of his episcopate, and also by comparing his views with those of Eusebius. Eusebius was already aged 65 when Constantine came to power in the east; he would live for another 14 years and there is evidence of his adapting at least some of his views in the light of recent events. Yet on this issue he retained his previous viewpoint. It was inappropriate to term Jerusalem a 'holy city', said Eusebius. Not so, said Cyril.

Throughout his lectures Cyril refers to this 'holy city'. On one occasion there may even be a conscious correction of the ideas of Eusebius and Origen before him. These scholars from Caesarea had interpreted the difficult verses in Matthew (27:52–3), which describe the resurrected saints appearing in the 'holy city', as a reference to their appearing in the *heavenly* Jerusalem.[9] No, says Cyril, this is plainly a reference to 'this city in which we are now'.[10]

Unlike Eusebius, he never refers to the city by its official pagan name of Aelia Capitolina.[11] Moreover, when interpreting Isaiah, he sees the prophetic visions for the future of Jerusalem as applying, not to the heavenly Jerusalem, but rather in a literal way to the physical Jerusalem of his own day. Perhaps the renaissance of the city, after 300 years of neglect, is precisely what Isaiah was predicting.[12]

So, for Cyril, Jerusalem's 'holiness' has not been denied by the coming of Jesus, or indeed by the Lord's strong words of judgment. Those words had related exclusively to the temple;[13] but nothing Jesus said casts aspersions on the *city* itself. This distinction between the city and the temple proves to be quite crucial in Cyril's argumentation. Eusebius too had noted the distinction, but argued that Jesus' words against the temple had a negative corollary for the city as well. Cyril now disagrees.

Having made this distinction he is then able to build up the case for Jerusalem's sanctity by appealing to the enormously significant events that occurred in the city during the time of Jesus' ministry. This is the city of the Incarnation, the scene of the Eucharist's institution, of the Cross, the Resurrection and the Ascension; it will also be the place of Christ's return.[14] As such Jerusalem should have for Christians a natural 'pre-eminence in all things'.[15] Each of these events is used by Cyril explicitly to bolster his arguments for Jerusalem as a 'holy city'.

It was a powerful argument. It remains the case, however, that the New Testament itself, which records these events, never used them to make this point. If anything, the New Testament portrays these events as happening not because of Jerusalem's sanctity but rather despite it. Certainly some of the ironies within the Gospel account are 'ironed out' in Cyril's reconstruction of these events.

This can be sensed, perhaps most powerfully, in his description of the Palm Sunday events. Within the Gospel, this is the moment when Jesus weeps over the city (note, not just the temple) and warns of its impending judgment: 'armies will come around you ... because you did not know the hour of your visitation' (Luke 19:41–4). It is the moment when Jesus is welcomed by the crowds, but soon the city will reject him. The City of God will reject the Son of God. The 'City of the Great King' (Matt.5:35) will reject that great King. Cyril glosses this point by saying that it was only the Jerusalem of old that rejected him: 'that Jerusalem crucified Christ, but that which *now* is worships him.'[16] For Cyril, Jesus had not been calling into question the underlying importance of Jerusalem. And the fact that there were now an increasing number of Christians in the city (even if not a majority) somehow legitimated the reintroduction of the idea of Jerusalem as a holy city. The city's rejection of Jesus in the past was not allowed to affect the status of the city; rather that status was affirmed by the existence of Christian residents and visitors in the present.

By the end of the fourth century, such ideas are well established within the Church. Jerusalem is once again on the map of the Christian conscience. In 451AD Bishop Juvenal will succeed in getting his see recognized as a fifth 'patriarchate'. And in Christian art the physical Jerusalem will increasingly come to be seen as a positive antitype of the true heavenly Jerusalem.

As a result, pilgrimage to the city came to be fostered by this sense that there was more to Jerusalem than just the sum of its special 'holy places'. And in later centuries there would come warriors from the west to reclaim this 'holy city' from the hands of the infidel. The idea of Jerusalem as a Christian 'holy city', despite its late start within Christian thought and some contrary voices in the New Testament, was set to become an enduring feature within Church history. It is a powerful sentiment, rich in potential, both for good and for ill.

The 'Holy Places' of the Incarnation

A similar pattern of development can be seen when we examine the different, but obviously related, question of pilgrimage to particular Gospel sites or 'holy places'. The legacy of the New Testament has been noted above, with its emphasis on spiritual worship and its silence as to how the first Christians expressed their value for the sites of Jesus' ministry. As we now move to the sub-apostolic period, one of the key questions becomes: did the Christian Church preserve an accurate memory of these sites?

With the sacking of Jerusalem in 70AD and the temporary exile of its Christian community, would the memory of particular Gospel sites have got lost? In Nazareth and Galilee the probable continuity of a Christian presence in the area makes it *a priori* likely that such memories would have been passed on;[17] but in the case of Jerusalem there is a real possibility of a major break within the 'tradition process'. A second such break occurs in the Second Jewish Revolt (135AD) when the Jewish believers are exiled from Jerusalem, never to return.

Almost certainly, however, the Christian community will have kept alive these site traditions – at least the most important ones, such as the site of Golgotha and the Easter Tomb, and the site of the Last Supper. As we saw above, Jewish Christians appear to have returned to Jerusalem soon after 70AD and it would not be impossible for Gentile Christians to inherit traditions from their exiled Jewish brethren after 135AD. Yet Jerusalem had twice been reduced to rubble since the time of Jesus. Things looked very different now. So, even if the *memory* of these sites was preserved, their *appearance* would have been irreversibly changed out of all recognition. For example, if the current church of the Holy Sepulchre marks the correct site, then the place of Jesus' crucifixion and resurrection had been covered by the Emperor Hadrian with a pagan forum;[18] and the site of the 'upper room' was now marked by a small church/synagogue, which lay in the derelict rubble of the former upper city, now stranded outside the southern edge of Aelia Capitolina.[19]

There are in fact some small signs that the Christian community within Aelia was interested in the historical aspects of the Gospel narrative, and saw themselves as custodians of these traditions. For example, not only did they use the building on the site of the 'upper room' as a place of worship (despite its odd location outside the town), they also had a library (which Eusebius consulted) and they preserved the original 'throne' of their first bishop, James, the brother of the Lord.[20] Their compiling a list of bishops (mentioned above) tells in the same direction. Even so, this community would have been very small until well into the third century and the number of visitors will also have been fairly minimal.

We do, however, know the names of a small number of the Christian visitors to Aelia/Jerusalem in the pre-Constantinian period. A man called Pionius in the third century, who was later martyred, mentions a visit he made to Palestine.[21] Melito, Bishop of Sardis, came to the land 'where these things were preached and done' to investigate the extent of the Old Testament canon.[22] And there was also Alexander, who came from Cappadocia around 200AD and was unexpectedly asked to be the bishop of Aelia. Alexander, however, had first come to the land, says Eusebius, 'in order to enquire about the places and to pray'.[23] This is the first explicit link between visiting Biblical sites and praying, that combination which would give rise to 'pilgrimage'. Meanwhile around 230AD Origen investigated Biblical sites such as Bethlehem and 'Bethany beyond the Jordan'.[24] Two generations later, Eusebius himself would also make the journey up from Caesarea, perhaps on several occasions, both as a historian and also when he became bishop of the province of Palestine.

Henry Chadwick once commented that 'the volume of devout tourism must have been much greater than these isolated examples suggest'.[25] Indeed, according to Eusebius' claims, visitors came from 'all over the world' to visit Bethlehem and to overlook the ruins of Jerusalem from the Mount of Olives.[26] Strictly speaking, however, Eusebius' exaggerated terminology gives us no real idea of how *many* such visitors there were, only that they came from a wide variety of places. Yet there were clearly more than just a handful.

Around 290AD, Eusebius himself composed a gazetteer (known as the *Onomastikon*) which listed most of the Biblical sites. Many of these, he said, were still being 'pointed out' to this day. In his *Ecclesiastical History* (7.18) he mentions a particularly intriguing item: a bronze statue of Jesus kept in a house in Panias (formerly Caesarea Philippi), which reputedly had belonged to the woman Jesus healed (Mark 5:34).

So by the year 300AD there was clearly in some quarters a real interest in the Land of Palestine, precisely because of its Biblical heritage. Nevertheless, in those days of continuing persecution, few had the luxury of going on such excursions. And there is no evidence of an emerging cult of 'holy places' as such. Jesus' words concerning 'worship in spirit and in truth' (John 4:24) will have had an enduring effect and made Christians reticent to reinvent the notion of particular places as 'holy' in themselves. But this is not the same thing as being interested in sites because of their historical significance within the life of faith. And this is precisely what we see in these early Christian visitors – a prayerful interest in these sites for reasons of history.

If we move the clock forward one hundred years, however, we will see an incredible contrast. By the year 400AD the Holy Land has been transformed out of recognition. Previous to Constantine, there had been little opportunity for significant Biblical sites to be earmarked in any public way. Worshippers had to be content with the natural surroundings. So, for example, a cave on the Mount of Olives had been frequented by Christian visitors, possibly used in the first instance just as a convenient, dry, discreet place in which to gather their thoughts.[27] With the coming of Constantine to power, however, all this changed. The Holy Land, and in particular the identifiable sites of the Gospels, were ripe for development.

The full story of what has been called 'Constantine's Holy Land Plan' is described elsewhere and is perhaps quite well known.[28] During Constantine's lifetime churches were commissioned over the three main Gospel sites, namely the places of Jesus' birth, death/resurrection and Ascension;[29] the Emperor also had work begun at the oaks of Mamre (Abraham's visitation in Genesis 18) and at Capernaum.[30] In the following decades more churches would be built (over the site of Pentecost, in Gethsemane, on Mount Tabor, in Nazareth and Cana and over Jacob's well) so that by the end of the 4th century there was a veritable pilgrimage trail. To read the accounts either of Egeria (the Spanish nun who visited in 381–4AD) or of Paula (a friend of Jerome who made her pilgrimage in the early 400sAD) is almost to be exhausted with the number of shrines which have now been built throughout the land.[31] Elaborate liturgies had been designed for residents and visitors alike. Holy Week was now a weeklong celebration of the Passion story with worshippers hearing Scripture readings appropriate to each place. Pilgrimage had 'come of age'.

Constantine himself never visited the Holy Land, though he said at his baptism shortly before his death that he had hoped to be baptized in the River Jordan (*Life of Constantine*, 4.62). Yet we learn that visitors came from all over the known world. Sizeable Armenian and Syrian communities became established within Jerusalem. Visitors from the Latin west were particularly frequent. One of the most famous was Constantine's British mother, Queen Helena, who visited in 326AD. Others that we know of include:

- the Bordeaux Pilgrim (333 AD), who wrote a useful travelogue;
- the heretic-hunting Epiphanius from Cyprus (393 AD);
- the godly Gregory of Nyssa (380 AD) who was unimpressed and raised questions about the whole enterprise of 'pilgrimage' (see his *Epistle* 2);
- the wealthy Poemenia who financed the building on the crest of the Mount of Olives, and Melania, who founded a monastery nearby, with Rufinus;
- various infamous Christians who came to Palestine for refuge (the heretics Arius and Pelagius, in 335 and 415 respectively).

The contrast between the years 300 and 400 could not be starker. Naturally it raises lots of questions for the modern reader. What theology of pilgrimage and 'holy places' was at work? And is it likely that any of the sites are authentic?

The Correct Locations?

On the latter point, some of the identifications are highly questionable by modern standards. Site traditions which emerge *for the first time only* in the fourth century are particularly suspect. These include Mount Tabor as the scene of the Transfiguration, the conglomeration of sites on Lake Galilee at Tabgha, and the locating of Cana at (what is now known as) Kefr Kenna. With each of these places the choice was reasonably appropriate but it was also influenced quite considerably by practical considerations of convenience. Given this sudden influx of pilgrims, all of whom wanted to be shown the *exact* spot, it would hardly be surprising if local people tried to meet their demands.

But the case looks quite different for those sites where there is evidence of some Christian tradition going back *before* the time of Constantine. This would suggest that we should treat very seriously the traditions, for example, concerning the cave in Bethlehem, the tomb of Christ and the homes of Jesus and Peter in Nazareth and Capernaum.

True 'Holy' Places?

On the more theological question, the concept of 'holy places' clearly came into vogue. Eusebius himself, despite his earlier qualms, begins to use 'holiness' language when describing the awesome event of the uncovering of the Easter tomb.[32] Bishop Cyril then takes this up, developing a conscious theology of 'holy places'. For Cyril, the Gospel sites 'all but showed Christ to the eyes of the faithful';[33] they had the power to 'shame', 'reprove' and 'confute' any who were tempted to disbelieve the message of Christ.[34] It was as though they were living witnesses to the Gospel events and had a power of their own. Egeria and Jerome likewise have no hesitation in constantly describing these places as 'holy'. No doubt there was some ambiguity as to what precisely this adjective denoted: were the places 'holy' simply in terms of association with historical events of a deeply religious kind? Or were they now in some sense charged with God's presence in a new and enduring way? But the step had been taken. If you like, historical tourism had been replaced by what can only be described as 'pilgrimage'. The Church had now sanctioned (or should we say, sanctified?) its own distinctive 'holy places'.

In some ways, this was but a part of a necessary adjustment that the worldwide Church needed to make as the era of persecution came to an end. Specifically Christian buildings were now possible, perhaps even necessary. The *invisible* Church now had *visible* churches (that is, buildings). This then raised all the questions as to how the Church's view of the sacred should affect the understanding of its church buildings set apart for the worship of the Christian God. This is the one 'holy' God who is transcendent and 'other', but who also in Christ and the Spirit is also accessible and immanent. How can physical buildings ever convey his otherness? But, equally, how can they also convey the truth that he is present and knowable anywhere by his Spirit, quite apart from any such building?

The New Testament had left a powerful message. The temple curtain, which previously had confined the Most Holy Place, had been torn in two. This meant that the presence of God was now realizable through Christ anywhere. The New Testament therefore had cast a vision in which Jesus Christ himself was the true Holy Place, fulfilling all that Bethel, the temple or Mt Gerizim were seeking to proclaim (John 1–4); in the words of W.D. Davies, holy space had been 'christified'.[35] Certainly the person of Christ outstripped the priority of place. In one sense, therefore, everywhere had been desacralized; in another sense, everywhere had been sanctified. Yet, whichever way you looked at it, what room did either of those visions leave for designated 'holy places', especially if that implied (as it seemed necessarily to do) a status of *non*-holiness for other parts of God's creation? Clearly the Church of the 4th century had to start using designated buildings. What was not so obvious was whether sacral language could rightly be used about them.

Christians ever since have answered this conundrum in different ways, with some endorsing a full-blown recognition of places as intrinsically holy. Others have understood this term more in human terms: as a 'holiness by association' with historical memories. Still others have been willing to see these places as 'holy' in a representational sense, not denying the universal sanctity of geography in the era of Jesus Christ, but rather seeing them as focused tokens of that universal sanctity.

With the scenes of the Incarnation, however, there has often been an extra line of argument; for these are the places which uniquely have been witnesses to the acts of the Divine Son on earth. This is where the Divine Presence has been known; perhaps that presence still mysteriously pertains to that place in the here and now?

Nevertheless the New Testament itself notably refuses to use this line of argumentation. Instead it manifests a high doctrine of the Incarnation without seeing that entailing a high doctrine of 'holy places', precisely because the Incarnate Son eclipses all holy places and himself becomes the ultimate holy place. There is no place on earth which mediates God's presence in an assured way; that can alone be found in Christ. Thus to be 'in Christ' is already to be in the holiest place. The places of the Incarnation cannot then be 'holy' in this fully theological sense of the term. If 'holy' is the correct category to use (and many would think it a category mistake), then on this reasoning it could only be a holiness of religious and historical association; that is, these places are holy to us for reasons of memory, but not 'holy' in the eyes of God. Any claim to this latter kind of holiness would ultimately be derogatory to Christ.

By and large, however, the Church of the 4th century came to adopt this sacral language, despite its inherent ambiguities. The rediscovery of the places of the Incarnate Christ was an important trigger, offering some seemingly indisputable legitimation. The Incarnation undergirded a sacramental view of the physical, a belief that the Creator God had used (and could use again) his created world to reveal his glory. Yet a critic might argue that the impetus came rather from an opposite source, namely the need as quickly as possible to baptize the religious instincts of newly converted pagans. Within paganism there was frequently a firm belief in the value of sacred groves and temples. Perhaps the Church, in trying to make evangelistic connections, was in danger of making Christian faith too similar to what its potential converts had known before?

Contrary interpretations such as these are common in analyses of the fourth century. Sometimes we can only ask what we ourselves might have done in similar circumstances. Could we have done any better? If the Church did not try to convert the pagans, then who would? If the Church did not gain acquisition of the Gospel sites and celebrate the life of Jesus, who else would do that? Into the vacuum the Church boldly marched, but there were costs involved. Was holiness effectively spread more widely, or instead more thinly?

Holy Places, Objects and People

As we have just suggested, the development of the Holy Land and its holy places in the 4th century is part of a larger picture. Not just in Palestine, but throughout Christendom there was a promotion of the sacred. In many places this was tied up with the building of churches and the celebration of the Eucharist according to more elaborate liturgies and ceremonial. Yet churches from this period (especially in the east) do not have any of the high icon screens or distant altars that will appear in subsequent centuries. These later developments would be justified by appealing to a doctrine of the holiness of the altar. Instead, in this earlier period, Christians built worship spaces which preserved a sense of open space (with the clergy seated in the apse and the table separated from the congregation only by a low *cancellum*). So, yes, there was in some ways a focusing of sacred space, but at the same time there was an evident accessibility into the holy. If you like, holiness, rather than being confined in precise locations, was shown to flow outwards into all the world.

In some regions, however, churches would be deliberately built over places of former pagan worship. In principle this stemmed not from a desire to blur the boundaries between Christianity and paganism, but from a strong theology which asserted that the goal of true religion was in Christ – a proclamation of Christ's kingship over other lords. Yet in the process there was a necessary acquiescence to the idea of 'sacred spaces' as something which was part of the shared heritage and discourse of Christianity and paganism.

Then again, in other parts of the Empire there were privileged locations which preserved the memory of apostles or martyrs. The great churches in Rome, which commemorate the martyrdom and tombs of Peter and Paul, are some of the first to be built in the Constantinian era. As with the tomb of Christ in Jerusalem, such building activity gave the opportunity to honour belatedly those who had died in weakness and shame. Not surprisingly Constantine, in seeking to give historical weight to his novel capital of Constantinople, also dedicated a church to the Twelve Apostles, trying to bring to this church memorabilia and relics associated with each apostle.[36]

The Growing Importance of Relics

This then raises the whole issue of relics, which also suddenly became so important during this period. The most famous relic was the first one to be 'discovered': the wood of the 'true cross'. Later legends have somewhat obscured the issue, but some wood was indeed found during those first excavations in the area of the modern Holy Sepulchre and immediately presented as part of Jesus' cross. Eusebius was quite sceptical about this, either doubting its authenticity or wary of how the Jerusalem church might develop a relic trade for its own purposes.[37] Yet within a few years Bishop Cyril was claiming that this relic had spread 'all over the world'.[38] By Egeria's day what remained of the relic in Jerusalem was displayed on Good Friday, but under careful observation by the clergy. Only a few years earlier a devotee had tried to bite off some of it to take home with her.[39]

In due course various other relics would be 'discovered' and would find their way to places far from the shores of Palestine. The Holy Land naturally had a monopoly on the bones of Old Testament characters (such as the patriarch Joseph and the prophets Zechariah, Habbakuk and Samuel). And there was a major sensation when the bones of St Stephen were uncovered in 415AD (in a tomb not far from the modern Ben Gurion Airport). Some years later the Emperor Theodosius II would pay vast sums to have the Empress Eudocia bring Stephen's bones back to Constantinople. It was all part of a movement whereby Christian visitors would try to take back with them a little bit of the Holy Land, what they referred to as *eulogiae* (or 'blessings').

At one extreme this might be tied up with a fair amount of superstition. Some pilgrims took home small 'tokens' of burnt clay (taken from the soil around the sites) and then ground them up, dissolved them in water and drank them for their supposed miraculous properties. On the other hand, some of it was not so dissimilar from modern tourists taking back various memorabilia of their trip, whether olive wood or Jordan water. In those days Jordan water was also a popular souvenir, but so too was oil from the lamps of the Holy Sepulchre, dried flowers from Gethsemane, or simply dust from Jerusalem's streets.

Once again, developments in the Holy Land were part of the wider picture, but also profoundly influenced that wider picture. Speaking of the privilege of being in Jerusalem, Cyril could boldly say: 'Others merely hear, but we see and touch.'[40] This was a strong promotion of pilgrimage and relics: come to Jerusalem and then take something of it back with you! As the Church sought to encourage faith, it tried to harness the senses of sight and touch. Paul had stressed that we 'walk by faith and not by sight' (2Cor.5:7) and Jesus himself had blessed those who believed without seeing (John 20:29). But now that blessing was sought in different ways.

Holy Saints

Finally this was the era of what might be called the cult of living saints or 'holy people', as seen in ancient monasticism. St Anthony had begun the desert monastic movement in the late 3rd century, and ever since people had had a strong desire to visit these austere holy men, to learn of God's ways and to sense God's presence. Monastic settlements burgeoned, especially in the eastern half of the empire, and the deserts were populated by monastic cells. So pilgrims to the Holy Land could visit not just holy places but holy people. In the 5th century, St Simeon Stylites would be perched on his pillar for over 30 years, a key attraction in western Syria. And when such saints died, their remains were treasured and often venerated as objects with peculiar power.

The lure of the desert and the contemplative life has been well discussed in other places.[41] For now we simply note that those not called to this life nevertheless felt the pull of the sacred, and journeyed out to meet these saints. In an age when the sacred was in danger of being cheapened, or perhaps too crudely identified with physical objects or places, here was a clear reminder that holiness within the Bible is properly a moral and personal category, something imbued by a holy God upon his people. The phenomenon of these holy men and women reminds us of this important Biblical challenge and asks us: if we have concerns about the wrong use of 'holy' categories as applied to places, are we as properly concerned for true holiness in ourselves?

Conclusion

So the first four centuries take us a long way from the days of the New Testament. Observers will sense appropriate development in some areas and questionable deviation in others.

As we conclude, it is worth noting that the fourth century was the century which celebrated the mystery of the Incarnation. The elevation of Jerusalem and the holy places, whatever the other political motivations, was justified *theologically* with reference to the Incarnation. Our evaluation of pilgrimage today will inevitably be affected by our understanding of the Incarnation. How do we appropriately celebrate the Incarnation? Does it legitimate a sacramental view of the physical? How do we affirm this unique history with its universal implications? And how can we appropriately proclaim in physical ways that he who once was 'without honour' (Luke 4:24) and 'crucified in weakness' (II Cor. 13:4) is now Lord of the world?

This focus on the Incarnation is clearly expressed by those who visited the Holy Land. 'No other sentiment draws people to Jerusalem,' said Paulinus of Nola around 400AD, 'than the desire to see and touch the places where Christ was physically present, and to be able to say, from their very own experience, "We have worshipped in the places where his feet have stood".'[42] It was indeed a 'God-trodden Land'.[43]

So, as we review this period of early Christian history on this theme, it raises important questions about the practice of pilgrimage. Is there a danger of idolatry? Is there a danger of seeing pilgrimage as essential? What would Jesus have made of this focus on the places where his feet had stood? These are important concerns for us today, and there were Christians in the 4th century who were aware of them too – at least to some degree. Thus Jerome actively discouraged some would-be pilgrims, assuring them that Christians in Britain had equal access to the door of Paradise.[44] Gregory of Nyssa thought the 'holiness' of the land was vastly exaggerated; if holiness was measured by the number of believing Christians per capita, then far better to stay in Cappadocia.[45]

In some ways the first four centuries reveal enough to highlight the potential of Christian pilgrimage, both for good and for ill. For it is a story of caution which then gave way to enthusiasm. Should we embrace the modern opportunities for Christian travel with equal enthusiasm?

There are many reasons for a positive approach. Of necessity the historical survey above, which has focused on the issue of what precisely pilgrims are visiting (are they holy cities or holy places?), has omitted many of the personal and communal aspects which make up the phenomenon of 'pilgrimage': the shared experience with other travellers who visit the same places (but somehow respond to them slightly differently); the task of ensuring that our visit is a benefit to the local population and not an example of 'irresponsible tourism'; the new perspectives we may gain on our everyday worlds to which we return, and so on. It may well be that what gives pilgrimage its appeal is precisely the way in which these and other factors converge simultaneously and in a focused way, both for individuals and for groups.

Yet, beneath all these factors, there lies a common core at the root of all pilgrimage experience: the opportunity to reflect on the historical roots of one's faith and to make an appropriate, personal response. This is what gives pilgrimage its rationale and validity. At its best pilgrimage is a seeking after 'roots that refresh'. We are 'creatures of time and space', empowered by memory, and living in a God-visited world. Pilgrimage is a geographical travelling (in 'space') which enables an imaginative travelling (in 'time'), which event can in turn be used by the God known there in the past to be known afresh in the present. It is historical enquiry bathed in prayer.

The story of the early Church above illustrates the existence of this proper historical instinct from the very outset. Of course, the first generation were in some senses more busy *making* history than studying it. Yet a work like Luke–Acts demonstrates how a concern with history may not be contradictory to (and indeed may complement) a fully-fledged commitment to the prior task of mission and evangelism. It is possible 'to retreat in order to advance', that is, to return (in historical enquiry and interest) in order to go forwards (in mission). So the Christians living before Constantine knew the importance of history; they just did not always have the luxury to travel to the places associated with that history. It is important that, whatever the potential abuses and pitfalls of pilgrimage, Christians do not react to the point of denying the value of history or the brute reality and particularity of the Incarnation. The Bible and Jesus are couched in history.

Yet a naive enthusiasm is also out of place. We do not have the luxury to forget the legacy of the Crusades and we would be unwise to ignore the Protestant reaction to abuses. This means that the notion of 'holy places', at least in my view, continues by and large to be inappropriate and unhelpful, both because of the way the Bible has focused the meaning of true 'holy space' onto Christ and also because of the way religious instincts so easily understand this phrase to imply some inherent theological status. These places are important, but not because of some divine *fiat* or election in the present, but simply because of history. Moreover, we must ensure that the object of our faith is God himself as revealed in Christ and not some object or place, however closely associated it may claim to be to the God who alone is to be worshipped. Holiness is not a quality to be touched, but a lifestyle to be lived.

As for Jerusalem itself, the heart-breaking era in which we live only confirms on a daily basis that this city (for all its genuine divine associations) can become an idol that demands awful sacrifices and which cannot deliver what it promises. Truly the 'glory has departed'. The greatest thing about Jerusalem is the Jesus who is no longer there, who once was there crucified and who continues to be rejected by the majority of its inhabitants. Of course, we can never treat Jerusalem as though it were not unique in the salvation-history of humankind (and for that reason we value it and 'pray for its peace'); but woe betide us if we ever think that Jerusalem itself is the answer to our problems or essential to our Christian identity. In contrast to Cyril's adulation of this 'holy city', which now seems so wistfully naive and out of place, we would do well to heed the instincts of the apostle: 'the present Jerusalem is in slavery with her children; but the Jerusalem that is above is free, and she is our mother' (Gal. 4:25–6).[46]

So, with regard to each of the three questions we raised at the outset, it can be sensed that the New Testament continues to have some vitally important lessons for us to heed, encouraging us to celebrate the Incarnation but also limiting some of the misguided or sentimental ways in which that celebration might occur. We value the examples of our forebears in the first four centuries; we also acknowledge that their contribution has played its own irrevocable role in changing the face of the Holy Land; but we also reserve the right to forge in our own day a theology of pilgrimage which pays a closer attention to the spirit of the New Testament.

Notes

1   Some of the material in this chapter has appeared in different format in *Walking in his Steps* (2000), co-authored with my Wycliffe colleague Graham Tomlin.
2   Walker, *Jesus and the Holy City*.
3   Eusebius, *Ecclesiastical History* (abbreviated *E.H.*) 4.15.44.
4   Ibid., 3.5.3.
5   Ibid., 4.5.3–5; 5.12.
6   Justin, *Dialogue with Trypho*, 80:5; 117:3; Irenaeus, *Against Heresies*, 5:32–5.
7   See, for example, Eusebius, *Commentary on Psalm 88* (*PG* 23:1064).
8   Eusebius, *Demonstration of the Gospel*, 6.18.
9   Origen, *Commentary on Matthew 17:1–2* (12:43; 169:5–7); Eusebius, *Commentary on Psalm 88* (*PG.* 23:1064b).

10   Cyril of Jerusalem, *Catechetical Lectures* (abbreviated *Cat.*) 14:16.
11   Eusebius can still use 'Aelia' of Jerusalem after 325 (for example in his *Theophany*, 4:20), as does Egeria much later, in 384 (*Egeria*, 9:7); significantly it was the term used in the Council of Nicaea (see its Canon 7).
12   *Cat.*, 18:34. Interestingly Eusebius seems to have begun to toy with such ideas, but applied the language of Isaiah exclusively to the church of the Holy Sepulchre (*Life of Constantine*, 3:33).
13   So, until the Muslims arrived in the 7th century, the temple platform area would be left desolate as a sure witness to Jesus' prophecy.
14   *Cat.*, 16:34; 14:23; 18:33; 15:15.
15   *Cat.*, 16:4.
16   *Cat.*, 13:7.
17   According to Eusebius, the grandsons of Jude lived in Galilee and the 'Nazarenes' continued for several centuries living as tiny communities in that region (*E.H.*, 3.20).
18   Apart from a passing reference in Acts 13:29, Jesus' tomb is never mentioned again in the 1st century. Despite later Christian conjecture, Hadrian's action was probably not consciously anti-Christian: see Eusebius, *Life of Constantine* 3:27 and my *Holy City, Holy Places?*, 244.
19   See Murphy O'Connor, 'The Cenacle'; and my *Holy City, Holy Places?*, ch. 8.
20   Eusebius, *E.H.* 7.19.
21   *Mart. Pionii*, 4:18.
22   Eusebius, *E.H.* 4.26.14.
23   Eusebius, *E.H.* 6.11.2.
24   Origen, *Against Celsus*, 1. 51; *Commentary on John*, 1:28.
25   Chadwick, 'Circle', 7.
26   Eusebius, *Demonstration of the Gospel*, 6.18.
27   Ibid.
28   See my *Holy City, Holy Places?*; Wilken, *Land Called Holy*; Hunt, *Holy Land Pilgrimage*.
29   For the vivid description of the discovery of a tomb identified as Jesus' and of the Constantinian churches built over the 'triad' of caves at Bethlehem, Golgotha and the Mount of Olives, see Eusebius, *Life of Constantine*, 3:25–43. For a full discussion of the questions of authenticity, see my *Holy City, Holy Places?* (chs 6–8) and *Weekend* (Chs 5–7).
30   See Eusebius, *Life of Constantine*, 3:53; and Epiphanius, *Against the Heresies*, 30:11.
31   For Egeria's diary, see the excellent translation and commentary by Wilkinson; for Paula's itinerary, see Jerome, *Epistle*, 108.
32   Eusebius, *Life of Constantine*, 3:25–8.
33   Cyril, *Cat.*, 14:23.
34   *Cat.*, 4:10; 12:32; 13:4; 13:38.
35   Davies, *Gospel and Land*, 367.
36   See *Life of Constantine*, 4.20.
37   See my *Holy City, Holy Places?*, 126–30; Drake, 'Eusebius'.
38   *Cat.*, 10:19.
39   *Egeria*, 37.2.
40   *Cat.*, 13:22.
41   See, for example, Chitty, *The Desert*; Brown, *Cult of the Saints*; also Walker and Tomlin, *Walking in his Steps*, ch. 10.
42   Paulinus, *Epistle*, 49:14.
43   As Palestine is described in an inscription at Amaseia in Pontus: see Wilken, *Land Called Holy*, p.192.
44   Jerome, *Epistle*, 58.
45   Gregory of Nyssa, *Epistle*, 2.

46   For a fuller exploration of how these Biblical perspectives should affect our approach to Jerusalem's problems today, see my 'Jerusalem: at the Centre?'; on this and the wider issue of pilgrimage and holy places, see *Walking in his Steps* (chs 2–3).

Bibliography

Barnes, T.D., *Constantine and Eusebius* (Cambridge, MA: 1981).

Brown, P., *The Cult of the Saints* (London: SCM, 1981).

Chadwick, H., 'The Circle and the Ellipse: rival concepts of authority in the Early Church' (inaugural lecture, Oxford: 1959), reprinted in *Variorum Reprints* (1982).

Chitty, D., *The Desert a City* (Oxford: Blackwell 1966).

Davies, W.D., *The Gospel and the Land* (Berkeley, CA: 1974 Second edition, NY: St Vladimir's Press, 1995).

Drake, H.A., 'Eusebius on the True Cross', *Journal of Ecclesiastical History*, 36 (1985), 1–22.

Hunt, E.D., *Holy Land Pilgrimage in the Later Roman Empire AD 312–460* (Oxford: Clarendon Press, 1982).

Murphy O'Connor, J., 'The Cenacle – Setting for Acts 2:44–45', in R.J. Bauckham (ed.), *The Book of Acts in its First Century Setting*, vol. 4 (Grand Rapids: Eerdmans, 1995), 303–22.

——, *The Holy Land*, 4th edn, (Oxford: Oxford University Press, 1998).

Taylor, J.E., *Christians and the Holy Places: the Myth of Jewish–Christian Origins* (Oxford: Clarendon Press, 1993).

Walker, P.W.L., *Holy City, Holy Places? Christian Attitudes to Jerusalem and the Holy Land in the Fourth Century* (Oxford: Oxford University Press, 1990).

——, *Jesus and the Holy City* (Grand Rapids: Eerdmans, 1996).

——, *The Weekend that Changed the World: The Mystery of Jerusalem's Empty Tomb* (London: HarperCollins, 1999); published in USA by Westminster John Knox Press (2000).

——, 'Jerusalem: at the centre of God's plans?', in M. Schluter (ed.), *Christianity in a Changing World: Biblical Insights on Contemporary Issues* (London: Marshall Pickering, 2000), 95–311.

Walker, P.W.L. and G.S. Tomlin, *Walking in his Steps: A Guide to Exploring the Land of the Bible* (London: HarperCollins, 2000).

Wilken, R.T., *The Land Called Holy* (New Haven, CT: Yale University Press, 1992).

Wilkinson, J., *Egeria's Travels*, rev. edn, (Jerusalem: 1981).

CHAPTER 6

Medieval Patterns of Pilgrimage: a Mirror for Today?

Dee Dyas

Nowhere have I received the grace of God in so large a measure as I did in the place where our redemption was wrought.

(*The Book of the Wanderings of Felix Fabri*, 4)

There is no need to run to Rome or Jerusalem to look for [Jesus] there, but turn your thought into your own soul where he is hidden.

(Walter Hilton, *Scale of Perfection*, I, 49)

Here is no home, here is but wilderness:
Forth, pilgrim, forth!
Know thy country, look up, thank God of all.

(Chaucer, *Balade de Bon Counseyl*, 17–19)

Introduction: a Continuing Conversation

It needs to be said: why on earth would any sane person look to the Middle Ages for perspectives on pilgrimage? Was this not the time when abuses connected with pilgrimage to holy places were at their height, with the roads of Europe crowded with the sick seeking healing from shrines which grew rich from their suffering, and gullible believers honouring relics of dubious provenance? It was, but it was much more than that. Within the medieval Church the multiple meanings of pilgrimage were explored with considerable commitment, insight – and creativity. Theologians, spiritual writers and ordinary Christians wrestled with the concepts of pilgrimage which they had inherited and embarked on their own pilgrim paths, consumed with the desire to seek God and know Him. They questioned the validity of holy places; they debated the ethics of pilgrimage; they strove to integrate inner and outer spiritual journeying; they sought to relate visits to shrines to the longer life journey which has as its goal the heavenly Jerusalem. In so doing, they were contributing to an ongoing conversation on the nature of pilgrimage which stretches back to the 4th century AD and beyond, a conversation continued within the pages of this volume.

It is, I believe, helpful for us to listen in to the medieval phase of that conversation for several reasons. Earlier chapters in this book examine the perspectives of the Old and New Testaments and developments in the early centuries of the Church. Looking at the attempts of medieval Christians to interpret and apply those perspectives offers us a chance to examine questions and experiences which closely mirror our own, yet at a distance which may allow a helpful degree of objectivity.

The appeal of journeying to 'holy places' has changed remarkably little in the intervening centuries, as the following quotations demonstrate:

> When April with its fragrant showers
> the drought of March has pierced to the root ...
> When the West Wind with his sweet breath
> has breathed life into the new shoots
> in every wood and field ...
> And small birds make melody ...
> Then people long to go on pilgrimages ...
> (···)
> At night there came into that hostelry
> Full nine and twenty in a company
> Of various sorts of people, fallen by chance
> Into fellowship and pilgrims were they all.

(Chaucer, *General Prologue to the Canterbury Tales*, c.1394)

> I began to walk. From this moment, when my heart leapt with joy, my discoveries began. Landscapes and marvellous skies, plants, flowers, trees with an incredible combination of colours, majestic flights of birds ... and diverse pilgrims of different ages, professions, nationalities, social classes, and beliefs.

(Pilgrim to Santiago de Compostela, 1994).[1]

A new awareness of the world, a sense of wonder, openness, discovery, adventure and entry into a new community of fellow travellers: all these elements are common to medieval and post-modern pilgrims. In both instances these experiences may or may not include a fresh encounter with God.

Furthermore, medieval spirituality offers a wealth of spiritual understanding which, properly contextualized and interpreted, can significantly enrich our own journeys with God. The years between the patristic period and the Reformation were not a time in which the Holy Spirit was inactive and from which contemporary believers have therefore little to learn, though neither, of course, was the medieval Church free from human error or questionable teachings and practice. Over a thousand years of spiritual journeying and exploration are laid out for us to study, interpret and compare with our own beliefs and experience and nowhere are the extraordinary riches of this resource more apparent than in the area of pilgrimage. Much of the discussion in this book centres upon the idea of journeying to Jerusalem but in medieval spirituality Jerusalem was not merely a single city. Medieval texts show Jerusalem functioning not as a single place but as a series of images, each of which explores a different strand of theological understanding and devotional practice. It is, by turns, an earthly city made holy by God, the heavenly city described in the Book of Revelation, the cloister and an inner place within the soul where God may be encountered. In Middle English spirituality we see these concepts developed in ways which both complement and contradict one another.[2] It is always necessary to ask which Jerusalem is in mind and how it may be reached. These questions are still of value today.

Patterns of Pilgrimage: the Medieval Inheritance

It is often assumed that journeying to holy places constituted the primary if not the sole meaning of pilgrimage in medieval thought. The reality is very different and highly relevant to our own time. Medieval Christianity was not a monolithic structure but a synthesis of competing discourses, each in its turn driven by the interaction of Biblical, patristic and contemporary preoccupations. The medieval debate about the nature of true pilgrimage both echoed and illustrated wider disputes within Christendom, addressing as it did the relationships between inner growth and external observance, theological understanding and popular religious experience. This debate was sustained by convictions passed down through the centuries, yet acquired a new urgency and resonance on the eve of the Reformation in England.

The first and most important point to be noted is that the primary understanding of pilgrimage inherited by the medieval Church was not that of journeying to holy places but the Biblical concept of Christians as pilgrims and strangers who travel through the exile of this world towards the heavenly Jerusalem. It would be hard to exaggerate the extent to which this perspective permeated medieval spirituality. For medieval Christians the expulsion of Adam and Eve from the Garden of Eden for disobedience meant that all human beings were in effect involuntary exiles, condemned to wander the world, separated from God and deprived of their true home. The material world was seen as essentially transient, its comforts, such as possessions and relationships, ultimately unreliable. It was therefore essential that individuals should choose to reverse this pattern, to recognize that this world was not their true home and to live with their hearts and minds set on reaching heaven; to be transformed from being a purposeless exile to becoming a traveller with a meaningful destination to reach.

Medieval Christianity was profoundly influenced by Old Testament paradigms of journeying with God drawn from the stories of Abraham and the Exodus, together with New Testament passages including Hebrews 11–13 and IPeter 1 and 2. Hebrews portrayed Abraham, Isaac and Jacob as role models who had sacrificed transient earthly benefits to win eternal security (11:8–10), offering in the process a cluster of connected concepts which included exile, living as a pilgrim/stranger in this world, desire for the heavenly homeland and the search for the security of the eternal city, faith expressed through venturing into the unknown (11:8) and willingness to relinquish transient secular wealth (11:25–6). In another key passage, Peter described Christians as 'pilgrims and strangers' (IPeter 2:11) and urged them, as citizens of another homeland, to resist the sins which warred against their souls.

Medieval Christians also found this understanding of life as a pilgrimage towards the heavenly homeland in the writings of many of the early Fathers,[3] such as the *Letter of St Clement* (Bishop of Rome c.90–99AD) which sent greetings from 'the Church of God which dwells as a pilgrim[4] in Rome to the Church of God in pilgrimage at Corinth',[5] and the second-century *Letter to Diognetus* which declared: '[Christians] live each in his native land but as though they were not really at home there [lit. as sojourners]. They share in all duties as citizens and suffer all hardships as strangers ... They dwell on earth but they are citizens of heaven.'[6]

This emphasis upon life as pilgrimage was transmitted to England through both the Roman and the Celtic churches and has remained a vital element in English spirituality to the present day. There were, however, other elements in the inheritance of the medieval Church which made discussion of the meaning of pilgrimage more complex – and more contentious – by far. The 4th century had witnessed two major developments, each offering a particular interpretation and expression of the Christian's pilgrim identity: the growth of Christian pilgrimage to holy places with its emphasis on physical travel, and the emergence of monasticism with its focus on stability and inner journeying. It is impossible to understand the fierce debates within the medieval Church (or indeed the questions which face Christians in the 21st century) without reference to these profoundly significant events.

As Peter Walker points out in Chapter 5, there are records of occasional visits to the Holy Land during the 2nd and 3rd centuries, but it was the Constantinian initiative, together with the parallel growth in the cult of the saints, which created a new sacred topography and added a new dimension of devotional experience. The theological paradox inherent in these developments did not go unnoticed then and remained a cause of serious concern for a number of medieval writers. If God was universally available through the Holy Spirit, then what was the point of making a dangerous, expensive and time-consuming journey to seek him in Jerusalem or other 'holy places'? As Jerome had argued in a letter to a would-be visitor: 'Access to the courts of heaven is as easy from Britain as it is from Jerusalem: "for the kingdom of God is within you." Nothing is lacking to your faith although you have not seen Jerusalem' (Letter 58). Similarly, Gregory of Nyssa had counselled 'Ye who fear the Lord, praise Him in the places where ye now are. Change of place does not effect any drawing nearer unto God' (Epistle 2).

Fourth-century writers had voiced other concerns: travel brought danger, both physical and moral, 'holy places' were not necessarily inhabited by holy people and fellow travellers were not always edifying companions. Moreover, there was more than a suspicion that the very idea of holy places, the pursuit of material benefits such as healing, the presentation of wax *ex voto* offerings, the practice of sleeping close to shrines to obtain revelations, all owed more to classical pagan religion than to New Testament Christianity. Ten centuries later, both orthodox churchmen and the Lollard followers of John Wyclif (c.1330–84) were still exploring the same questions. The Dominican preacher John Bromyard complained that 'There are some who keep their pilgrimages not for God but for the devil. Those who sin more freely when away from home or who go on pilgrimage to succeed in inordinate and foolish love, those who spend their time on the road in evil and uncharitable conversation ... make their pilgrimage away from God to the devil.'[7]

The subject of pilgrimage comes up frequently in Lollard testimonies, though Wyclif wrote little himself on these topics. Their complaints were threefold. Firstly, there was no merit in so-called 'holy places'.[8] Secondly, travelling to such shrines was, they alleged, all too often a pretext for immorality out of sight of the local community as well as a misuse of resources which should be used instead to help those in need.[9] Thirdly, and most importantly, true pilgrimage was a moral journey of obedience, lived out day by day in the calling assigned by God: 'I call them true pilgrims traveling towards the bliss of heaven which, in the state, degree or order to which God calls them, busy themselves ... to keep faithfully the commandments of God, hating and fleeing all the seven deadly sins.'[10]

The 4th century had also seen the emergence of monasticism in the deserts of Egypt and Palestine. Monks, whether solitary hermits or living in community, renounced their homes and families to enter into a life of prayer and discipline, suffering exile on earth in order to win citizenship in heaven.[11] From the start this way of life was understood as a highly specialized expression of the pilgrimage of life, in which interior journeying took priority. It was of course essentially a paradoxical kind of journey in which progress could only be made by staying still and stability became, both for monks who lived in community and for anchorites who adopted a more solitary life, an essential part of their calling. Indeed in many monastic texts commitment to physical stability is equated with obedience. In reality the principle of *stabilitas* was frequently honoured more in the breach than in the observance and there is documentary evidence of many attempts, by both Councils of the Church and individual monastic leaders, to correct the tendency of religious to wander outside their cloisters.[12]

Of particular concern was the question of what I shall call 'place pilgrimage'. While it was accepted that some monks and nuns occasionally needed to travel, either to conduct essential business or when directed to move from one community to another, influential figures such as Anselm and Bernard of Clairvaux consistently opposed the idea that those vowed to a life of monastic pilgrimage should be permitted to leave the cloister to engage in pilgrimage to holy places. Leaving aside such pragmatic considerations as the increased risk of exposure to temptation, arguments tend to focus on the relationship between the heavenly and the earthly Jerusalem. Geoffrey of Vendôme urged: 'we should not stray from the journey of our profession in order to make a journey to Jerusalem'.[13] Bernard of Clairvaux went even further, insisting that the cloister itself prefigured the heavenly Jerusalem[14] and that the monastic life was a pilgrimage where the monk travelled with his heart while remaining stable with his body.[15] Writing of a cleric who gave up a pilgrimage to the earthly Jerusalem to enter a monastery, he claimed: 'Your Philip, wishing to set out to Jerusalem, found a short cut and quickly arrived where he wished to go ... His feet are already standing in the courts of Jerusalem ... He has entered the holy city ... This is Clairvaux. She herself is Jerusalem, the one which is in heaven' (Letter 64).

It can now be seen that the multifaceted understanding of pilgrimage inherited by the medieval Church included one overarching theological concept (which I term 'life pilgrimage'), together with three strands of practical interpretation which I classify as 'moral pilgrimage', 'interior pilgrimage' and 'place pilgrimage'. The elements associated with each strand are set out in Table 6.1. The concept of life pilgrimage, reinforced by the comments of Augustine of Hippo (354–430)[16] and Gregory the Great (c.540–604),[17] was transmitted to the Anglo-Saxon Church by both Roman and Celtic missionaries and featured strongly in sermons and saints' lives, poetry and prose. A 10th-century homily comments: 'we are pilgrims in this world ... and now must seek another homeland'[18] while the Old English poem, *The Seafarer*, urges

> Let us think where we have our real home,
> And then consider how we may come thither;
> And let us labour also, so that we
> May pass into eternal blessedness.[19]

This concept continued to shape the landscape of medieval spirituality throughout the Middle Ages. Towards the end of the 14th century Chaucer

6.1   Life Pilgrimage

'pilgrims and strangers on earth' (Hebrews 11:13)
'pilgrims and strangers in the world' (1Peter 2:11)

exiles →	obedience →	citizens of heaven
Place Pilgrimage	Moral Pilgrimage	Interior Pilgrimage
mobility	stability	stability
shrines	calling	withdrawal/solitude
saints	obedience	anchorites/monks/mystics
relics	responsibility	prayer/meditation
indulgences	community	encounter with God
danger	service	visions
temptation	love	anticipation of heaven

can still assume the pre-eminence of the journey to the 'Jerusalem celestial' and William Langland states, without further explanation, that 'pilgrims are we all'.[20] This was and remained the primary understanding of pilgrimage inherited and explored by the medieval Church. Poets, preachers and spiritual writers all reflect on the motif of Christians as pilgrims and strangers, people whose whole life was played out in a place of exile, whose values and behaviour sprang from their identity as a citizen of another land, whose desire was not the temporary pleasures of their current place of sojourn but the eternal security of heaven.

The central, non-negotiable expression of life pilgrimage was to live in daily obedience to God in the place of one's calling, resisting sin and serving others whether as labourer, lord of the manor, merchant or priest. Integrity in business, the exercise of privilege and power for the benefit of the needy, a turning away from personal fulfilment to service of the community: these were all hallmarks of the daily life of moral pilgrimage, explored and spelled out by the church to its members. Stability and responsibility were essential components of this life, and both orthodox Christians such as Chaucer and Langland and the Lollard followers of John Wyclif are scathing in their criticisms of those who wander away from their calling for whatever reason. Medieval Christianity set great store on love for neighbour as a necessary expression of love for God. Sin is frequently defined in terms of failure to love, so that the primary evil of a sin such as gluttony is not the effect on the individual but the fact that overindulgence deprives others of their necessary sustenance. For many this concept of daily obedience as journey towards the heavenly Jerusalem was immensely helpful. Its weaknesses lay in a tendency to emphasize works over grace and the danger that in practice the horizontal displaced the vertical, love for other human beings taking precedence over loving and relating to God.

To this life of 'moral pilgrimage' some medieval Christians added 'interior pilgrimage', which roughly corresponded to what the Middle Ages knew as the Contemplative Life and played a significant role within monasticism, anchoritism, mysticism and meditation. Stability, focus and perseverance were essential. Walter Hilton (d.1396) used an extended metaphor based upon the geographical pilgrimage to Jerusalem, to illustrate the need for sacrifice and single-mindedness: '[A pilgrim] going to Jerusalem leaves behind him house and land, wife and children: if you want to be a spiritual pilgrim you must make yourself naked of all you have ... Now beware of enemies that will be trying to hinder you if they can ... keep on your way and desire only the love of Jesus.'[21] Despite the positive lessons that he draws from the practice of place pilgrimage, Hilton advocates spiritual rather than physical journeying. In the first Book of the Scale he wrote: 'there is no need to run to Rome or Jerusalem to look for [Jesus] there, but turn your thought into your own soul where he is hidden' (I.49). Those who retreated from the world, whether to a monastery or an anchorite's cell built into a church or city wall, searched, in Bonaventure's phrase, for an 'interior Jerusalem'.[22] This was the experience of Julian of Norwich (c.1342–c.1416) who wrote, 'Then our good Lord opened my spiritual eye, and showed me my soul in the midst of my heart. I saw the soul as wide as if it were an endless citadel ... In the midst of that city sits our Lord Jesus.'[23] It is also vital to note that ultimately the goal of the contemplative was, in fact, not a place but a person: 'According to our spiritual proposition, Jerusalem is as much to say *sight of peace* and stands for contemplation ... for contemplation is nothing other than a sight of Jesus, who is true peace.'[24]

Towards the end of the 14th century, Christians who had not embraced monastic or anchoritic callings were also seeking ways to add contemplative prayer to their life of active service in the world. Meditation on the Scriptures of the kind recommended in the pseudo-Bonaventuran *Meditations on the Life of Christ* offered them and others a pilgrimage of the imagination in which they could enter into the events of the Nativity and the Passion:

> The shepherds also came to adore him ... You too ... kneel and adore your Lord God ... beg his mother to let you hold him a while. Pick him up and hold him in your arms. Gaze on His face with devotion and reverently kiss Him and delight in Him. You may freely do this, because he came to sinners to deliver them.[25]

The various modes of interior pilgrimage too had their temptations, problems and detractors. Monasticism had long been considered the only sure route to heaven, an assumption which presented the medieval Church with two substantial problems: such an approach implicitly devalued the lives of the majority of Christians and it patently did not guarantee holiness, since physical withdrawal from the world did not mean escape from temptation. It was easier to retreat to the cloister than to focus on seeking God once there and, despite successive attempts at reform, the monastic movement was much criticized in the later Middle Ages as many found their vows of stability, chastity, poverty and obedience burdensome or even irrelevant. There were similar problems for those who chose the anchoritic pathway, often seeking to lead a 'solitary life' in the middle of a bustling medieval town where the temptations of gossip, materialism and even sexual misconduct were never far away.[26] Much of the material written for those who would indeed learn how to focus body, mind and soul in the quest for the interior Jerusalem is highly technical and in the case of the author of the *Cloud of Unknowing* unashamedly exclusive. Small wonder that ordinary Christians, struggling to pursue their more mundane pilgrim way, wondered whether opting out of the world should be read as achieving the pinnacle of spiritual experience or as an act of irresponsibility and self-centredness, a failure to follow God's law of love.

The third strand, 'place pilgrimage', included journeying to saints' shrines or other holy places to secure general pardon or forgiveness for specific sins, to seek healing and other material benefits, to grow in spiritual understanding and to express devotion. Successful completion of the journey was marked by external signs such as the acquisition of pilgrim badges and relics which would allow some kind of transfer of the experience to their home environment. The earthly Jerusalem was the supreme pilgrimage goal, offering enhanced understanding of the Scriptures and, above all, the chance to walk in the footsteps of Christ. There were official tours in which 'Pilgrims are led through the localities of Christ's passion in such an order that they meet their Lord, and go to meet him as he comes towards them'.[27] Here doctrine became tangible; as Cyril had said centuries earlier, 'Others only hear; we see and touch.' Jerusalem, it seemed, was the ultimate 'holy place', where Christ had walked, taught, died and risen from the dead. But the theological paradox remained: how could an omnipresent God be especially available in one location? And if He was in truth more accessible in Jerusalem or Rome or Canterbury than elsewhere what did that say about the rest of a pilgrim's existence or the lives of those who never had the chance to go on pilgrimage?

Moreover, the Holy Land, and the Holy City, were patently not places where holiness held sway: then, as now, churches squabbled over territorial rights and pilgrims were subject to violence and robbery. Nor was holiness of character or behaviour automatically conferred on those who visited. Friar Felix Fabri noted with horror that 'Some nobles were led by vanity to write their names ... on the walls of the church [of the Holy Sepulchre] ... on the pillars ... on the slab which covers the tomb of our Lord',[28] while another traveller, Arnold von Harff, seems to have regarded as an essential part of a (male) pilgrim's vocabulary the phrase, 'Woman may I sleep with you?' which he helpfully supplies in Greek, Slavonic, Arabic and 'the Jewish speech'.[29]

Pilgrimage offered an opportunity to escape from the responsibilities and constraints of life in the home community and often resulted in enhanced status within that community upon return. Ideally such journeys would be accompanied by an experience of inner growth and thus, in theory, were a valuable way of expressing and resourcing the life pilgrimage of an individual. In practice, place pilgrimage was often seen as a distraction from, or a substitute for, genuine devotion. There was also a real sense in which the popularity of place-oriented pilgrimage and devotion to the saints threatened to diminish the true scale of the Christian life. Both trends may have expressed genuine devotion but they also facilitated a kind of spiritual 'reductionism' as the demands of a direct relationship with God and the requirement to make the whole of life a pilgrimage were gradually scaled down to something a little more manageable. A journey to Canterbury or Jerusalem, though hard, was nevertheless a measurable achievement; steps forward on the longer journey towards heaven were less easy to discern. Moral and interior pilgrimage emphasized commitment and stability, experiencing God in the place of one's calling and service. Place pilgrimage, on the other hand, was possibly unnecessary, involved expense and sometimes physical if not moral danger, and meant leaving one's daily responsibilities, usually for long periods of time. Pilgrimage was an excuse, for many the only excuse, to see the world; those who travelled to Canterbury, Rome or the earthly Jerusalem were therefore open to the charge of 'curiositas', of being in fact tourists rather than pilgrims, pursuing adventure and stimulus rather than experience of God.

It may well seem that the Middle Ages almost suffered from an embarrassment of riches in terms of pilgrimage options. Yet, as the brief summary above indicates, it was far from easy to reconcile the different goals and priorities inherent in each approach. All agreed on the overall understanding of the Christian life as a pilgrimage towards heaven: the question faced by practitioners of each strand of expression was essentially about integration. Did their chosen path resource or distract from that longer journey which all must make?

Integrating our Pilgrimages: the Challenge for Today

The issues raised by medieval approaches to pilgrimage are once more high on the spiritual agenda. At the beginning of the 21st century we see again an extraordinary resurgence of place pilgrimage among people of all faiths and none, a burgeoning interest in contemplative prayer and a strong desire among many believers to relate their faith to everyday living. The impulses and debates of earlier centuries are not as far away as we may imagine. So can the experience of medieval Christians, both positive and negative, shed light on our multiple pilgrimages? Used carefully, I believe that it can.

Rediscovering the Pilgrimage of Life

I want to suggest that the key to integrating the various spiritual journeys which we make is to reclaim this New Testament concept of the Christian life as a purposeful journey towards heaven which permeated the whole of medieval spirituality. It gave perspective to human life, with its unpredictable joys and sorrows; it offered an eternal security which liberated men and women to risk all for God; it challenged Christians to live and worship with integrity on a daily basis. Today this concept not only offers a 'sojourner' identity which enables Christians to combine community involvement with a detachment which safeguards their prophetic role, but gives value and direction to daily living. It provides a context into which spiritual experiences of all kinds can be incorporated and against which they need to be measured. It is also a meta-narrative which still makes sense to many inside and outside the Church because the idea of journey is so deeply ingrained within the human psyche. It needs to be reclaimed from the slightly old-fashioned associations of Bunyan's 'Pilgrim's Progress' because this is not quaint allegory but profoundly challenging spiritual reality. To be pilgrims and strangers means that the growing, journeying, adventuring is never done. There is always more. Too many Christians, too many churches, grow for a while and take a rest, sometimes a very long rest. They cease to ask, 'What is next? Where are we going?' The pilgrimage of life offers a continuing story into which our shorter journeys are woven; it also provides, I suggest, the only way to reconcile those who stand on different sides of the place pilgrimage debate.

Recognizing the Power of Place

The history of the Church demonstrates clearly that the human instinct to identify and revere 'holy places' is remarkably strong, even in a religion which is theoretically resistant to such concepts. As E.D. Hunt remarks in a recent essay: 'There should by rights, of course, be no such thing as Christian pilgrimage ... None the less ... whatever the Gospel injunctions, Christians from the start have gone on pilgrimage.'[30] There has been a continual process of oscillation between what Hunt identifies as the 'purist' position of those who maintain that holy places are not a necessary, or even helpful, constituent of Christian spirituality, and an apparently irrepressible human desire to identify places where God may be especially accessible.

Anthropologists contend that this instinct is universal, that all societies have a concept of sacred space and that the process of pilgrimage has many functions within the life of the individual and the society to which they belong.[31] The appeal of the pilgrimage experience is an intriguing blend of the medieval and the post-modern, which sit remarkably well together. Pilgrimage sites offer stories of saints and of God interacting with ordinary people; they provide an intensely visual environment; they draw the pilgrim into an atmosphere of corporate spirituality which yet allows infinite scope for individual response. Small wonder that Christian pilgrims also have many fellow travellers. Those who travel to traditional Christian sites such as the Holy Land, Compostela, Glastonbury and Iona may well have no clearly articulated religious faith at all. They may be simply exploring the world and their own identity within it, investigating the experience of journey and using Christian shrines as a convenient goal. So are they tourists or pilgrims? Or the former in the process of becoming the latter? A tourist may occupy the same space as a pilgrim, may travel for relaxation and new experiences, and will usually return with objects which recall those experiences. A significant number of those on vacation make visits to the churches and monasteries and other sites of religious significance because of their artistic and historical interest. Figures published in 1989 noted the presence of more than 6000 pilgrimage centres in Western Europe, generating over 60 million 'religiously motivated' visits per year. Total annual visits, including casual tourists, curiosity seekers and 'art history pilgrims', were thought to exceed 100 million annually.[32]

So where does the tourist end and the pilgrim begin?[33] The answer seems to be when the observer becomes a participant, when the experience of travel becomes infused with recognition of the need for change. A 26-year-old Swiss (nominal) Protestant comments on her journey to Compostela:

> To compare the pilgrimage with other travels, I think that the main difference is that the pilgrimage changed me as a person ... It was an inner and an outer way. Other travels are mostly outer ways ... to educate yourself, see new things, culture, people, environment. But I've never heard of anybody saying, 'I'm going on three weeks' holiday to search for something more, to answer some questions' – as you do as a pilgrim.[34]

The Church should not ignore the openings presented by the quest to find spiritual reality in special places. We should be concerned to make available places which offer quiet, beauty and peace to those who are searching for God. We also need to take the opportunity to show that the God whom they have found in a special place is also available in every place.

Rejecting Imitation without Discrimination

We need to be aware that imitation without discernment will simply lead to a replication of medieval problems rather than an appreciation of medieval solutions. The fact that a belief or practice is 'medieval' does not necessarily mean that it is right or helpful. Medieval spirituality needs to be understood in its original context, and evaluated against Biblical principles and wider Church tradition. The current interest in topics such as pilgrimage, the medieval mystics, 'Celtic spirituality' and the use of labyrinths manifests two serious flaws: the uncritical acceptance of medieval practice and the promotion of inadequately researched 'discoveries' which bear little relation to historical reality but lend a spurious authority to present-day spiritual preoccupations.[35] The latter point is particularly apparent in discussion of holy places and pilgrimage. The Celtic churches which played such a major role in the conversion of 7th-century England actually focused on a specialized form of life pilgrimage which meant literal exile and emphasized the 'leaving' of home and security rather than travelling towards shrines or other special places. In marked contrast, many proponents of 'Celtic Christianity' today, even those from evangelical or charismatic backgrounds, are demonstrating an increasingly place-centred approach to spirituality, focusing on ancient Christian sites[36] and even embarking upon a re-evaluation of the concept of relics.[37] Ian Bradley has recently voiced his concern that 'Celtic Christianity' has in fact been 'hijacked by the New Age movement and neo-paganism', particularly in attitudes towards spirituality and place.[38]

Re-examining the Relationship between Physical and Spiritual Journeying

The medieval experience of place pilgrimage was often strong on experience but weak on theology. Too frequently it became a substitute for daily closeness to God rather than an aid to it, failing to feed back into everyday life. Too many of those who travelled were in effect tourists first and pilgrims second – if at all. The post-modern fascination with pilgrimage is similarly driven by experience rather than by any substantial reconsideration of the Protestant objections to pilgrimage expressed at the Reformation.[39] Christians of all traditions are going on pilgrimage to the Holy Land, to Rome and to a variety of smaller, local shrines, simply because they find it helpful.[40] As pilgrimage once again becomes a significant feature of Christian spirituality, we need to ask whether there is any Biblical warrant for such a revival and why the human instinct to identify and visit holy places should be so persistent. Are the perceived benefits of journeying to holy places a result of taking time out to be open to God, to reflect on our lives, to receive new information and experiences which will undergird our daily Christian living, or are they qualitatively different from the interaction with God which we may expect at home? If God is as accessible at home as he is in Jerusalem, what justification is there for spending time and resources on travelling to the Holy Land? If such journeys do make a significant contribution to Christian experience, what does this say about 'everyday life'? How does locating God in a particularly 'holy' space, whether an internationally recognized shrine or simply a local church, affect everyday expectations of experiencing His presence and power?

The experience of the medieval Church suggests that to treat place pilgrimage as an isolated experience is potentially profoundly unhelpful. It may produce a temporary spiritual high but may equally well be followed by the spiritual equivalent of post-vacational dysphoria. What is needed is integration and I want to offer two medieval examples which may provide useful perspectives.

Those embarking on lengthy pilgrimage would have gone to church to pray, not just for a safe arrival at their destination, but for a spiritually enhanced return to their community and daily responsibilities. The *Service for Pilgrims* contained in the *Sarum Missal* included several such prayers referring to the homecoming of the prospective pilgrim:

> *V*. The good angel of the Lord accompany thee;
> *R*. And dispose thy way and actions aright, that thou mayest return again to thine own place with joy.

> *Collect*:
> O God ... we beseech thee that thou wouldest grant unto these thy servants ... that having prosperously accomplished the course of their appointed journey, they may return unto their own homes; and having been received back in safety, may pay due thanks unto thy name.[41]

Lincoln Guild records show that members were not only required to support those who went on pilgrimage but also to share in their homecoming:

> If any brother or sister wishes to go on pilgrimage to the Holy Land, every brother and sister shall give him one penny ... And when he returns, and his fellows know it, they shall go and meet him, and go with him to the mother church.[42]

Pilgrimage was prepared for physically and spiritually and both departure and return were celebrated. Perhaps, as Henry Carse suggests, modern pilgrims might benefit from more preparation before they travel and more guidance on how to integrate their experiences into daily living upon return.

The second example is taken from the *Book* of Margery Kempe (c.1373–c.1438), the irrepressible laywoman from King's Lynn, who more than any other individual of her time has left us an example of integrated pilgrimage. A strong-willed, highly emotional woman, Margery infuriated and baffled her contemporaries by her refusal to be pigeonholed – or excluded from any kind of spiritual experience. She longed for (and claimed) mystical experience; she also visited every major shrine, including Rome, Compostela and Jerusalem. She almost drove her fellow-pilgrims insane, yet the record of her visit to Jerusalem is qualitatively quite different from any other extant pilgrimage narrative in English. Margery's relationship with God is the same whether she is in a holy place or at home. She is told by God that she is forgiven without the need for indulgences or pilgrimage at all. And as she approaches the earthly city she makes a connection which I have not found in any other contemporary narrative: she asks God 'that, just as he had brought her to see this earthly city of Jerusalem, he would grant her grace to see the blissful city above, the city of heaven'.[43] Her visits to Jerusalem, Rome and Compostela, which begin midway through her own development, are presented as enhancing her spiritual journey, however strange that journey may appear; they are not regarded as a substitute for it. In this sense she is returning to the understanding of life as pilgrimage which characterized the Early Church, yet also seeking to use place pilgrimage as a means of growth in understanding and devotion.

Redefining the Metaphor

It is a commonplace to speak of '*literal* journeys to holy places' and of the '*metaphor* of life as pilgrimage'. I want to suggest that these statements in fact invert both Biblical and medieval perspectives since the supreme significance of pilgrimage lies in seeking the heavenly Jerusalem, the eternal reality of which the earthly city is but a shadow. Within medieval spirituality, it was the 'geographical' pilgrimage which was the metaphor, a miniature version of that longer, more complex journey which every soul must choose to undertake. Place pilgrimage, rightly undertaken, functioned as a microcosm of life: bringing insecurity, even danger, as familiar surroundings and relationships were surrendered, if only for a short time. It offered a chance to enter into community with others from different backgrounds, frequently united only by a common faith and a common goal. It provided challenges, encouragements, time to focus on God and opportunities for new experiences of God. I would suggest that, if we hold to the overarching Biblical concept of life as journey, the process of journeying to places where we can learn more of and focus more completely on God can be more readily encompassed and incorporated.

Conclusion

The history of the Church demonstrates with uncompromising clarity that holding in tension the truth of God's omnipresence and the human instinct towards holy places is far from easy. It also makes it clear that to fail to hold the balance can lead to distortion of worship, spirituality and mission, as expectations of God are limited by wrong concepts of his presence and availability. Medieval spirituality suggests that there are three main ways of pursuing our pilgrimage through life: through practical service, developing our inner relationship with God and through special places and experiences. It also suggests that these both can and should be held together as individuals explore their own journey according to vocation, opportunity and temperament.

We also need to recognize that the aim of all true medieval pilgrims was not in the final analysis to see Jerusalem but to see Jesus. Each Jerusalem, whether interior, earthly or heavenly, was only of importance as the setting in which God could be encountered and it is that encounter which we need to pursue. The God of the Bible is a God who interacts with real people in real geographical settings. Remembering and revisiting places which have witnessed such events is not necessarily wrong. What is vital is that such acts of recall lead to an ever-increasing awareness that the God who has acted 'somewhere' is to be encountered everywhere.

Notes

1 Frey, *Pilgrim Stories*, 71.
2 For a fuller discussion see Dyas, *Pilgrimage*.
3 Ladner, 'Homo Viator', 237, observes: 'The topoi of *xeniteia* and *peregrinatio*, of pilgrimage, of homelessness, of strangeness in this world, are among the most widespread in early Christian ascetic literature.'
4 This phrase is also used in greetings to churches in the *Epistle of Polycarp to the Philippians* and *The Martyrdom of Polycarp* in *The Apostolic Fathers*.
5 *The Apostolic Fathers*. See also *Epistle of Barnabas*, ch. 19.
6 *Letter to Diognetus*, 5, in *The Apostolic Fathers*.
7 *Summa Praedicanti Feriae*, I. 6. Cited Davies, *Pilgrimage*, 83.
8 *Selections*, 117.
9 Ibid., 86.
10 *Two Wycliffite Texts*, 61–2.
11 'Depuis ses origines, le monachisme avait été considéré par certains de ses représentants, et des plus authentiques, comme une forme d'exil' (Leclercq, *Aux Sources*, 35).
12 See Constable, 'Opposition'.
13 *Patrologia Latina*, 157, 162BC; cited Constable, 'Opposition', 134.
14 Leclercq, 'Monachisme', 68–9: 'St Bernard defines the monk as a dweller in Jerusalem: *monachus et Ierosolymita*. Not that he must be bodily in the city where Jesus died ... For the monk this might be anywhere. It is particularly in a place where, far from the world and from sin, one draws close to God ... The monastery is then *a Jerusalem in anticipation*' [my italics].
15 Constable, 'Opposition', 136, n.41. See also Leclercq, *Aux Sources*, 82–4.
16 See, for example, Augustine's suggestion that Christians should make use of earthly things 'like a pilgrim in a foreign land, who does not let himself be taken in by them or distracted from his course towards God' (Augustine, *City*, XIX:17).
17 See Gregory, *Morals*, Bk. 18.
18 *Blicking Homilies*, 23.
19 Hamer, *Choice*, 195.
20 *Langland*, XI.240
21 *Scale of Perfection*, II, 21, 22.
22 *Itinéraire*, VII,1.
23 *Showings*, ch. 68.
24 *Scale of Perfection*, II, 21.
25 *Meditations*, 38–9.
26 See, for example, *Ancrene Wisse*, the early 13th-century guide for anchoresses.

27   Fabri, *The Book*, I, 472.
28   Ibid., II, 86.
29   *The Pilgrimage*, 77, 91, 131, 220.
30   Hunt, 'Christian Pilgrims', 27.
31   See, for example, Eliade, *Myth*.
32   Nolan and Nolan, *Christian Pilgrimage*, 1–2.
33   Morinis, *Sacred Journeys*, 10–14, suggests that there are six main types of pilgrimage which may coexist within traditions: devotional, instrumental (seeking a worldly benefit such as healing), normative (as part of a ritual cycle), obligatory, wandering and initiatory (seeking transformation).
34   Frey, *Pilgrim Stories*, 27.
35   See Bradley, *Celtic* and Meek, *Quest*, for a critique of this movement.
36   See, for example, Raine and Skinner, *Celtic*, 440–42.
37   Mitton, *Restoring*, 78, 81–2.
38   See Bradley, *Celtic*, 201.
39   Davies, *Pilgrimage*, 167ff.
40   See Robinson, *Sacred*, for examples.
41   *Sarum Missal*, 167–8.
42   *English Gilds*, 172.
43   Kempe, *The Book*, ch. 28.

Bibliography

The Apostolic Fathers, trans. Francis X. Glimm, J. M-F. Marique and G.G. Walsh, *The Fathers of the Church*, vol. 1. (Washington, DC: Catholic University Press of America, 1969).

Augustine of Hippo, St, *Concerning the City of God against the Pagans* (Harmondsworth: Penguin, 1972).

Bernard of Clairvaux, St, *Letters of St Bernard of Clairvaux* (London: Burns & Oates, 1953).

The Blickling Homilies of the Tenth Century, in R. Morris, (ed.), *EETS OS* (London: Trubner & Co, 1880).

Bonaventure, *Saint Bonaventure: Itinéraire de l'esprit vers Dieu*, ed. H. Duméry (Paris: Bibliothèque des Textes Philosophiques, 1990).

Bradley, I., *Celtic Christianity: Making Myths and Chasing Dreams* (Edinburgh: Edinburgh University Press, 1999).

Chaucer, G., *Riverside Chaucer*, ed. L.D. Benson (Oxford: Oxford University Press, 1988).

Constable, G., 'Opposition to Pilgrimage in the Middle Ages', *Studia Gratiana*, 19 (1976), 123–46.

Davies, J.G., *Pilgrimage Yesterday and Today: Why? Where? How?* (London: SCM Press, 1988).

Dyas, D., *Pilgrimage in Medieval English Literature, 700–1500* (Cambridge: D.S. Brewer, 2001).

Eliade, M., *The Myth of the Eternal Return, or Cosmos and History* (Princeton: Princeton University Press, 1971).

English Gilds, in T. Smith, (ed.), *EETS OS* (London: Oxford University Press, 1870).

Fabri, F., *The Book of the Wanderings of Brother Felix Fabri* (London: Palestine Pilgrims' Text Society, 1896).

Frey, N.L., *Pilgrim Stories On and Off the Road to Santiago* (Berkeley: University of California Press, 1998).

Gregory the Great, St, *Morals on the Book of Job*, in *Library of the Fathers of the Holy Catholic Church* (Oxford: John Henry Parker; F. & J. Rivington, 1845).

Gregory of Nyssa, St, *Select Writings and Letters of Gregory, Bishop of Nyssa*, in W. Moore and H.A. Wilson (eds), *Select Library of the Nicene and Post-Nicene Fathers of the Christian Church* (Grand Rapids, Michigan: Eerdmans, 1954).

Hamer, R.A., *Choice of Anglo-Saxon Verse* (London: Faber & Faber, 1970)

Hilton, W., *Walter Hilton: The Scale of Perfection*, in J.P.H. Clark and R. Dorward (eds), *Classics of Western Spirituality* (New York: Paulist Press, 1991).

Hunt, E.D., 'Were there Christian Pilgrims before Constantine?', in J. Stopford (ed.), *Pilgrimage Explored* (Woodbridge and Rochester: York Medieval Press/The Boydell Press, 1999), pp.25–40.

Jerome, St, *Letters and Selected Works*, in *Select Library of the Nicene and Post-Nicene Fathers of the Christian Church* (Grand Rapids, Michigan: Eerdmans, 1954).

Kempe, M., *The Book of Margery Kempe*, trans. B.A. Windeatt (London: Penguin, 1985).

Ladner, G.B. '*Homo Viator*: Medieval Ideas on Alienation and Order', *Speculum* XLII (2) (1967), 233–9.

Langland, W., *William Langland, The Vision of Piers Plowman: A Critical Edition of the B-text based on Trinity College Cambridge MS B15.17*, ed. A.V.C. Schmidt (London: J.M. Dent, 1995).

Leclercq, J., 'Monachisme et Pérégrination du XI au XII Siècle', *Studia Monastica*, 3 (1961), 33–52.

——, *Aux Sources de la Spiritualité Occidentale: Étapes et Constantes* (Paris: Les Éditions du Cerf, 1964).

Meditations on the Life of Christ, 2nd edn, trans. Isa Ragusa and Rosaline B. Green (Princeton: Princeton University Press, 1977).

Mitton, M., *Restoring the Woven Cord: Strands of Celtic Christianity for the Church Today* (London: Darton Longman and Todd, 1995).

Morinis, A. (ed.), *Sacred Journeys: The Anthropology of Pilgrimage* (Westport and London: Greenwood Press, 1992).

Nolan, M.L. and S. Nolan, *Christian Pilgrimage in Modern Western Europe* (Chapel Hill and London: University of North Carolina Press, 1989).

Raine, A. and J.T. Skinner, *Celtic Daily Prayer: A Northumbrian Office* (London: Marshall Pickering, 1994).

Robinson, M., *Sacred Places, Pilgrim Paths: An Anthology of Pilgrimage* (London: Marshall Pickering, 1997).

Sarum Missal in English, ed. V. Staley (London: Alexander Moring, 1911).

Selections From English Wycliffite Writings, ed. A. Hudson (Cambridge: Cambridge University Press, 1978).

Two Pilgrim Itineraries of the Later Middle Ages, ed. R.B. Tate and T. Turville-Petre (Santiago: Xunta de Galicia, 1995).

von Harff, A., *The Pilgrimage of Arnold Von Harff* (London: Hakluyt Society, 1946).

CHAPTER 7

Protestants and Pilgrimage

Graham Tomlin

Protestants do not go on Pilgrimages – at least that is the common perception. In fact, many Protestants do go on pilgrimage, although they do not tend to call it that. The majority of visitors to the Holy Land, for example, are Protestants from North America, Great Britain or Europe, yet many of them feel uncomfortable with the word 'pilgrimage' to describe what they are doing. Confronted by the language of 'holy places', 'shrines' and the tendency to erect ornate churches on any spot with a claim to Christian antiquity or significance, many Protestants feel a little awkward, choosing politely to ignore the ideology of pilgrimage, calling their trip instead a 'study tour' or something equally neutral.

Much of this originates of course in the strong critique of pilgrimage mounted by the 16th-century Reformers themselves, although it is important to realize that criticism of pilgrimage did not begin with them. Even at the very origins of Christian pilgrimage in the patristic period, Gregory of Nyssa voiced loudly his doubts about the whole exercise,[1] and, in the Middle Ages, figures as diverse as Thomas à Kempis,[2] Jan Hus[3] and Erasmus of Rotterdam[4] all had critical things to say about the theological inconsistency and moral sleaze associated with medieval pilgrimage.

Delving into the works of Luther, Calvin or any other of the magisterial Reformers, it does not take long to find a very negative estimation of pilgrimage. A typical case is Luther's trenchant opposition to the practice in *To the Christian Nobility of the German Nation* of 1520:

> all pilgrimages should be dropped. There is no good in them: no commandment enjoins them, no obedience attaches to them. Rather do these pilgrimages give countless occasions to commit sin and to despise God's commandments. This is why there are so many beggars who commit all kinds of mischief by going on these pilgrimages.[5]

Or even more briefly: 'There is no need at all to make a distant pilgrimage or to seek holy places.'[6] Faced with such an apparently total rejection of the practice, subsequent Protestantism has inherited a deep suspicion of the idea, which is hard to shake off, and persuaded many to avoid pilgrimage altogether, as at best unnecessary, at worst downright dangerous. Yet is there more to be said about the Protestant critique of pilgrimage? What in fact lay behind the

Reformers' objections to the contemporary pilgrimages with which they were familiar? Can pilgrimage be rehabilitated within the structure of Protestant theology? This chapter seeks to examine the basis of the Reformation critique of pilgrimage, a task which (perhaps surprisingly) has seldom been done in any depth.[7] It asks why the Reformers rejected pilgrimage, and whether their anxieties about late medieval pilgrimage amount to a total rejection of going on pilgrimage altogether.

Owing to the short compass of the chapter, there is only space to examine the arguments of Luther and Calvin as the two strongest and clearest critics of medieval pilgrimage in the Reformation. However, on the basis of such an analysis, this chapter also seeks to explore what the theology of the Reformation might have to say, both positively and negatively, about the practice of pilgrimage in the 21st century. As it looks at these very questions, it tries to re-evaluate the Protestant suspicion of the practice. It seeks to identify the 16th-century evangelical critique as an enduringly valid warning about abuses that can creep into notions of pilgrimage, and yet put forward a positive understanding that might inform a responsible approach to pilgrimage for those who stand today within the tradition of the Reformers.

Luther and Pilgrimage

While the Reformation spread far and wide beyond the limits that Martin Luther wanted to place upon it, the German Reformer remained, as long as he lived, the instigator and inspiration for the rest of the movement. So any analysis of a 'Reformation perspective' on most issues must start with him. In his early writings, Luther displays a fairly ambivalent approach to pilgrimage, verging on mild approval. In 1518, the year after the storm had broken over his publication of the *95 Theses on the Abuse of Indulgences*, Luther felt he needed to explain his position more fully to guard against misinterpretation. The result was the *Explanations of the 95 Theses*, in which he raises the contemporary practice of pilgrimage to sites such as Santiago de Compostela in Spain, Aachen or Trier in Germany, and Jerusalem in the Holy Land. Luther proceeds to discuss the issue in fairly neutral tones. He outlines a number of false reasons why people go on pilgrimage, including idle curiosity (thoroughly bad), seeking indulgences ('bearable' but not a very good idea) and 'a longing for affliction, and labour for one's sin', which Luther considers a rare, but worthy reason for going on pilgrimage. Finally, he offers a valid reason for setting out, namely 'if a man is motivated by a singular devotion for the honor of the saints, the glory of God, and his own edification'.[8] What distinguishes good pilgrimage from bad is motivation. If a pilgrim sets off with the desire to glorify God, or even to edify his own faith, then pilgrimage can be a good and helpful exercise. If he undertakes a pilgrimage in order to gain merit of any kind before God, then it is downright harmful.

Later in the same treatise, Luther goes on to indicate that he does not condemn pilgrimage to sites where relics of Christ and the saints are kept, but at the same time laments the fact these are often done to the exclusion of centring devotion on the best relic which Christ has left behind, the experience of suffering. This is a common theme of Luther's writing at this early stage of his theological development, and reflects the significance of the theology of the Cross in his early work. To prepare for God's grace sinners must not try to multiply works of devotion, instead they must allow God to do his work – to humble them through despair, doubt and suffering until they reach the point when they realize their own emptiness before God and cry out for mercy. Hence suffering is the most excellent relic of all, the place where we find God's grace.

All this certainly falls short of an enthusiastic recommendation of pilgrimage. However, Luther does not condemn it out of hand. In subsequent years, however, as his controversy with the papacy gathered pace and significance, he began to distance himself sharply from many practices of late medieval piety, and his statements on pilgrimage soon become more polemical and negative. Luther's developing critique consists of four broad objections.

The chief reason why Luther recommends the abolition of pilgrimages is that, in his own time, the practice had become inextricably linked with a theology of merit and 'works' which was the primary and lifelong target of his theology. One of the chief expressions of that mistaken theology was the doctrine common among the theologians of the *via moderna*, among whom Luther gained his early theological training, that if a sinner does what he can, God will not deny the reward of his grace.[9] In a comment on Genesis 8:22 ('While the earth remains, seedtime and harvest, cold and heat, summer and winter, day and night, shall not cease') Luther cites this mistaken belief as the reason why pilgrimages have multiplied:

> From this perverse opinion have originated many dangerous assertions, even some that are clearly false and ungodly, as, for instance, when they maintain: 'When a man does that of which he is capable, God gives grace without fail.' With this trumpet signal, as it were, they have urged men on to prayers, fastings, bodily tortures, pilgrimages, and the like. Thus the world was convinced that if men did as much as they were able to do by nature, they were earning grace, if not by the merit of condignity, then by the merit of congruity.[10]

The main distinguishing mark of Luther's thought over against that of most late medieval theology was his denial that human merit had anything to do with salvation. No late medieval theologian believed in 'justification by works' if that is taken to mean justification by human works alone. All theological systems, whether Thomist, Scotist, Humanist or Nominalist, offered some variation on the theme that justification was the result of some form of cooperation between God's grace and human endeavour, which transformed individuals and enabled them to progress towards salvation. Luther broke from this altogether, insisting that justification was granted by God, not on the basis of human merit, no matter how much it was assisted by God's grace, but instead, on the basis of the merits of Christ – an external, not an internal righteousness. Pilgrimage had become closely intertwined with the very theological system that Luther opposed, so that to go on pilgrimage had become one of the works which was deemed meritorious or advantageous before God:

> that is the reason for so many monastic orders, cloisters, temples, pilgrimages, and much more. At the bottom of this lies the false notion that these works justify and save. They are steeped in the illusion that such works and the monastic life merit eternal life and redemption from sin and death.[11]

For Luther, such a theology was pastorally and soteriologically disastrous. It led to an anxious uncertainty about salvation, never at rest, never satisfied, whereas the Christian's true birthright was a confident and sure knowledge of God's good will to justify and save, despite human sin and failure. For him, the practice of late medieval pilgrimage, whether within his native Germany or wider afield to the great shrines of Christendom, had become almost inextricably entwined with what he felt was a damaging and dangerous theology. Pilgrimages undertaken as part of penance or in fulfilment of a vow were seen, in the popular mind at least, as a meritorious work which would be rewarded with grace, and the desire to acquire such grace had become the dominant motivation for undertaking such journeys. Contemporary pilgrimage had become so infected with 'works righteousness' that it was better to discontinue the practice altogether.

A second reason why Luther rejected pilgrimage was that, in focusing on particular geographical locations, it could end up distracting attention from the places where God had chosen to make himself known. Luther laments the fact that so many Christians of his day troop off to Compostela or Rome, as if they will find God there, and as if he cannot be found within their own local church. On one level, Luther's point here is eschatological. Since the coming of Christ and the Holy Spirit, God is no longer confined to one place as he was under the old dispensation. It is therefore unnecessary to visit Jerusalem or any other specific geographical location to find God, as had been necessary in Old Testament times. Luther is eloquent on this point, as he writes of

> the villainy which lured us to Rome, Compostela and Jerusalem, thinking up one pilgrimage after another. This is where the people were to go and pray, just as though we could not find God at home, in our bedroom or

wherever we happened to be. God is no longer confined to one place, as He was when He chose to dwell in Jerusalem before the advent of the true temple, Christ the Lord. Thus we read: 'The hour is coming when neither on this mountain nor in Jerusalem will you worship the Father in spirit and in truth' (John 4:21–3). The temple in Jerusalem is no more, and now God must be worshiped wherever one happens to be ... For if Christ is sitting at the right hand of His Father, why, then, should we seek Him in Rome, in Compostela, in Aachen, or at the Oak? You will not find God there; you will find the devil. For God will not let Himself be found in a place of our own choice and choosing.[12]

Luther's point here moves from the eschatological (in the new age, God can now be encountered anywhere) to the sacramental (God has in fact told us where to find him). While it is true that God can be found anywhere, his presence is focused in particular places; however these are not so much geographical but theological locations. For Luther, creation acts like a mask (*larva*), which both conceals and reveals the presence of God. Fallen human reason, however, is liable to misread the signs of God's presence behind creation, so God has designated certain places where he is specifically to be found, and where his will and purpose can be made plain for all to see and understand. These particular sacramental places are identified as the Word, the water of baptism, the bread and wine of the Eucharist, and the people of God. It is to these places that he has directed people to go if they are to find him. As Luther points out in 'The Babylonian Captivity of the Church' of 1520, all that is needed for living the Christian life is found in the local church:

> Let every man stay in his own parish; there he will find more than in all the shrines, even if they were all rolled into one. In your own parish you find baptism, the sacrament, preaching and your neighbour, and these things are greater than all the saints in heaven ... Let him stay at home in his own parish church and be content with the best; his baptism, the gospel, his faith, his Christ, and his God, who is the same God everywhere.[13]

As Luther saw it, the medieval pilgrimage industry was both fuelled by, and in turn fed, dissatisfaction with the local church. It fostered a sense of spiritual restlessness and ingratitude, where, not content with the gracious provision God had made for Christians in the normal practice of a local church, the pilgrim was always looking for something else, something extra, beyond what God had provided. More than this, though, it was a refusal to look for God in the very places where he has committed himself to be found, and instead insisting that God be found in places of human choosing.

Luther's third objection to pilgrimages was that not only had they become a distraction from the ways in which God had revealed himself in Word, Sacrament and Church, they also encouraged escapism from the true duties of the Christian life. Luther often cites the tendency to spend vast amounts of time and money on pilgrimages (which are not commanded in Scripture), which would have been better spent on helping the poor, one's own family or neighbour (which is). Luther depicts an ordinary penitent going to confession with his local priest, and finding himself commanded to go on a (relatively expensive) barefoot pilgrimage to Rome as part of his penance for sin. On returning home after confession he sees his neighbour's family in poverty and pain, in dire need of food and finance. Luther's advice is unequivocal: 'he should look to the love of Christ, help him, and let the pilgrimage go.'[14] Commenting on the story of Abraham and Sarah in Genesis 18, Luther contrasts St Jerome's pilgrimages to desert places, normally viewed as meritorious and praiseworthy, with Sarah's ordinary hospitality towards guests from her own hearth. For Luther the latter, much more 'ordinary' task is of much greater value in the eyes of God.[15]

The Reformation was characterized to a large degree by a move away from specifically religious activities towards social ones, and much of this can be traced back to Luther himself. He could even describe the sum of Christian life as 'faith ... directed towards God and love towards man and one's neighbour'.[16] A central aspect of the Reformation critique of late medieval piety concerned its excessive focus on religious works, which took up valuable time, energy and money which would have been better spent on relief for the poor or ordinary acts of generosity and kindness towards one's neighbours or family.[17] For Luther, one of the great benefits of the doctrine of justification by faith alone was that it freed the Christian from the necessity of religious works which needed to be performed in order to aid the process of justification. In this way, Christian energies could be liberated for true acts of service and kindness to others. Works motivated in this way also had greater integrity. They were no longer performed out of a desire for individual salvation, using the neighbour as an instrument to acquire personal piety or merit. Instead they could be performed out of genuine love and compassion for the neighbour, now that the question of justification was settled elsewhere, through faith.

Pilgrimages were one of the many time- and money-consuming activities of late medieval religion that Luther felt had become a serious distraction from acts of true Christian service. They had become a diversion from the real focus of Christian life, in the building up of other people and the Christian community.

A fourth reason why Luther decided against pilgrimages concerns the financial corruption which so often clung to pilgrimage sites. As a relatively young friar, Luther had visited Rome on a small business errand, connected with the inner working of his own Augustinian order. On several occasions, he remembered how disappointed he had been with what he had found there: 'At Rome, men do not find a good example, only pure scandal.'[18] Pilgrimage to the famous centre of the Christian world actually did more harm than good as visitors saw for themselves the decadence and filth of the place. The experience seemed to colour his view of pilgrimage from then on. In his *To the Christian Nobility of the German Nation* of 1520, Luther repeats the charge that one of the main results of pilgrimage is to 'strengthen greed' and to fill the coffers of avaricious bishops.[19] Over time, his views did not change. In his Commentary on John's Gospel in 1537, the same note is sounded. Commenting on the commodification of religion under the papacy, Luther complains: 'This has degenerated into extortion. Special letters of dispensation are issued, brotherhoods and communities are organized, pilgrimages are undertaken, and all sorts of fairs are instituted – all of which nets a great amount of money.'[20]

Again, contemporary pilgrimage has fallen into serious disrepute. It has become associated with some very unsavoury company. And again, because of the seriousness of this charge of severe corruption within medieval pilgrimage, most of which Luther interprets as a money-making scam by avaricious priests and prelates, and which brings little if any benefit to the participants, he recommends, as a result, that wise Christians will desist from going on pilgrimage altogether.

Calvin on Pilgrimage

John Calvin strikes similar notes when he comments on pilgrimage. His comments on the practice are not as numerous as Luther's, and seldom does he dwell on the practice long enough to mount a thorough critique of it. Characteristically, 'pilgrimage' occurs in long lists of other aspects of late medieval piety which Calvin wants to turn away from, such as masses for the dead, candles lit in front of shrines or sprinklings of holy water. As a second-generation Reformer, Calvin was less clearly in the forefront of the attack on pilgrimage than Luther, and there is a sense in Calvin's writings of this as a battle which has already been fought, and no longer a central issue.

Nevertheless, Calvin does have some charges to make against pilgrims and medieval pilgrimage. Like Luther, he comments on the corruption and licentiousness that often accompany pilgrimage,[21] and stresses that pilgrimage is nowhere commanded in Scripture.[22] He goes beyond this, and even beyond Luther, in suggesting that a scriptural text such as John 4:21 actually prohibits pilgrimage, though it is significant that the target of his attack in this and on many other occasions is specifically *votive* pilgrimages (pilgrimages undertaken as a result of a vow). Another aspect of contemporary pilgrimage which Calvin dislikes is the idea that a pilgrimage remains meritorious or valid, regardless of the state of the heart:

> And thus, if a monk rise from the bed of his adultery to chant a few psalms without one spark of godliness in his breast, or if a whoremonger, a thief,

or any foresworn villain, seeks to make reparation for his crimes by mass or pilgrimage, they would be loath to consider this lost labour. By God, on the other hand, such a disjunction of the form from the inward sentiment of devotion is branded as sacrilege.[23]

A particular aspect of pilgrimage considered at some length by Calvin is the widespread medieval interest in relics of the saints and apostles in his *Treatise on Relics* of 1543. Implicit within this critique is an attack on pilgrimage to holy sites possessing such collections of relics, which was an integral part of the whole industry. This piece is a remarkable catalogue of the location of various collections of relics across Europe, not of course as a guidebook for those who would wish to visit, but as a piece of subversive detective work to destroy such interest. Calvin takes great delight in pointing out how an arm of St Antony, formerly kissed and venerated in Geneva, turned out to be the bone of a stag; how there are at least 14 nails from the Cross being exhibited in different places, and how most of the apostles must have had two or three bodies to provide the scattered catalogue of bones and skulls on show in the various pilgrimage centres of Europe. The treatise is designed to uncover the unscrupulousness of those who put forward such fakes for veneration, and the credulity of those who visit them. More important, however, are Calvin's cautionary remarks about the relic trade, which have a primarily theological rather than ethical focus.

> But the first abuse, and, as it were, beginning of the evil, was, that when Christ ought to have been sought in his Word, sacraments, and spiritual influences, the world, after its wont, clung to his garments, vests and swaddling clothes; and thus overlooking the principal matter, followed only its accessory.[24]

His point is similar to that of Luther mentioned above, that pilgrimage to sites where relics of Christ and the saints are on display has an inbuilt tendency to deflect attention away from the places where God has chosen to make himself known and available to us – most notably in the Word and sacraments – and onto lesser things. His fear is that a preoccupation with trivia will lead to the worship of trivia, rather than adoration of the true God. Calvin is fully aware of the positive motivation which lies behind much devotion to relics, namely the desire to keep alive memory of and devotion to Christ and the saints. However, 'the desire for relics,' he concludes, 'is usually the parent of idolatry.' An intense focus on these items will almost inevitably, he thinks, lead to a fascination with them. Such fascination inevitably draws attention and devotion onto the relics themselves (which in most cases are bogus anyway) and away from a devotion to Christ, who alone is worthy of worship. To call such objects 'sacramental' and to validate devotion to them in this way is, for Calvin, to miss the point. True sacraments are those places where God has directed us to find him. For Calvin, the water of baptism and the bread and wine of the Lord's Supper enjoy a special status as means of grace, as spaces where the unity between Christ and the believer is both demonstrated and enacted, precisely because they enjoy divine institution. We are not at liberty to create our own sacraments: 'all divine worship of man's devising, having no better and surer foundation than his own opinion, be its semblance of wisdom what it may, is mere vanity and folly.'[25] For Calvin, this is a cardinal theological principle: it safeguards the freedom and initiative of God, and is an expression of the fundamental futility of human attempts to establish means of approaching God on our own terms.

It is perhaps characteristic of Calvin's theology that it is he rather than Luther who mounts a sustained attack on pilgrimage to collections of relics. Calvin's theology always had a tendency to assert the spiritual nature of worship of God, whereas Luther was more cautious about dividing physical from spiritual reality, so much so that he could write that 'The Spirit cannot be with us except in material and physical things such as the Word, water and Christ's body and in his saints on earth.'[26] In addition, Luther always had to be a little careful about relics, as his chief patron in the early years, Frederick the Wise, possessed a very large collection of them, kept in the Castle Church at the other end of the main street in Wittenberg from Luther's Augustinian friary. However, Luther's and Calvin's positions are not very far apart and they combine to sound a rigorous and robust note of caution about the practice of pilgrimage which has had a huge influence upon the history of pilgrimage since the 16th century, and remains influential on the many Protestants who visit pilgrimage sites today, yet feel that they do not quite belong there.

The Reformation and Pilgrimage Today

This survey of the thought of the two major figures within the Protestant Reformation of the 16th century presents a common front, but for different reasons. As we might expect, given the different cast of their theologies, Luther and Calvin focus on different aspects of pilgrimage as they mount their critique. Luther condemns the exercise primarily because it has become tied up with a theology of merit, an attempt to justify oneself by religious works, thus compromising the central article of justification by faith alone. For Calvin, on the other hand, given the centrality in his theology of the proper worship of Christ, as the place in which God makes his benefits available to us, it is the tendency of pilgrimage to attract worship to irrelevant accessories, rather than to the main thing itself, which is its Achilles' heel. It might be said that, for Luther, the chief sin was unbelief, whereas for Calvin it was idolatry. These theological perspectives are reflected clearly in their respective (and complementary) objections to pilgrimage.

Of the two, Calvin's is the more fundamental objection. His critique rests on a more basic problem, that focusing on a particular object or place has the potential of distracting attention from Christ himself. As we have seen, in other (sacramental) contexts, Luther stressed quite emphatically the capacity of physical things to convey the real presence of God, and so in principle has fewer difficulties with the idea of particular places or objects as being helpful or beneficial to faith. Similarly, Calvin tends in general to take a stricter line on Scriptural permission – what is not in Scripture tends to be frowned on – whereas Luther could often permit practices not explicitly outlawed by the Bible.

Although different in focus, there is a large degree of overlap in the two theologians' evaluation of pilgrimage. Put together, their arguments also sound fairly conclusively like a comprehensive denial of the value of the practice altogether, yet, on closer inspection, the attack on pilgrimage found in these Reformation thinkers is more strictly speaking an attack on the abuse of pilgrimage, rather than on pilgrimage itself. Luther's arguments focus on the close connection between contemporary pilgrimage and a theology of justification by meritorious works. His additional arguments, that pilgrimages distract attention from the designated place of God's revealed presence, from works of true Christian love and piety, and his protest at the financial corruption entailed, all have a similar character. In other words, Luther's critique does not argue that pilgrimage in itself is fundamentally wrong, just that it has become so entangled with damaging and dangerous habits of thought and life that it would be better to desist altogether. In fact, Luther says as much in his treatise *To the Christian Nobility* of 1520: 'I say this not because pilgrimages are bad, but because they are ill-advised at this time.'[27]

In context, this statement refers to pilgrimage to Rome, and Luther adds an instruction that 'no-one should be allowed to make such a pilgrimage for reasons of curiosity or his own pious devotion, unless it is first acknowledged by his parish priest, his town authorities, or his overlord that he has a good and sufficient reason for doing so'.[28] There is no evidence that such an arrangement was ever formally instituted, yet the point is that Luther does acknowledge here the possibility of 'good and sufficient reason' for going on pilgrimage. Luther is clearly concerned to prevent the damage caused by embarking on pious journeys for the wrong reasons, yet he leaves open the possibility of doing so for the right reasons. Unlike indulgences, where Luther's initial attack was on their abuse, but which he later condemned altogether, Luther never goes this second step with pilgrimage. For him, it remained a practice damned by association.

As we have seen, Calvin comes closer than Luther to a total ban on pilgrimage. However the main lines of his case can also be understood as primarily aimed at the abuse rather than the practice. In his robust critique of the relic trade, he attacks not so much pilgrimage in itself, as pilgrimage to pious souvenirs, which are often bogus, and a severe distraction from true faith and piety. The fact that many of his cited references to pilgrimage are to 'votive pilgrimage' indicates that one of his principal objections is to the element of compulsion involved. For him, as for Luther, pilgrimage is nowhere commanded in Scripture, and Calvin sees the performance for vows to undertake such journeys as an infringement of the liberty of a Christian and a mistaken attempt to earn merit or fulfil legal requirements which had no place in a theology of faith. Again, Calvin too is eloquent on the sexual and financial abuse that sometimes accompanied pilgrimage, and was a strong critic of pilgrimage undertaken where the heart was not engaged along with the body and the feet. Pilgrimage which detracts from spiritual attention to and worship of Christ is, in Calvin's mind, to be resisted. However again this leaves open the question of whether a form of pilgrimage can be found which avoids such a tendency.

It might be useful to think of the Reformation critique of medieval pilgrimage by imagining a delicate flowering plant which has become tightly entangled with some aggressive and dangerous weeds. The weeds are so dangerous, and so inextricably tangled up with the plant, that the only remedy is to pull up plant and weeds together. Better to have nothing at all than a pleasant flower which has merely become a climber for poisonous weeds, especially as the plant is not essential to the garden in the first place. The question remains, however, of whether, with some distance of time, when conditions are very different, the plant can be re-rooted in good soil which can be kept clear of the weeds which damaged it so much in the past.

Reforming Pilgrimage?

If it is true that the main focus of Luther's and even Calvin's attack on medieval pilgrimage was strictly speaking on abuses rather than the thing itself, another series of questions presents itself. In the light of their critique of the practice, what might a responsible Reformation approach to pilgrimage look like? What might Reformation theology have to say to the contemporary understanding and conduct of pilgrimage today?

It hopefully goes without saying that any introduction to pilgrimage or teaching on the subject needs carefully to avoid any suggestion that the exercise earns any particular merit towards salvation, or indeed affects the constancy of God's compassion or faithfulness in any way. Whereas the *hajj* in Islam enjoys the status of one of the five pillars of that faith, pilgrimage can never become in any sense compulsory for Christians, either by declaration or by implication. Despite the close association between pilgrimage and a theology of merit in the late Middle Ages, it is perfectly possible to engage in pilgrimage without any sense that this curries any kind of special favour with God, or places the pilgrim on any special new spiritual plane not enjoyed by those who stay at home. More positively, however, four further points might be made.

Ethical Responsibility

Luther and Calvin, not to mention the countless other less well-known reforming figures of the 16th century, all drew attention to the corruption which had seeped into the pilgrimage industry. It is perhaps a tendency which always lies close at hand when such sensitive and personal subjects as faith and devotion are present. It is very easy to prey upon religious desire and affection, and the space between open-hearted faith and simple credulity is one that many unscrupulous traders looking for a quick profit are happy to fill. In the 19th century, on his visit to the Holy Land, Mark Twain complained of how the pilgrim's 'life is almost badgered out of him by importunate swarms of beggars and pedlars, who hang on the strings to one's sleeves and coat-tails, and shriek and shout in his ears'. It is a description which will sound very familiar to any modern pilgrim who has visited the main sites in Israel at the height of the tourist season. Pilgrimage has attracted its fair share of unscrupulous trade and, at times, pilgrimage guides have often been tempted to stretch credulity by claiming more than is warranted for particular sites or objects. Open-minded and open-hearted faith is necessarily vulnerable to abuse. If it becomes cynical and jaundiced from the outset, it loses something essential to its own character. The Reformation critique of the ethics of pilgrimage comes as a healthy and necessary reminder of the openness of faith to exploitation, its susceptibility to being taken for a ride, and the need for simplicity and honesty on the part of both host and visitor to enable the experience to be as beneficial as possible.

Holy People and Holy Places

Luther's concern that pilgrimage encouraged dissatisfaction with the local church, allied with his insistence that it should not replace acts of kindness and generosity to one's neighbour, friend or fellow-Christian, serves as a reminder that pilgrimage needs to take with the utmost seriousness the Christian community which the pilgrim leaves, and which he or she visits. It is sadly common for western visitors to the Holy Land to visit all the main Biblical sites, but never to exchange a word with a local Christian, Arab or Jew. Visitors can equally be rushed in and out of pilgrimage sites with no thought for the impact that their visit has upon the local area or the need to support the local Christian community, whether economically or in prayer. Luther's insistence on the necessity that pilgrimage contribute to, rather than detract from, local Christian communities might serve as a reminder to Christian tour companies to design itineraries which deliberately enable supportive contact with local Christians. Similarly, pilgrimage needs to ensure that it does not detract from or create dissatisfaction with home churches.

There is a paradox to be found at the heart of pilgrimage. A pilgrim goes in search of a closer knowledge, experience or relationship with God. However, a common outcome of good, healthy pilgrimage is a renewed and strengthened sense that God can in fact be found, not just in so-called 'holy places', but anywhere. Since the coming of the Spirit, God can now be found wherever his people meet. The temple where he is pleased to dwell can be found wherever the body of Christ now meets (ICorinthians 3:16; 6:19). Responsible tour leaders will bear this in mind constantly, crafting the expectations and outcomes of a tour plan to strengthen rather than weaken attachment, commitment and practical action within and from local churches back home.

Focus on Christ

Calvin's cautionary remarks about relics and Christian gullibility may strike us as unnecessarily scathing. The relic industry is nothing like as widespread today, and a certain healthy scepticism is fairly common about some of the more outlandish claims made for pilgrimage sites or artefacts. Nevertheless, it is hard to deny that it remains distinctly possible to encourage an unhealthy, voyeuristic fascination with places and objects in present-day pilgrim tours. Many Christian visitors to the Holy Land have found themselves wondering whether or not this really was the cave where Jesus was born, the mountain where he fed the five thousand, or the route he took through Jerusalem carrying his cross. It is possible to spend one's entire time in the Church of the Holy Sepulchre worried about questions of architectural and archaeological authenticity and to miss completely the opportunity to reflect on the nature and meaning of the Cross and resurrection of Christ in the place where Christians have come for centuries to recall and experience, in some extended way, those very epochal events. Fascination with precise locations can do precisely what Calvin was afraid of – lead subtly away from the worship of Christ, to attention to trivias which, however interesting, fail to promote holiness or transformation.

Again, one of the effects of good pilgrimage to the Holy Land is a renewed sense of the true humanity of Christ. Some popular Christianity can verge uncomfortably on the fringes of Docetism. In other words, Jesus is worshipped and sung to as a spiritual, almost imaginary being who bears little relationship to real life, or to the historical figure who lived in the middle of the complex ferment of 1st-century Palestine. Visiting the land of Jesus brings home to many a Christian traveller the emphatic earthiness of the real Jesus, that here was a figure deeply engaged with the political, religious and economic issues of his own time, and who died on a real cross in a real city in real history. In other words, responsible pilgrimage can strengthen faith in the reality of the

Incarnation, in the depth of divine involvement in and commitment to the world in Christ. In this way, far from distracting from Christ in the way which Calvin feared, good, theologically informed pilgrimage can in fact refocus attention upon and strengthen faith in him.

A Metaphor for Life

By far the majority of Calvin's references to *peregrinatio* do not in fact refer to medieval journeys to holy places, but to the Christian life, lived in anticipation of arrival at the heavenly city, from cradle to grave.[29] Pilgrimage as a metaphor for the Christian life has a very long pedigree, and in restoring this as its primary usage Calvin was only returning to an ancient and respected Christian meaning. The Protestant tradition beyond Luther and Calvin explored this metaphor, often in great detail, most notably of course in Bunyan's *Pilgrim's Progress* of 1678.

The idea of life, or more specifically *Christian* life, as pilgrimage gives it shape and direction, and orients it decisively towards its future rather than its present, the destination rather than travelling for its own sake. It is perhaps a metaphor which needs to be rediscovered in a post-modern age which has lost any sense of purpose or destination to life, and where Christian existence is liable to take its lead from the surrounding culture rather than its Biblical roots. A Church living in a culture which does not see any direction in the future, but instead celebrates the aimlessness of wandering, needs good Christian imagery which reminds it again and again of its true calling to live in anticipation and hope, not complacency and contentment.

Again well-led pilgrimage can use the experience of travel to places of special spiritual or historical interest as a means of restoring this sense of the whole of Christian life as a journey. Travelling to new and disturbing places can be an unsettling and disorienting experience, just what is sometimes needed to help re-evaluate 'normal' life which has become stuck in a debilitating routine. Sleeping in a different bed each night can become a reminder that, in a very true sense, Christians, like their Lord, have nowhere to lay their heads. Travelling with the hope of a climactic arrival at Jerusalem, or wherever the goal of the journey lies, can become a reaffirmation of the hope of arrival one day in the 'heavenly Jerusalem', the promised new world order – a new heaven and a new earth.

In these small ways, tour leaders can help pilgrims reappropriate the important role that the notion of pilgrimage has played, not least in the Reformation, as a metaphor for Christian life. Calvin's disdain for pilgrimage which fails to change the heart and the behaviour of participants reminds us of the need for pilgrimage today not to become like a holiday which is designed to enable us to forget and escape from the realities awaiting us at home, but instead, to become an experience which enables the pilgrims to reassess their 'regular' Christian existence, and reorient it to its true identity and goal. It can restore a sense of proper Christian ambition which is dissatisfied with the status quo, and instead determines to anticipate and hope towards the day when the earth will be renewed and the kingdom of God will come in all its fullness.

The Reformation critique of pilgrimage still needs to be heard today. It still stands as a caution against some of the theological and spiritual pitfalls into which the exercise can fall in the 21st as well as in the 16th century. Yet at the same time, as we have seen, the critique falls short of a total prohibition on the practice, and in an age where the theological battles have moved onto other grounds, there is scope for the rediscovery of pilgrimage as ethically responsible, supportive of local Christian communities, renewing faith in and understanding of Christ and rooted in Christian life as pilgrimage towards the goal of a new heaven and a new earth.

Notes

1 Gregory of Nyssa, 'On Pilgrimage', 382–3.
2 À Kempis, *Imitation*, 216 (IV.I).
3 See Hus's treatise 'On Simony', which he defines as 'trafficking in holy things', with its implied critique of indulgences and pilgrimages to holy sites.
4 Erasmus, 'Enchiridion', 337f, 348.
5 *LW*, 44.171.
6 *LW*, 44.40.
7 An example can be found in Davies, *Pilgrimage*, 96–108, which gives a useful overview but does not delve very deeply into the theological objections to pilgrimage in the Reformation.
8 *LW* 31.199.
9 The Latin phrase usually ran *'facientibus quod in se est, Deus non denegat gratiam'*.
10 *LW*, 2.123 (Gen.8:21).
11 *LW*, 23.171 (John 6:63).
12 *LW*, 22.250 (John 2:22).
13 *LW*, 44.187.
14 *LW*, 51.107.
15 *LW*, 3.216.
16 *LW*, 51.75.
17 See Gerrish, 'By Faith Alone', 89.
18 *LW*, 44.170.
19 *LW*, 44.184.
20 *LW*, 22.220 (John 2:14).
21 Calvin on Hosea 4:14 (*Twelve Minor Prophets*).
22 See for example Calvin on Acts 14:3 (*Acts*, 3), and on Jonah 1:16 (*Twelve Minor Prophets*, 69–70).
23 Calvin on Psalm 50:16 (*Psalms*, 275).
24 Calvin, 'Treatise on Relics', 289.
25 Ibid., 290.
26 *LW*, 37.95.
27 *LW*, 44.169–70.
28 *LW*, 44.169.

29 For the NT roots of this imagery, see for example Galatians 4:26, Hebrews 11:10, Revelation 21:2.

References

À Kempis, T., *The Imitation of Christ* (Glasgow: Fount, 1977).

Calvin, J., *Calvin's Commentaries on the Book of Psalms, vol. 2*, trans. J. Anderson (Edinburgh: Calvin Translation Society, 1844).

——, 'Treatise on Relics', in *Tracts and Treatises on the Reformation of the Church by John Calvin*, trans. H. Beveridge (Edinburgh: Oliver & Boyd, 1844).

——, *Calvin's Commentaries on the Twelve Minor Prophets, vol. 1*, trans. J. Owen (Edinburgh: Calvin Translation Society, 1847).

——, *Calvin's Commentaries: The Acts of the Apostles*, ed. D.W. Torrance and T.F. Torrance (Edinburgh: Oliver & Boyd, 1966).

Davies, J.G., *Pilgrimage Yesterday and Today: Why? Where? How?* (London: SCM, 1988).

Erasmus, 'Enchiridion', in M. Spinka (ed.), *Advocates of Reform*, Library of Christian Classics, vol. XIV (London: SCM, 1953), pp.295–379.

Gerrish, B.A., 'By Faith Alone: Medium and Message in Luther's Gospel', *The Old Protestantism and the New: Essays on the Reformation Heritage* (Edinburgh, T&T Clark, 1982), pp.69–89.

Gregory of Nyssa, 'On Pilgrimage', in P. Schaff, and H. Wace (eds), *Nicene and Post-Nicene Fathers, 2nd series, vol. V* (Grand Rapids: Eerdmans, 1892).

Hus, Jan, 'On Simony', in M. Spinka (ed.), *Advocates of Reform*, Library of Christian Classics, vol. XIV (London: SCM, 1953), pp. 196–278.

Luther, M., *Luther's Works*, 55 vols (Philadelphia: Fortress and St Louis: Concordia, 1955–75).

CHAPTER 8

Louis Massignon, the Seven Sleepers of Ephesus and the Christian–Muslim Pilgrimage at Vieux-Marché, Brittany

Anthony O'Mahony

Distinguer pour unir – Distinguish in order to unite.

(Jacques Maritain)

Louis Massignon (1883–1962), who was a dominant presence in the field of Islamic studies, and whose career which began in 1900 spanned more than 60 years, was arguably one of the most important Orientalist scholars in the European tradition of the 20th century.[1] However, distinguished as his career was, today his name would probably be known only within the scholarly world as related to Islamic studies, were it not for a life whose range defies easy categories. He made a special contribution to our knowledge of Islamic mysticism, Sufism, and sociology, and had a deep and lasting influence upon Islamic studies in general, particularly in France,[2] and upon understanding of Islam within the Christian tradition.[3] By the force of his personality and the originality of his ideas Louis Massignon was perhaps the only Islamicist scholar who was a central figure in the intellectual life of his time. Abbé Harpigny, in his landmark study *Islam and Christianity according to Louis Massignon*,[4] divides Louis Massignon's itinerary into three episodes: *le cycle hallagien*, which ended with the submission of his doctoral thesis, *La Passion d'al-Hosayn-ibn Mansour al-Hallâj, martyre mystique de l'Islam*, in 1922; *le cycle abrahamique*, until his ordination as a priest in the Greek Catholic Melkite church in Cairo in 1950; and *un cycle gandhien*, a period of political activism which ended with his death in 1962. It was during the last episode of his life that he grafted a Christian–Muslim pilgrimage onto a traditional Breton '*Pardon*' at Vieux-Marché.

Massignon established the Christian–Muslim pilgrimage during the period of the Algerian war, which at that time, it seemed, would bring about destabilizing civil conflict within metropolitan France itself. The original *pardon* was centred on the tradition of the Seven Sleepers of Ephesus whose feast was traditionally celebrated at Vieux-Marché in Brittany. Mention of the seven sleepers is found in both the Christian and Muslim traditions, and for the latter an entire Qur'anic sura is dedicated to their memory, whilst the Christian East honoured their feast from the early centuries onwards. Massignon, who was always interested in the confluence of Christianity and Islam, saw this ancient feast, celebrated in his beloved Celtic west of France, as an opportunity to bring about an encounter that would witness to the deep bond which held the two traditions together in a fraternal theological witness, which he could only reason would be understood at the end of eschatological time.

Louis Massignon's Theological Vision and the Challenge of Pilgrimage

Louis Massignon would find, in the witness of the west, a profound affirmation of his Christian theological vision, which informed his very public political life and witness. Massignon held a view of history which sees the handing on of knowledge of God from one individual to another as the only significant process and therefore most deserving of study. His mystical encounter in Iraq in 1908 was for him an intensification of the Christian consciousness to which Muslims witnessed. He developed this concept of history in a series of letters to Paul Claudel between 1908 and 1909 in which the meaning of history is to be found, not in the impersonality of social evolution, but in the divine word in the individual soul.[5] Encounters such as these can take place within the ordered framework of an established tradition, but they can also be sudden confrontations: the unexpected 'Other' breaks in on ordinary life, shattering and transforming it. In a moment of illumination a man can transcend his worldly images and see, beyond them, another beauty. History is a chain of witnesses entering as carriers of a truth beyond themselves, and a chain which can run across the habitual frontiers of different religions. Massignon believed that he himself had been drawn into this chain, in an event which is difficult to comprehend. It is perhaps also difficult to accept all the details as he has described them, but the event certainly decided the direction of his life. The event was his initiation as a witness, a participant in the mystery of substitution, by which a man can provide for others what they cannot obtain for themselves.[6] Having acquired through Muslims the knowledge of transcendence, how could he himself serve as a channel through which they could come to knowledge of incarnation?[7]

Massignon stood in conscious opposition to the kind of historical approach which was common in the 19th century: the view, that is to say, which saw history as having a meaning inside itself, moving by its own inner dynamism towards a goal which it could achieve in this world, and one which thought of great collectives (nations or races or classes) as carriers of this movement. For Massignon, the meaning of history was to be found rather in the working of the grace of God in individual souls, crossing all barriers between human communities – even religious communities – and its end was a goal that lay beyond the limits of the perishable world. The process revealed itself above all in the lives of certain individuals who had been touched by grace in some special way and had responded to it fully, by being witnesses to the presence of God and, if need be, by martyrdom.[8] Martyrdom is more than a religious act; it is a political statement: martyrdom is a political act affecting the allocation of power between two societies, or between a subgroup and the larger society.[9] That is why, during the first three centuries of Christianity, Roman authorities increasingly considered the movement a direct threat to their authority and acted accordingly. And that is why Massignon felt such an attraction towards the cult of the seven sleepers.

At the level of theology Massignon believed passionately that somehow the Christian Church had to include Islam within its understanding. He identified Islam as a particular theological statement:

> The goal of Qur'anic revelation is not to expose or justify supernatural gifts so as to be ignorant of them, but, in recalling them to the name of God, to bring back to intelligent beings the temporal and eternal sanctions – natural religion – primitive law, the simple worship that God has prescribed for all time – that Adam, Abraham and the prophets have always practised in the same way.[10]

For Massignon, Islam is 'the faith of Abraham revived with Muhammad'. He therefore firmly believed that Islam has a positive, almost prophetic mission in the post-Christian world, albeit that one might, in his terms, describe it as an 'Abrahamic schism'. He put the matter forcibly in the following statement:

> Islam is a great mystery of the divine will, the claim of the excluded, those chased into the desert with Ishmael, their ancestor, against the 'privileged' ones of God, the Jews, and especially the Christians, who have abused the divine privileges of Grace. Islam is the divine lance, which, by the Holy War, has stigmatised Christianity.[11]

Massignon was fond of this image of the lance as an expression of the role of Islam in history in regard to the Church, especially in conjunction with the evocative imagery of the stigmata. In the *Hijrah of Ishmael* he spoke of the 13 centuries during which Islam confronted Christianity and he said that for these hundreds of years Islam has been 'the angelic lance which has stigmatised Christianity'. However we understand Massignon's thought, he wished to be understood as an Orthodox Christian thinker and he was careful and prudent to seek the advice of others within the Church regarding his theological statements towards Islam. He had an overall passion for the unity of the Church, for he considered that unity existed as a reality, though it needed to be witnessed to. Christianity for him was the cosmic consummation of all humanity. It was not only a historical event, but also a pilgrimage which needed to include the other. Christian witness has been characterized as 'Walking in the Pilgrim City':

> Therefore Jesus also suffered outside the city gate in order to sanctify the people by his own blood. Let us then go to him outside the camp and bear the abuse he endured. For here we have no lasting city, but we are looking for the city that is to come. (Hebrews 13:12–14)

Blessed and cursed by a peculiar 'hopelessness', Christians claim fellowship with Christ who suffered outside the city gate, and are called to follow him into that wilderness beyond the camp, that region other than the earthly *civitas*, from which we might discern another city. This other city shows the structures of this world, which seem so solid and so real, to be afflicted with an ephemeral quality, a kind of unreality, so as to make them a source of anxiety rather than a resting place for our restless hearts (Luke 12:11–34). And so we exist in a state of perpetual pilgrimage to our true *patria*, following 'Jesus the pioneer and perfecter of our faith, who for the sake of the joy that was set before him endured the cross, disregarding its shame, and has taken his seat at the right hand of the throne of God' (Hebrews 12:2).

Dwelling 'outside the camp' need not entail a removal to a place apart. Christianity was from its earliest days a predominantly urban phenomenon, enacting its peculiarly homeless form of existence within the institutional confines of the late ancient city. Though there have been within Christianity from its earliest times monastic institutions which would locate themselves in a withdrawing to uninhabited places, for the vast majority of Christians in the first four centuries physical withdrawal from the city was not an option, nor was it held up as an ideal. At the same time, the Gospel call to homelessness is not a purely internalized indifference to this life, nor an invisible kind of pious detachment. When Paul speaks of those 'who walk not according to the flesh but according to the spirit' (Romans 8:4), he is not contrasting a spiritualized Gospel, which asks only for faith, to the carnal law which demands specific, visible actions. The Gospel, no less than the Law, requires actions, gestures and rituals: collection for the poor in Jerusalem, baptism, faithful participation in the Eucharist. What are called for are actual, concrete social practices by which the community of the Church is manifested as 'a chosen race, a royal priesthood, a holy nation, God's own people'. That which marks out the Church as a distinctive community of people, a 'nation', must be visible so it may 'proclaim the mighty acts of him who called you out of darkness into his marvellous light' (1Peter 2:9).[12]

The *Oxford English Dictionary* defines pilgrimage as 'a journey (usually of considerable duration) to some sacred place as an act of religious devotion'. In this definition the salient elements of the modern concept of pilgrimage are contact with the sacred and displacement.[13] Massignon saw pilgrimage as an intensely political act. His journeying to Jerusalem he saw as a witness to the nature of unity and that the Incarnation made the political possible to enact and fulfil.[14] The mystical thought of Massignon turns upon the concept–symbol *déplacement* (change of place). This notion, and its corollary, *la personne déplacée* (a personal shift), animates the thought and action of Massignon at all levels, be it scholarship, political or mystical. Considering the meeting between God and Man as the height of the human experience, Massignon is so profoundly Christian, despite what one could call his understanding of the temptation towards Islam – which he rejected, that he could not conceive of God and the relationship of God to humanity except as movement, *déplacement*, incarnation.

Never before has history known so many frontiers as in our modern world, and at no period has there been such a frequent violation of frontiers as happens today. It would seem that the establishment and removal of frontiers is the order of the day. This contradictory process is a window into the plight of humanity in these times: a dialectical tension between demarcation of particular identities and crossing over to the other shore. It is important to note, however, that the crossing of frontiers and the birth of the new are a sheer necessity for a new historical period or a particular context. The reality of the search for authentic renewal from within tradition outgrows the bounds and frames in which it was set up and forces the crossing of frontiers and the breaking of the frame. A remapping of the territory and a redrawing of the frontiers follow it: tradition is an ever-emerging source of theological creativity, rooted identity and wise compassion.[15]

However, crossing, of course, is not simply an external event. It is also a spiritual experience. The American Catholic theologian, David Burrell, has taken up this journey as an enriching spiritual endeavour:

> We are invited, in our time, on a voyage of discovery stripped of colonizing pretensions: an invitation to explore the other on the way to discovering ourselves. The world into which we have been thrust asks nothing less of us; those of us intent on discovering our individual vocations cannot proceed except as partners in such a variegated community. And as that journey enters the domain of faith, our community must needs assume interfaith dimension. What once were boundaries have become frontiers, which beckon to be broached, as we seek to understand where we stand by expanding our minds and hearts to embrace the other. Put in this fashion, our inner journey can neither be syncretic nor procrustean, assimilating or appropriating. What is rather called for is mutuality of understanding and of appreciation, a critical perception which is already incipiently self-critical. Rather than reach for commonality, we are invited to expand our horizons in the face of diversity. The goal is not an expanded scheme, but an enriched inquirer: discovery of one's own faith in encountering the faith of another.[16]

How it all Began

A fire burning in the night in late July of each year after the feast of Mary Magdalene: it is the evening of the Breton pilgrimage, the *tantad* a fire of joy, near the old chapel after the divine office. The procession moves to the rhythm of the *Gwerx*, this old Breton 12th-century canticle which narrates the adventure of the seven cave dwellers of Ephesus,[17] those seven young Christians who were persecuted under the Roman Emperor Decius (c.250) and returned in witness of the resurrection. The Qur'an gives an identical version of this story in *Sura* 18 of the Cave.[18]

The legend of the Seven Sleepers of Ephesus, according to the most common form, is of Syrian Christian origin. The first reference to the legend in western literature is by Gregory of Tours.[19] The story is told that Emperor Decius went to Ephesus to hold a great pagan celebration and slaughter the Christians there. Seven youths prayed for God to save the Christian people. They were accused before the Emperor, so they hid in a cave on Mount Ceolian outside Ephesus. Their hiding-place was discovered and its entrance blocked. The martyrs fell asleep in a mutual embrace. Nearly 200 years later a herdsman of Ephesus rediscovered the cave on Mount Coelian, and letting in the light, awoke the inmates, who sent one of their number to buy food. The lad was astonished to find the Cross displayed over the city gates, and on entering to hear the name of Christ openly pronounced. By tendering a coin of the time of Decius at a baker's shop he roused suspicion, and was taken before the authorities. He confirmed the truth of his story to his accusers by taking them to the cavern where his six companions were found, youthful and beaming with a holy radiance.

During the reign of Theodosius II, Roman emperor of the east, there was some controversy over the resurrection of the dead and Theodosius prayed that God would reveal the truth to the people. On hearing what had happened at Ephesus, he hastened to the spot, in time to hear from the young men themselves that God had wrought this wonder to confirm his faith in the resurrection of the dead. This message delivered, they again fell asleep. According to some sources Theodosius wanted to build golden coffins for them, but they appeared to him in a dream and told him to leave them in the earth, as they had been, to await the General Resurrection.

Located in the heart of the Breton country, nothing distinguishes the pilgrimage of this hamlet of the seven saints in Vieux-Marché from the other Breton pilgrim sites, except that, since 1954, this pilgrimage is the place where the Orient and the Occident, Christians and Muslims, meet. It all happens in respectful silence. Any traces of folklore were banished from the gathering and the only concessions in the first years were the tea and the crêpe served to welcome pilgrims in a barn, and a couscous before departure. All this was done with the greatest simplicity. Even during the most difficult moments of the

French–Algerian drama a Muslim delegation came to take part in the pilgrimage. The 'presence of Louis Massignon the apostle of peace alone served to avoid any equivocation'. He created this Muslim–Christian pilgrimage in this place where for centuries the Seven Sleepers of Ephesus have been venerated. Massignon invited everyone present to pray 'for serene peace between the peoples', between 'believers, sons of Abraham'.[20]

Since 1965, after the end of French Algeria, the bell from the Catholic cathedral in Algiers has hung in the church at Vieux-Marché.[21] It would seem that right up to his final years the tradition of the Seven Sleepers of Ephesus was an important element in the spirituality of Louis Massignon. The Islamo-Christian pilgrimage that he had grafted onto the tradition of a Breton '*pardon*' dedicated to the Seven Sleepers of Ephesus at Vieux-Marché had the meaning of a sign for him; in his eyes it seemed to be a sign announcing the spiritual encounter which he sought among the sons and daughters of Abraham; and Christians could doubtless specify that this spiritual search, as far as it concerned Islam, looked back to the period when Muhammad could find a new Barnabas with the potential to make him into a new St Paul.[22]

The Chapel of the Seven Sleepers was built between 1703 and 1704. It is in the shape of a Latin cross, with the two side-chapels built on a higher level. The one on the south side is built over the dolmen of Stiffell, which forms the crypt. The dolmen is itself listed as a 'monument historique' (1875–7). It is oriented east–west and is formed of four uprights and two capstones measuring 14'6" by 6'6". The Seven Sleepers, who have been venerated here for several centuries, are also known as the Seven Sleepers of Ephesus (modern Selçuk in Turkey), all young men: Maximilien, Marc, Martini, Denis, Jean, Séraphim and Constantin.[23]

Why did Massignon choose this place? The chapel had already caught the attention of historians and of orientalists. Renan mentions the chapel. Massignon made it known. The middle aisle is built on a crypt, evoking the cave of the seven walled up alive in Ephesus, formed by a heavy dolmen. The chapel was built on the same spot as an old sanctuary that since the 6th century has been dedicated to the Seven Sleepers of Ephesus. This cult is found in Christianity and Islam. Near the chapel on the hill is the Stiffell, a granite fountain from which water gushes at seven different points. Massignon considered that the cult of the oriental saints came to Brittany through the intermediary of Greek missionary monks who landed together with navigators on the tin route in the small port of Yaudet in the bay of Lannion, which then opened up for trade with the Orient. Here are also venerated other oriental saints such as St Thècle at Ploubezre, which is in the same valley leading to the sea.[24]

Massignon loved the valley of the seven saints where natural beauty and symbolism unite. The Breton writer Louis-Claude Duchesne reflects, years after: 'It is a privilege to accompany him. With the belt of his rain coat knotted his creases in his face still showing the tan of incessant trips and missions to the orient, and with a Basque beret on an ascetic face with a look of fire.' Herbert Mason, now Professor of History and Religion at Boston College and the principal translator of Massignon into English, vividly recorded his encounter with Massignon.

> My most vivid recollection of his humility was his participation in the Muslim–Christian pilgrimage at Vieux-Marché, Brittany. Though then a complete stranger to the Muslim world, I participated with him and the other pilgrims in this unusual 'fraternal witness' of peace and common prayer in July of 1959. I had witnessed firsthand in France atrocities and near atrocities that grew out of that Algerian war, and then I saw a few people from both sides at peace, in prayer, in talk, able to eat and converse together. I saw a revelation of what could be. Massignon was in a sense the host at the pilgrimage, and it has not stopped with his death, as some said it would, but rather has grown in size each year as others have seen and attached to its validity. He took pains to try to make strangers feel at home, to include some whom others would exclude. He made links between the guests, the different pilgrims. I was fascinated and deeply touched seeing him during a crowded candlelight procession on Saturday night come up and calm an old handicapped Algerian who was momentarily lost from his son and fearful of being trampled by the crowd. That was the kind of gesture he could make without thinking. And I recall him sitting on a wall near the chapel telling a group of Bretons, awed and attentive, about the history of their own Vieux-Marché and the cult of the Seven Sleepers that had existed there over the centuries, in a place they had known all their lives and assumed to be more or less insignificant. But it was less with Massignon that any of us were involved than with the meaning of being there – at once so strange and unheard of in those days and yet so plausible. It was a renewing experience that, without his special hospitality, I might have missed.[25]

Duchesne records Massignon's statement of 1 February 1962 that 'the friends of our pilgrimage are more in number than would be believed by the old reactionaries who in this ecumenical day and age ought to be pleased about our pilgrimage instead of keeping ignoring it!'

July 1962 was Massignon's last Breton pilgrimage, the 'pilgrimage of Islamo-Christian reconciliation'. Massignon wrote (letter, 4 August) to the pilgrims as they were gathering: 'For about nine years we have prayed and fasted (eighty-ninth fast last Friday), suffered. Behold the timid dawn of peace.' During this last pilgrimage Massignon welcomed Muhammad Taki[26] and the President of the Students from Comoros who during the ceremony of the *source* read Sura 18: 'His Arabic psalmody was moving, a cry of resurrection which though our seven [sleepers] walled up alive joined with the cry of Magdalene (buried on their thresh hold) for Lazarus.'[27] Resurrection! This was for Massignon the key word. No encounter is without this reference. On 27–8 July 2002, the 38th Pardon 'Islamo-Chrétien des Sept Saints Dormants' took place at Vieux-

Marché. In recent years a colloquy has formed part of the pilgrimage around a central theme of concern to Christians and Muslims. For 2002 it was the spiritual value of hospitality in an era of globalization. Père Roger Pèrez represented Breton Catholicism, Muhammad Loueslati represented the Muslim community and recited the Sura 18; Mgr Pierre Boz, the patriarchal exarch for the Melkite Catholics,[28] was also present.

Louis Massignon as Political Mystic and Christian Islamicist

However we understand or measure the work and personality of Louis Massignon, there was a deep symmetry between his writings, his acts and his beliefs. At the centre of Massignon's scholarly endeavour was the search for what was, or is, original in a person, a society or a work. Authenticity, where present, was one of the qualities he sought: there took place what was worthwhile and essential. Such authenticity could lie in the subject matter which was expressed, or in the way in which such subject matter was expressed. His interest was aroused by the particular traits pointing to a certain authenticity. Behind such originality or authenticity Massignon could detect, in some cases, a testimony or *témoignage* (witness). This sensitivity was at the root of his never-ending attention to expressions of the human soul, especially those of a religious connotation.

Massignon's research constantly faced the methodological difficulty of proving that something was or was not a borrowing from something else. However, if Massignon could not present strict evidence, he always attempted to discover other hypotheses than those of direct literary or historical derivation, in order to explain similarities between different phenomena without any apparent relationship. For example, he showed considerable interest in such coincidences as existed both in Islam and in Christianity and sought to link them with each other or find some connection between them at a deeper level.[29]

A clear record of how Massignon reconciled his scholarly work on Islam with his Christian beliefs is found in *Les trois prières d'Abraham: Seconde prière* (The three prayers of Abraham: Second prayer), which is a meditation on Abraham's prayer for Ishmael, as reported in Genesis. He stresses that Ishmael's exile took place after he had been circumcised and had received God's blessing in response to Abraham's prayer (Gen.17:18–20). Massignon sees in Muhammad's own forced emigration, or *hijra*, from Mecca a repetition of Ishmael's banishment at the instigation of Sarah. He suggests that, when Muhammad encountered the Jews in Medina, he therefore declared before God that he drew his inspiration from Abraham and claimed Abraham's entire spiritual and temporal heritage for the Arabs alone.[30] In later years, he became particularly interested in those phenomena which show a convergence or dialogue between Islam and Christianity: the meeting of Muhammad and the Christians of Najran, the cult of Fatima as a parallel to the veneration of the Virgin Mary, the veneration of the Seven Sleepers of Ephesus by Christians and Muslims alike, and vocations within Islam of mystical compassion and substitution like that of al-Hallâj. Al-Hallâj, the martyr mystic of Islam, was crucified for his theological views regarding the possibilities of God, which resembled a Christian understanding. Massignon, who was very interested in biography and liked to plot on the graph of what he called 'the curve of life', found the life stories interesting. He also thought that there are Christic figures within Islam who could ultimately play a role in bringing Muslims to confess the divine sonship of Jesus, the Christ, if only at the last judgment. Such figures included Salmân Pâk,[31] al-Hallâj,[32] al-Ghâzali and others.

The renewal of Massignon's Christian religious consciousness was directly linked in his own mind to Islam. Al-Hallâj, particularly, had moved forever beyond the realm of mere academic interest to become an actual guiding fraternal force. Their extraordinary friendship 'filled the heart of Massignon and shaped his mind so thoroughly that he can be seen as the greatest Muslim among Christians and the greatest Christian among Muslims'.[33] Massignon, with his involvement in the political issues of his time (Jerusalem, Palestine, Morocco, Algeria), was not just a radical activist, but a radical exemplar of a Hallâjian synthesis, old but little known in our world, of the heart and mind, *qalb* and *'aql*, unalienated from one another. This was his full achievement as a human being and the simplest, profoundest fruit of his friendship with al-Hallâj. In a letter to the American mystic and Trappist monk Thomas Merton, he wrote:

> My case is not to be imitated; I made a duel with our Lord, and having been an outlaw (against nature in love), against law (substituted to Moslems), and Hierarchy ... (leaving my native proud Latin community for a despised bride and insignificant Greek Catholic Melkite church), I die lonely in my family, for whom I am a bore ... I am a gloomy scoundrel.[34]

He died during the night of 31 October–1 November 1962.

The Seven Sleepers of Ephesus in Islam

The word 'cave' describes a hollow space in a mountain or hill. The term 'cave' (*kahf, ghar, magharat*) is used in the Qur'an to designate a place of refuge for the faithful or a locus of intimate contact with God; kahf occurs six times in the Qur'an (18:9, 10, 11, 16, 17, 25). 'The Cave' (*sura al-Kahf*) is the title of Qur'an 18, which consists of 110 verses. It refers to the story of the Companions of the Cave (vv.9–26), an Arabic version of widely circulated Christian accounts about the Seven Sleepers of Ephesus. This version tells of a group of youths who, fearing persecution or death for their faith, fled to a cave with their dog. God sheltered them there in a slumberous state for perhaps 309 years. When they awoke, they were discovered by their townspeople who decided to build a mosque over them and their hiding place.

Muslim commentators and traditionalists debate over the meaning of the ambiguous Qur'anic narrative and embellish it with details from Christian accounts. According to these sources, after the youths discovered that their religion had finally prevailed in their homeland, they blessed Theodosius, the faithful ruler, and returned to their death-like sleep to await the final resurrection. In the Qur'an and its subsequent interpretation, this cave was understood to be a sanctuary for the faithful and a place where they enjoyed God's mercy. It also represents the tomb from which the dead were to be resurrected. Ibn Ishaq, the important and early biographer of Muhammad, said that this story was revealed to him to show the prophet of Islam's authenticity. The background to this was the growing opposition to him and his movement in Mecca. Caves were also the locations of pivotal moments in the life of Muhammad. After periods of spiritual retreat, Muhammad received his first revelations from the angel Gabriel in a small cave. For Sufi commentators, it came to represent a place of spiritual retreat for the worldly body awaiting illumination from the divine spirit. Muslim exegetical and geographical literature ordinarily followed the Eastern Christian location of the 'Companions of the Cave' at Ephesus.[35]

The Seven Sleepers in the Life and Thought of Massignon

On 19 September 1951, Massignon visited the site of Ephesus in Turkey. He was less interested in the ruins of the famous city of antiquity than in the holy places scattered nearby, particularly the House of the Virgin, a small house which Anne Catherine Emmerich, the 'visionary' from Dülmen, described with such precision that its ruins were eventually found in the mountains in 1881: 'Just as Ephesus is certainly the place where Saint John lived and meditated his Gospel (so full of the intimacy of Christ) and his Apocalypse (written very nearby, on the island of Patmos) until he found himself in a more and more poignant union with the Compassion of Our Lady, it is also almost certainly the place where he let the Holy Virgin live (who became increasingly suspect and threatened in Palestine); and this small house in the mountains ... where Saint John isolated himself in order to pray "for the people" might be the one where the Holy Virgin had her Dormition.'[36]

There is a whole tradition that Mary, whom Christ had entrusted to Saint John, came to live in Ephesus. There are, of course, Church theologians and historians who do not believe that the Virgin Mary left Jerusalem for Ephesus at a very early date and quite obviously before the first serious persecutions struck the budding Christian community. Massignon, it has to be said, was not absolutely sure of it himself and publicly considered the possibility that the Virgin's house was at Ephesus to be 'plausible', while adding: 'I refuse to go any further.'[37] In private, however, and in the letters of the Badaliya, he showed himself to be more affirmative. It is indeed hard to imagine that Saint John should have left the mother of his Saviour in Jerusalem where her life was in danger, when Christ on the Cross had entrusted his beloved disciple with the task of looking after his mother.

But as Ephesus is, in the eyes of Massignon, primarily the place of the communion of life between the Virgin and Saint John, it took on a great significance in his life as Ephesus constituted a link between the Dormition, the Resurrection and the three witnesses of Christ being pierced by the lance (Mary, John and Mary Magdalene), on the one hand, and the seven young people from the cave, the so-called Seven Sleepers, on the other.

Who are the Seven Sleepers for Massignon? These seven young Christians from Ephesus who were immured alive were probably the victims of a religious persecution who miraculously woke up from their sleep for one moment in 448, at the very moment when the Eastern Church was split between Melkites, The Church of the East, Armenians and Copts.[38] It was during his studies on Qur'anic exegesis that Massignon became interested in their history. Under the cover of his research on al-Hallâj, he had already noted that al-Hallâj was tortured in 309 of the Hijra (922), and that 309 was also the Muslim figure to indicate how long the Seven Sleepers' slumber lasted. In Massignon's eyes, this was a patent sign. After his pilgrimage, the story of the Seven Sleepers was to hold an increasingly important place in his spirituality. As he wrote to Mary Kahil on 26 January 1956: 'Let us penetrate into this path which is so wide, in this night which is so dark, into the cave where the Seven Sleepers, who are before God immured in his Holy Will, are cradled in the Dormition of love.'[39]

The Qur'an dedicated a sura to them, *Ahl al Kahf* (Qur'an 18:9–26), in other words, 'the People in the Cave': 'Do you understand that the men in the Cave of Al-Raquim constitute a marvel amongst our signs?' According to Massignon, these verses form the Apocalypse of Islam. Indeed, the Seven Sleepers appear in both Islam and Christianity as the early witnesses of Resurrection: 'Their amorous impatience made them appear inordinate, so that they would be witnesses [of the Resurrection] for one short moment.' Their cave is 'the place where the first call of the Last Judgement will resound', and their mysterious slumber is a cradling, 'like that of a small boat on the ocean'. The Qu'ran records, 'You would have thought they were awake, even though they were asleep; and we turned to the right and to the left whereas their dog stayed on the threshold, with his forelegs stretched out' (18:18).

The legend of the Seven Sleepers would thus seem to constitute a bridge between Christianity and Islam. As Mgr Charles Molette was to say later on,

'We have to be clear about this: for Christianity, the cult of the Seven Sleepers is only of marginal importance ... Nevertheless, this legend is a significant parable: it confirms that the belief in the resurrection concerns all those who will be entrusted to God until death. ... As Islam joins Oriental Christianity in its veneration of the Seven Sleepers, it thereby witnesses its faith in God, who will mysteriously let all life blossom into resurrection on the Last Day; life which will be dedicated freely to the power of His will which is beyond comprehension – can any Christian remain insensible to this encounter?'[40]

Finally, like the Seven Sleepers of Ephesus, they who were 'immured alive for Justice', Massignon, during the last few years of his life on earth, was to feel that he had been immured alive, incarcerated on earth. Like them, the expectation of the arrival of the Master of life remained in his heart, of which the waking of the Seven Sleepers is a sign: 'The bursting open of those seven buds before the eternal spring, the blossoming which makes the rosebud open up before the evening dew, is Jesus who, from the bottom of his heart, burst the seals to the cave where they were immured. Like them, let us call him so that he can burst open our prison.'[41]

Across the world there are numerous sanctuaries dedicated to the Seven Sleepers of Ephesus, both on Christian and on Muslim soil, and Massignon visited all the major ones. One of them is in Damascus, where he went on 6 January 1954; this crypt is unusual in that it has seven *qibla* (prayer niches), one for each of the Sleepers. Nadjmoudine Bammate reported an astonishing anecdote on Massignon's visit to this sanctuary: 'I climbed up to the cliff, which is so yellow, absolute and smooth and dominates Damascus, and I visited the caves. The guide told me: "One day a man, a man whom I admire, whom I respect, came to visit this cave. Ever since then, it has not been the same for me." And he showed me the photograph: it showed Louis Massignon bent over an inscription engraved on that wall.'[42] In Guidjel in Algeria (southeast of Setif), the discovery of which Massignon owes to his friend Lounis Mahfoud, Massignon visited the seven pillars dating back to the Fatimid period; and finally, in 1957, he visited a church in Rotthof near Passau in Bavaria, which is dedicated to the Seven Sleepers.

After Ephesus, however, the sanctuary most dear to Massignon was the crypt of the Seven Sleepers at Vieux-Marché, the discovery of which he owed to his daughter Geneviève. This sanctuary held an important place in Massignon's spirituality because of the Muslim–Christian pilgrimages that the orientalist initiated; they were modelled on the traditional Breton pilgrimages and continue to be held there, enjoying varying fortunes. On 27 June 1952, mass was said at Vieux-Marché and also in Rotthof in honour of the Seven Sleepers. Massignon was clearly struck by the presence of this ancient Christian tradition in the heart of Brittany, as well as by the site's resemblance to that in Guidjel.[43] He subsequently set up an annual Muslim–Christian pilgrimage that was launched in 1954. In 1955, about a dozen

Muslims were invited, and Mgr Nasrallah, the Melkite priest and scholar who asked Breton helpers to recite the Creed and Our Father in the Celtic language, celebrated the high mass in the Byzantine rite. Massignon noted, 'the Greek Catholic rite has thus affirmed its ecumenical vocation in its highest form, by uniting Greek and Arab, Celtic and French elements in front of Christians and Muslims'.[44] In 1950, Massignon was ordained a Catholic priest, although he was married, in an old Anglican church, which had been acquired by his collaborator Mary Kahil in Egypt for the Melkite church in the heart of Cairo. In 1956, about a thousand people took part in the pilgrimage, amongst them 20 Muslim workers, and received the support of four African archbishops and bishops. In the following year the death of Hajj Lounis Mahfoud was commemorated: he was assassinated in Sétif by 'freedom fighters', because he believed in reconciliation in Algeria. The *Fatiha* was said for him, and red roses were put on the altar slab of the crypt.

It was after his pilgrimage to Ephesus on 19 September 1951 and his discovery of the tomb of Mary Magdalene that Massignon's meditation on the destiny of whom he called the first witness of Ephesus was most intense. The life of Mary Magdalene bears a triple witness for Massignon. Together with the Virgin Mary and Saint John, at the foot of the Cross, she witnessed Christ being stabbed with the lance; in the Resurrection Garden the Master showed himself to her: it is the encounter with the Only beloved; and finally, in Ephesus, she kept guard, all by herself, not far from the House of Mary: she was buried there on the step of the Cave of the Seven Sleepers.

Massignon is well aware of the fact that legend says that, in 1279, the tomb of Mary Magdalene was moved to Saint-Baume where, according to the *Légende dorée* (golden legend), it arrived miraculously in Sainte-Marie-de-la-Mer. But either these relics were transported from Constantinople (where they were moved to in the 10th century) to Provence after 1204, or Mary of Bethany, the sister of Lazarus, was confused with Mary Magdalene: in Massignon's eyes 'it is undoubtedly the latter who was buried in Ephesus and subsequently came to be considered the guardian of the cave of the Seven Sleepers and of the great necropolis of believers buried around the cave'.[45]

On 19 September 1951, Massignon spotted the tomb, or rather the niche, where the pilgrims laid out the body of Mary Magdalene for veneration. The presence of this sepulchre in the basilica built in the mid-5th century on the cave of the Seven Sleepers is, at least for the orientalist, a subject of profound meditation: he believed that 'She who kept guard at the door of the Sepulchre found herself at the door of another tomb, that of the Seven Sleepers who were immured alive, for the sake of Justice, awaiting Resurrection. It is thus in close relation to Magdalene that the Seven Sleepers make us realise the inexhaustible significance of the Encounter to which God invites us, to meet up with those we have loved, after leaving them and having "lost" them, without even doubting that this will happen, in Him and for Him.'[46]

Finally, Mary Magdalene is recognized in the Christian tradition as the first hermit of those who later on were to imitate, in the desert, her forsakenness in Love. This is why Massignon considers her amorous asceticism to be 'imitable and exemplary', 'this deprivation of a vestal waiting, in the fire of expiating absence, for the return of the moment which has forever made her into the first Witness of the Truth, of victory, of the life of the eternal Lover: happier than Thomas'. Massignon was to attest to the importance of Ephesus once again in 1961, in a grandiose and prophetic vision, a true act of faith: 'Ephesus must, for all Christian and Muslim groups, become, before the final gathering in Jerusalem, the place of reconciliation in *"hzarat Meryem Ana"* (Our Mother, in Turkish), while waiting for Israel to finally recognise it as the glory of Sion before joining in this so much sought for unanimity.'[47]

The cult of the Seven Sleepers started in Ephesus in about 448AD, a little after the proclamation at the Third Ecumenical Council on the divine maternity of Mary. And it was possible to write 'that Ephesus the spiritual world of primitive Christianity received an undeniable structure where Mary was found with John, Mary Magdelene and the Seven Sleepers – linked together in the same perspective of dormition and resurrection'.[48] This is why Massignon saw in the mystery of Ephesus the desire and the waiting for the resurrection: the assumption of Mary ascribed to Ephesus affirmed the resurrection promised to all humans; also at Ephesus St John waited for the Lord to fulfil his promise at Lake Tiberias in 'coming to find him'.[49] And Mary Magdalene interceded in the same place to the Lord for the seven entombed Lazaruses whose memories are preserved in Islam as well as Christianity. According to the tradition of the Seven Sleepers of Ephesus, as already related, some two hundred years later[50] they appeared living in the town of Ephesus and after their language and ancient coins had convinced the inhabitants of the unusual character of their appearance they died again.

Certainly Massignon notes that the invention of the Seven Sleepers must be understood in terms of the religious psychology of inventions of bodies of saints and relics which appeared in the 4th and 5th centuries in the Christian Orient following the victory of Constantine and the searches of Helena. However, according to the tradition 'the originality of the Seven Sleepers is that the institutive did not come from the Ephesians of that time who had forgotten them, but from the martyrs themselves, in order to find and witness to the pagan Ephesians and convince them'. This brutal fact, concludes Massignon, 'like the resurrection of Lazarus the reality is a shock, its very absurdity, which is very unpleasant to our reason. And which confounded the sadducian Greeks of the time, as the sadducian Jews, at the time of Lazarus'.[51]

Was it due to this Ephesian mystery that, since 1951, this place has become a site of international pilgrimage common to Muslims and Christians? Since then the almost instinctive influx of pilgrims who come to pray in the Marian sanctuary of the 4th century that has been discovered and restored has become an undeniable fact. In fact this Breton *pardon* attracted some 100 000 pilgrims in the 1960s.[52] For Massignon this movement could only be something of the Holy Spirit working in the hearts of believers. In his eyes it was a response to the act of faith of Pius XII proclaiming the dogma of the Assumption in 1950.[53]

The Development of the Ephesian Tradition in Christianity and Islam

The Seven Sleepers of Ephesus are venerated in the ancient liturgy of the Byzantine Church on 22 October and 4 August, the feast of their translation. In the Syriac-speaking churches, the theme of the Seven Sleepers is used in the sermons of Jacques de Saroug at the beginning of the 6th century. Two hymns in the divine office of the Maronite Church celebrate the Seven Sleepers in two feasts dedicated to them. There are also two feasts witnessing to the Seven Sleepers in the Armenian Church, as well as the Coptic and Ethiopian Churches. In the Mozarabic rite, as in the rite of the Latin Occident, their memory is commemorated on the 27 July. In the 6th century, St Gregory of Tours translated the Syriac legend into Latin. It is without doubt that, through a Celtic translation from the Latin version of St Gregory of Tours, the legend has come into Breton tradition. And to use as a Christian crypt this place of burial while respecting the dolmen which is encased in the right branch of the chapel, the veneration of the Seven Sleepers must have been part of the very beginnings of the evangelization of the Celtic lands before the local councils of the 6th and 7th centuries forbade centres of Christian worship to be associated with such tombs.

In all, the memory of the Seven Sleepers is found in some 45 Christian sites apart from the Roman sanctuary. In France, as well as the Breton Pardon we may mention Arras, Marseilles, Orleans, Noirmoutiers: above all at Marmoutier since here, at the Latin place of the Seven Sleepers, St Odilion de Cluny inspired the commemoration of the dead faithful, 'the Sleepers' – according to St Paul's own expression[54] – a celebration which became the Latin feast of the Day of the Dead on the day following All Saints' Day. In Islam remembrance of the Seven Sleepers is kept in a particular way. The Maronite priest–monk–scholar Youakim Moubarac stated: 'so that the worship is not repugnant to the intransigent monotheism of Islam, in the Koran where the Seven Sleepers are the witnesses anticipating the resurrection, it is said that a mosque is dedicated to them.'[55]

It seems that it was the Syriac tradition of Jacques de Saroug that is found in the Muslim tradition in Sura 18: that Sura, as Moubarac notes, 'is the start of Friday public rite as used throughout Islam'.[56] And 'it is the only one cited on Egyptian radio on every Friday at mid-day prayer'.[57] Regarding the Ephesian locality, three themes of the announcement of judgment are brought together: the resurrection of the Seven Sleepers who were buried alive, the scandal of the divine conduct of events underlined by the dialogue between the heroes and God, and finally the discovery of the source of life and the breaking of the wall which protected the community of believers.[58]

According to Moubarac, 'for Muslim tradition the cave of Ephesus is the place where the first call of the last judgment will be sounded. The Seven brought to life will be the avant-garde of the Messiah.'[59] In their waiting they sleep a mysterious sleep in which God speaks to them. This is an exaltation of life given up to God. Those who give themselves up to it are not dead but living. And already 'they are walled up, in absolute faith and love, their resurrection'.[60]

Thus in Islam as well as in Christianity the cult of the Seven Sleepers of Ephesus is linked to what is important. For Christians it is a sign of the resurrection. For Muslims it is a type of parable, teaching which suggests abandonment to the will of God until the end, the day of judgment and the resurrection. And at the same time as being a sign it is a gauge of the resurrection for it was given to the Seven who had been walled up to reveal themselves in the town of Ephesus; it is 'so that we know that the promise of God is true'.[61]

The Value of the Point of Encounter between Christianity and Islam

As has already been made clear, however, for Christians the cult of the Seven Sleepers of Ephesus is a marginal tradition and, for whoever reflects on it, it must be like that. But this legend is a significant parable as it confirms that everyone who trusts in God until their death must be concerned with the resurrection. So if one is interested in the faith of which this tradition is the sign a question immediately suggests itself: is there a Christian who could 'say so much' if he rejects the apostolic faith 'in the resurrection of the flesh and life everlasting'? [62] In picking up the oriental Christian veneration of the Seven Sleepers of Ephesus, Islam witnesses to its faith in God. For Massignon, the Christian resurrection on the last day can only be understood as Christ's abandonment to his Father's incomprehensible will. Can a Christian be insensible to this encounter?

Louis Massignon did not think so. His studies and his faith linked together with his experience so that he took up 'the defence of the act of *theologal*[63] Abrahamic faith', whose presence he discovered in the Muslim tradition referring to Abraham: on the one hand because of the contents of the act of faith of Abraham towards God who was revealed to him and on the other hand because of the confident abandon by Abraham to God which revealed it. This confident abandonment to God continued up to and including the sacrifice of Isaac; so Abraham was led to believe that 'God is powerful enough to revive the dead and that is why he recovered his son and was a symbol'.[64] Also

Massignon – and for him this second aspect surpassed the first – took up 'the defence of Abrahamic abandonment of the Seven Sleepers of Ephesus' because of the spiritual message it carries, even if it is limited to those who maintain the tradition in Islam as well as in Christianity.

The third and final point is more important than the other two. This meeting in Massignon's eyes promotes or even hastens the great understanding between Christianity and Islam, Christians and Muslims. History has not yet allowed this to be realized but it should become ineluctable on the day when Christians imitate St Francis at Diametta, and Muslims, who until now have certainly refused,[65] accept the ordeal. The repercussions of this test would help millions of believers by bringing them to a purification which is an abandonment to God, who enables them to experience spiritually both death and resurrection. A grandiose vision, in the style of Massignon, was both a theological and a spiritual pilgrimage which came together for him at Vieux-Marché, a continuing vindication of the witness to the Seven Sleepers of Ephesus. The pilgrimage still continues each year, gathering Breton Catholics, Muslims and Melkite Catholics together in the spirit of Massignon and out of the knowledge that eschatological unity is the consummation of pilgrimage.

Notes

1 On Louis Massignon, see the following studies: Moncelon, 'Louis Massignon'; C. Destremau and J. Moncelon, *Massignon, Louis Massignon: mystique en dialogue*; Borrmans, 'Louis Massignon'; and Mary Louise Gude's important study in English, *Louis Massignon: The Crucible of Compassion*.

2 Edward Said made numerous critical references to Louis Massignon; unfortunately, as with much of Said's work, religion is rarely taken sufficiently seriously or engaged as a tradition; see 'Islam, the Philological Vocation and French Culture', and *Orientalism*, 263–74.

3 Robinson: 'Massignon, Vatican II and Islam as an Abrahamic Religion'; Caspar: 'La vision de l'Islam chez Louis Massignon et son influence sur l'Église'.

4 Harpigny, *Islam and Christianity according to Louis Massignon*, 19–25.

5 Malicet, *Paul Claudel – Louis Massignon (1908–14)*.

6 Hourani, *Islam in European Thought*, 97–8.

7 Rocalve, *Place et rôle de l'Islam et de l'Islamologie dans la vie et l'Œuvre de Louis Massignon*.

8 Hourani, *Islam in European Thought*, 44. On Christian martyrdom, see de Andia, 'Martyrdom and Truth'. On how Massignon influenced the Iranian Shi'a thinker and political activist of the Islamic revolution whom some consider a martyr, see O'Mahony, 'Mysticism and Politics'.

9 Bill and Williams, *Roman Catholics and Shi'I Muslims: Prayer, Passion and Politics*, 66.

10 Massignon, *Examen*, collection 'Studi arabo-islamic del PISAI', 38, and O'Mahony, 'Islam *face-à-face* Christianity'.

11 Quoted in Griffiths, 'Sharing the Faith of Abraham', 202.

12 Bauerschmidt, 'Walking in the City'.

13 Bowman, 'Contemporary Christian Pilgrimage to the Holy Land'.

14 O'Mahony, 'Le pèlerin de Jérusalem'.

15 O'Mahony, 'Christians and Muslim–Christian Relations'.

16   Preface to Arnaldez, *Three Messengers for One God*, vii.

17   D. Massignon, 'Les Septs Saints'; see pp.693–8 for the 54 verses of the Gwerz, and Louis Massignon (text), 'Les Sept Dormants d'Éphèse (*Ahl al-Kahf*)'.

18   For the legend in Muslim tradition, see the work of the Italian Jesuit, Dall'Oglio, *Speranze nell'Islam. Interpretazione della prospettiva escatologia di Corano XVIII*, who has established a centre for Christianity and Islam at the monastery of Dar Musa in the Syrian mountains. He and the monastery are of the Syrian Catholic rite. For an in-depth study of the whole question of the Seven Sleepers of Ephesus, see Jourdan, *La tradition des sept dormants*.

19   See in this regard, van Esbroeck, 'La légende'. I would also like to acknowledge here help with sources from Sebastian Brock, the Oriental Institute, Oxford and the Jesuit liturgist, Andrew Cameron-Mowat, SJ, Heythrop College, London. For an echo of the legend of the Seven Sleepers in Judaism, see Heller, 'Eléments, parallèles et origines'.

20   Duchesne, 'Chemins Bretons'; Rozelet, 'Massignon et les pèlerins de Sept Dormants à Vieux-Marché'.

21   The Algiers Cathedral bell was erected originally in 1868 by Cardinal Lavigerie and sent to Vieux-Marché in July 1965. The bell is engraved as follows: 'Venez chrétiens et musulmans, adorons le Seigneur. Je l'ai chanté à la cathedrale d'Alger jusqu'en 1963; je continuerai à le chanter au Vieux-Marché. Appelez-moi cloche de l'Unité.' See Duchesne, 'Le Pardon'.

22   Certainly a spiritual encounter has been sought from the time when Sarah made Abraham send away the Egyptian servant Hagar and her son Ishmael (Gen.8:21). But to be clear one must say that it is unacceptable for the Christian faith to see the divine promise regarding Ishmael as a prophecy of Islam. At least that page of Genesis is the gauge not only of the prayer of the father of believers for all those whose faith is part of his line but also of the divine response. Also we have a double certitude: on the one hand the prayer of Abraham constantly accompanies his spiritual descendants wherever they are and by which ever way they are linked to him, but on the other hand the water which restores life to Ishmael can be seen as a parable of the merciful fidelity of the God of Abraham: this mysterious water, because it derives from a divine source, represents eternal life. Elsewhere the Bible refers to Abraham's descendants through Hagar (Gen.25:5–18; IChronicles 1:29–31), but also those of his concubine Qetvra (Gen.25:1–4; IChronicles 1) and one finds even Madian and Epha, who are his issue in the vision of Isaiah, celebrating the astonishing resurrection of Jerusalem (Isa.56:4–8). See Molette, 'La tradition des Sept Dormants d'Éphèse chez Louis Massignon'.

23   Molette, 'Les Sept Dormants d'Éphèse'.

24   G. Massignon, 'Le culte des Sept Dormants d'Éphèse', 170–74.

25   Mason, 'A Memory of Massignon', 321; poem by Mason, 'The Seven Sleepers'.

26   Taki, 'Hommage à Mohamed', 51.

27   Duchesne, 'Chemins Bretons', 28.

28   *Bulletin de l'association des Amis de Louis Massignon*, no. 12 (2002), 45–6.

29   Louis Massignon's bibliography as a scholar is impressive. For the complete bibliography, see Moubarac, 'L'Œuvre de Louis Massignon'. Amongst his studies, the first place must go to his double doctoral theses of 1922. *La Passion d'al-Hosayn-ibn Mansour al-Hallâj, martyre mystique de l'Islam*. Massignon continued to work on a new edition of this work until his death in 1962. After his death, the new edition was assembled by a group of scholars working together with the Massignon family and friends, which was published as *La Passion de Husayn ibn Mansur Hallâj, martyre mystique de l'Islam*. The second edition was translated into English by Herbert Mason as *The Passion of al-Hallâj: Mystic and Martyr of Islam*. An abridged version appeared as *Hallâj: Mystic and Martyr*, edited and translated by Herbert Mason. And *Essai sur les origines du lexique technique de la mystique musulmane*. First Edition: Paris: Geuthner 1922; Second Edition: Paris: Vrin 1954; Third Edition: Paris: Vrin 1968. Now translated into English by Benjamin Clark as *Essays on the origins of the technical language of Islamic mysticism* (University of Notre Dame Press, 1999).

30   See the studies by Arnaldez: 'Abrahamisme, Islam et christianisme chez Louis Massignon', and 'Figures patriarcale's et prophétiques'.

31   Moncelon, 'Salmân Pâk dans la spiritualité de Louis Massignon'.

32   Arnaldez, *Hallaj ou la religion de la croix*; Mason, *Al-Hallaj*, and *The Death of al-Hallaj: a dramatic narrative*.

33   Madkour, 'Louis Massignon', *L'Herne Massignon* (Paris: edition L'Herne, 1962); 68.

34   Louis Massignon to Thomas Merton, 31 December 1960, Thomas Merton Study Centre, Bellarmine College, Louisville, Kentucky quoted in Griffiths, 'Thomas Merton, Louis Massignon and the Challenge of Islam'.

35   Campo, 'Cave'.

36   Louis Massignon, letter to *Badaliya*, 1–2.

37   Louis Massignon, letter to *Badaliya*, 3.

38   Louis Massignon devoted the following studies to the tradition of the Seven Sleepers of Ephesus: 'Les Sept Dormants: apocalypse de l'Islam', 'Les fouilles archéologiques d'Ephèse et leur importance religieuse', 'Les sept dormants d'Ephèse (Ahl al-Kahf) en Islam et en chrétienté'.

39   Keryell, *L'Hospitalité sacrée*, 297.

40   Molette, 'La tradition des Sept Dormants d'Éphèse chez Louis Massignon'.

41   Destremau, Christian and Moncelon, Jean, *Massignon*, 327.

42   Nadjmoudine Bammate, conference, 28 October, 1963; Massignon, *Mystique en dialogue*, 178.

43   Morillon, *Louis Massignon*, 75.

44   Massignon, letter to *Badaliya*, 5–6.

45   Massignon, 'La maison de la Vierge et le tombeau de Marie-Madeleine', 6.

46   Massignon, 'Le culte des Sept Dormants', 125.

47   Destremau and Moncelon, *Louis Massignon*, 19.

48   Geschwind, *Wider erwachendes Ephesos, Fruhchristliche Turkei* (1953), 18–19, cited in *REI*, 1954, 61.

49   John 21:22.

50   Qur'an 18:24 speaks of 309 years.

51   Massignon, 'Les sept dormants d'Ephèse (*Ahl al-Kahf*) en Islam et en chrétienté', 94.

52   72 000 (1961), 135 000 (1962), 200 000 (1963).

53   Louis Massignon himself reported to Charles Molette in 1962 the words spoken early in 1950 in an audience with Pope Pius XII when he spoke about his intention to define the dogma of the Ascension: 'Holy Father, even if no one listens to you on earth, there is someone who will approve your act of faith and give it an unimaginable fecundity and that is Mary. And Islam who venerates her will benefit.' 'La tradition des Sept Dormants d'Éphèse chez Louis Massignon', 177.

54   IThessalonians 4:13.

55   Moubarac, 'Le culte liturgique et populaire des Sept Dormants martyrs d'Ephèse (Ahl al-Kahf)'. Cf. Qur'an 18:21. Moubarac was Massignon's principal collaborator and interpreter for some years: 'Hommage: Père Youakim Moubarach', (Islamo Christiana, 1991) 41–3.

56   Ibid., p.30.

57   Ibid.

58   cf. Ibid., p.28; cf. *Review Etudes Islamique*, 1954, pp.71–2.

59   Moubarac, ibid., p.35.

60   Ibid., p.35.

61   Qur'an 18:21.

62   The Creed of Nicea.

63   To acquire knowledge about God is one thing; to commit oneself to him is another. Though these actions are obviously related, they constitute discrete moments in the development of the Christian life. In order to maintain this distinction, spiritual authors of the classical French tradition distinguish between the terms 'théologique' and 'théologal'. The former term describes

what pertains to theological study and learning, whereas the latter denotes what pertains to the devotional life and practice of the Christian believer. Interestingly the English poet John Donne wrote that the 'Theologall virtues, Faith, Hope and Charity, are infus'd from God'. See the Dominican theologian Romanus Cessario, *Christian Faith and the Theological Life*, 1.

64 Hebrews 11:19.

65 The ordeal is alluded to in Qur'an 3:54. See also Massignon, 'La Mubahala de Médecine et l'hyperdulie de Fatima'. Without doubt, for it is perhaps to an 'ordeal' that an allusion is made in the Qur'an 3:54. Cf. Massignon, *Opera Minora* 1, 550–72 (see above). The marian cult and the mystical, apocalyptic city of the Seven Sleepers of Ephesus are linked. Indeed in Qur'anic tradition the dormition of the Seven Sleepers is only comprehended in connection with the dormition of Mary. According to Massignon, 'hyperdulia of the souls of grief in Islam for Fatima of the Marian hyperdulia, from this anguish of mystical and apocalyptic parturition which should not be underestimated', *Opera Minora*, 1, 572.

References

Andia, Y. de, 'Martyrdom and Truth: From Ignatius of Antioch to the Monks of Tibhirine', *Communio: International Catholic Review*, 29 (2002), 61–88.

Arnaldez, R., 'Abrahamisme, Islam et christianisme chez Louis Massignon', *L'Herne Massignon*, (Paris: edition L'Herne, 1962) 123–5.

——, *Hallaj ou la religion de la croix* (Paris: Plon, 1964).

——, 'Figures patriarcales et prophétiques', *Lumière et Vie*, 188 (1988), 81–96.

——, *Three Messengers for One God* (Notre Dame and London: University of Notre Dame Press, 1994).

Bauerschmidt, F.C., 'Walking in the City', *New Blackfriars: special edition – Michel de Certeau, SJ*, 77 (1996), 504–18.

Bill, J.A. and J.A. Williams, *Roman Catholics and Shi'I Muslims: Prayer, Passion and Politics* (Chapel Hill and London: University of North Carolina Press, 2002).

Borrmans, M., 'Louis Massignon, Témoin du dialogue islamo-chrétien', *Euntes Docete*, XXXVII (1984), 383–401.

Bowman, G., 'Contemporary Christian Pilgrimage to the Holy Land', in A. O'Mahony, Göran Gunner, Kevork Hintlian (eds) *The Christian Heritage in the Holy Land* (London: Scorpion/ Melisende, 1995), pp.288–310.

Campo, J.E., 'Cave', *Encyclopaedia of the Qur'an*, vol. 1, pp.292–4.

Caspar, R., 'La vision de l'Islam chez Louis Massignon et son influence sur l'Église', *L'Herne Massignon*, (Paris: edition L'Herne, 1962) 126–47.

Cessario, R., *Christian Faith and the Theological Life* (Washington, DC: The Catholic University of America Press, 1996).

Dall'Oglio, P., *Speranze nell'Islam. Interpretazione della prospettiva escatologia di Corano XVIII* (Genoa:1991).

Destremau C. and J. Moncelon, *Massignon* (Paris: Plon, 1994).

Duchesne, L., 'Chemins Bretons. De N.D de Liesse aux Sept Saints d'Ephèse', *Louis Massignon. Mystique en dialogue* (Paris: Éditions Albin Michel, 1992), pp.27–30.

——, 'Le Pardon des Sept Dormants d'Ephèse en Vieux-Marché', *Bulletin de l'association des Amis de Louis Massignon*, 8 (1999), 34–42.

Esbroeck, M. van, 'La légende des Sept Dormants d'Ephèse selon le Codex Syriaque N.S. 4 de Saint-Pétersbourg', *VI Symposium Syriacum*, ed. R. Lavenat (Rome: Pontificio Istituto Orientale, 1992).

Griffiths, S.H., 'Thomas Merton, Louis Massignon and the Challenge of Islam', *The Merton Annual*, 3 (1990), 151–72.

——, 'Sharing the Faith of Abraham: the "Credo" of Louis Massignon', *Islam and Christian–Muslim Relations*, 8 (1997), 193–210.

Gude, M.L., *Louis Massignon: The Crucible of Compassion* (Notre Dame: University of Notre Dame Press, 1996).

Harpigny, G., *Islam et Christianisme selon Louis Massignon* (Louvain: Université Catholique de Louvain, 1981).

Heller, B., 'Eléments, parallèles et origines de la légende des Sept Dormants', *Revue des Études juives*, XLIX, 98 (1904), 190–218.

Hourani, A.H., *Islam in European Thought* (Cambridge: Cambridge University Press, 1991), pp.97–8.

Jourdan, F., *La tradition des sept dormants. Une rencontre entre chrétiens et musulmans* (Paris: Éditions Maisonneuve & Larose, 1983).

Keryell, J., *L'Hospitalité sacrée* (Paris: Nouvelle Cité, 1987).

Malicet, M. (ed.), *Paul Claudel – Louis Massignon (1908–1914)* (Paris: Fayard, 1973).

Mason, H., 'A Memory of Massignon', *The Muslim World*, LVII (1967), 321–2.

——, *The Death of al-Hallaj: a dramatic narrative* (Notre Dame: University of Notre Dame Press, 1979).

——, *Al-Hallaj* (Richmond: Curzon Press, 1995).

——, 'The Seven Sleepers', *Bulletin de l'association des Amis de Louis Massignon*, 8 (1999), 50.

Massignon, D., 'Les Sept Saints Dormants d'Éphèse: Rencontre islamo-chrétienne à la crypte dolmen', *La vie spirituelle*, 725 (1997), 687–701.

Massignon, G., 'Le culte des Sept Dormants d'Éphèse', *L'Herne-Massignon*, 170–74.

Massignon, L., *La Passion d'al-Hosayn-ibn Mansour al-Hallâj, martyre mystique de l'Islam*, 2 vols (Paris: Geuthner, 1922).

——, *La Passion de Husayn ibn Mansur Hallâj, martyre mystique de l'Islam*, 2nd edn, 4 vols (Paris: Gallimard, 1975).

——, *The Passion of al-Hallâj: Mystic and Martyr of Islam*, 2nd edn. 4 vols, trans. Herbert Mason, Bollingen Series XCVIII (Princeton: Princeton University Press, 1982). An abridged version appeared as *Hallâj: Mystic and Martyr*, ed. and trans. Herbert Mason (Princeton: Princeton University Press, 1994).

Massignon, Louis, *Essai sur les origines du lexique technique de la mystique musulmane*, 1st edn (Paris: Geuthner, 1922); 2nd edn (Paris: Vrin, 1954); 3rd edn; (Paris: Vrin, 1968, reprinted Paris: Cerf, 2001). Translated into English by Benjamin Clark as *Essays on the origins of the technical language of Islamic mysticism* (Notre Dame: University of Notre Dame Press, 1999)

——, 'Les Sept Dormants: apocalypse de l'Islam', *Analecta Bollandiana*, 68 (1950), 245–60.

——, 'La maison de la Vierge et le tombeau de Marie-Madeleine', *Samedi Soir*, 6 (1951), 6.

——, 'Les fouilles archéologiques d'Ephèse et leur importance religieuse (pour la chrétienté et l'Islam)', *Mardis de Dar es-Salem* (Paris–Cairo: 1952), pp.3–24.

——, 'Les sept dormants d'Ephèse (*Ahl al-Kahf*) en Islam et en chrétienté: Recueil documentaire et iconographie réuni avec le concours d'Emile Dermerghem, Lounis Mahfoud, Dr Suheyl Ünver, Nicolas de Wit et Mathias Zender', *Revue des Etudes Islamiques* (1954, 59–112; 1955, 93–106; 1957, 1–11; 1958, 1–10; 1959, 1–8; 1960, 107–19; 1961, 1–18, 1962, 1–5).

——, *Examen du 'Présent de l'Homme Lettré' par Abdallah ibn Torjoman* (Rome: Pontifical Institute of Arabic and Islamic Studies of Rome, 1992), following the French translation published in *Revue de l'Histoire des Religions*, XII (1886).

——, *Mystique en Dialogue*, Collection 'Question de', no. 90 (Paris: Albin Michel, 1992).

——, 'La Mubahala de Médecine et l'hyperdulie de Fatima: La Mubahala. Etude sur la proposition d'ordalie faite par le prophète Muhammad aux chrétiens Balhârith du Najrân en 'an 10/631 à Médine', *Opera Minora*, 1, 550–72.

Molette, C., 'La tradition des Sept Dormants d'Éphèse chez Louis Massignon', *L'Herne-Massignon*, ed. J-F. Six (Paris: l'Herne, 1970), pp.175–81.

——, 'Les Sept Dormants d'Éphèse', *Bulletin de l'association des Amis de Louis Massignon*, 8 (1999), 13–33.

Moncelon, J., 'Louis Massignon', *La Vie Spirituelle*, 680 (1988), 363–79.

——, 'Salmân Pâk dans la spiritualité de Louis Massignon', *Luqmân* (Tehran), automne–hiver (1991–2), 53–64.

Morillon, J., *Louis Massignon* (Paris, Éditions universitaires, 1964).

Moubarac, Y., 'Le culte liturgique et populaire des Sept Dormants martyrs d'Ephèse (Ahl al-Kahf), trait d'union Orient–Occident entre l'Islam et la Chrétienté', *Studia Missionalia* (Rome), 11 (1961), 136–92.

——, 'L'Œuvre de Louis Massignon', *Pentalogie Islamo-Chrétienne*, I (Beirut: Éditions du Cénacle Libanais, 1972–3).

O'Mahony, A., 'Mysticism and Politics: Louis Massignon, Shi'a Islam, Iran and Ali Shari'ati – a Muslim–Christian Encounter', *University Lectures in Islamic Studies*, 2 (1998), 113–34.

——, 'Le pèlerin de Jérusalem: Louis Massignon, Palestinian Christians, Islam and the State of Israel', in A. O'Mahony (ed.), *Palestinian Christians: Religion, Politics and Society in the Holy Land* (London: Melisende, 1999), pp.166–89.

——, 'Christians and Muslim–Christian Relations: Theological Reflections', in A. O'Mahony and A. Siddiqui (eds), *Christians and Muslims in the Commonwealth* (London: Al-Tajir, 2001), pp.90–128.

——, '*Islam face-à-face* Christianity', *The Way: review of contemporary Christian spirituality*, supplement, 104 (2002), 75–85.

Robinson, N., 'Massignon, Vatican II and Islam as an Abrahamic Religion', *Islam and Christian–Muslim Relations*, 2 (1991), 182–205.

Rocalve, P., *Place et rôle de l'Islam et de l'Islamologie dans la vie et l'Œuvre de Louis Massignon*, Institut Français de Damas, Collection Témoignages et Documents, no. 2, 1993.

Rozelet, A., 'Massignon et les pèlerins de Sept Dormants à Vieux-Marché', in J. Keryell (ed.), *Louis Massignon et ses contemporains* (Paris: Éditions Karthala, 1998), pp.339–53.

Said, E., *Orientalism: Western Conceptions of the Orient* (London: Routledge & Kegan Paul, 1978), pp.263–74.

——, 'Islam, the Philological Vocation and French Culture: Renan and Massignon', in M.H. Kerr (ed.), *Islamic Studies: A Tradition and its Problems* (Malibu, CA: Undena Publications, 1980), pp.53–72.

Taki, 'Hommage à Mohamed', *Bulletin de l'association des Amis de Louis Massignon*, 8 (1999), 51.

III
THEOLOGICAL
PERSPECTIVES ON
PILGRIMAGE

CHAPTER 9

A Theology of Eucharistic Place: Pilgrimage as Sacramental

Peter Scott

Jerusalem: a City of Conflict

A theology of pilgrimage cannot today avoid the issue of Jerusalem as a city of conflict. If Jerusalem as a site of pilgrimage has anything to teach Christians, it must be by reference to the realities that God's world pushes towards us. If pilgrimage is always pedagogical, no arbitrary restriction can be placed on what it has to teach us. If the authority of the 'new Jerusalem' is somehow drawn from and renewed by pilgrimage, then the circumstance of contemporary Jerusalem cannot be ignored. Places are always sites of power and sometimes conflict. Somehow, the authority of the new Jerusalem, as the authority of God, must be sought through a city in conflict.[1] That is the only route to receiving the truth of Jerusalem, and thereby the truth of pilgrimage to Jerusalem.

In the face of Jerusalem's seemingly intractable political circumstance, a certain type of Protestant response seems congenial. In *Spaces for the Sacred*, Philip Sheldrake summarizes this Protestant position thus: 'The physical world, images and ritual need to be questioned because they tend to divert people from placing their security in God alone.'[2] Characterizing the Calvinist position, Rosemary Radford Ruether puts the matter more strongly still: 'Calvinism dismembered the Medieval sacramental sense of nature.... Only the disembodied Word, descending from the preacher to the ear of the listener, together with music, could be bearers of divine presence.'[3] Such a view cannot be said to support pilgrimage to particular places. This view also connects with certain Scriptural injunctions regarding mission. In Luke's Gospel, Jesus urges his disciples to proclaim his name, 'beginning from Jerusalem' (Luke 24:47 NRSV). At Acts 1:8, Jesus seemingly commands the disciples to fan out from Jerusalem 'to the ends of the earth'. On such a view, the place of Jerusalem is decentred by the imperative of mission. The conclusion of the Revelation to John of Patmos, with its famous vision of the descent of the new Jerusalem (Rev.21:1–2), may also function to direct attention away from the 'old' Jerusalem. The heavenly city of Jerusalem is not to be confused with the earthly city of Jerusalem. Furthermore, the heavenly city is to be sought, so to speak, through the expansionary movement of mission. Kenneth Cragg partly understands the matter in this way. Early Christianity is best interpreted, he argues, as a missionary movement that, by its Scripture and practice of Eucharist, is self-sufficient. It does not need to seek the blessing of place except for those places of the preaching of the Gospel and the breaking of bread at which the name of Christ is proclaimed and received.

Such a relativizing of Jerusalem can find some support from Israel's construal of its formation through an Exodus journey. As Robert Jenson notes:

> Gods whose identity lie in the persistence of a beginning are cultivated because in them we are secure against the threatening future. The gods of the nations are guarantors of continuity and return, against the daily threat to fragile established order; indeed, they *are* Continuity and Return. The Lord's meaning for Israel is the opposite: the archetypically established order of Egypt was the very damnation from which the Lord released her into being, and what she thereby entered was the insecurity of the desert. Her God is not salvific because he defends against the future but because he poses it.[4]

Attention to the fixed place of Jerusalem, as appears to be required by pilgrimage, seems at first sight to be an attempt to guard against a future given by YHWH. Nor can the Davidic covenant easily be appealed to in support of pilgrimage. The establishment of the Davidic covenant does not directly contradict the emphasis on God's future. Israel's empty temple stands as criticism of the temples of other gods: 'what other nations said of the fixed presence of God in holy places and images Israel with her empty temple said instead of God's occurring word: "The grass withers, the flower fades; but the word of our God will stand forever" [Isaiah 40:7–8].'[5] It may then be true that 'The desert's portable sanctuary tent was replaced with a proper temple of the region and period'. To this description, nonetheless, must be added further: 'this [sc. temple], however, lacked that for which such temples were normally built, the boxed-in and thereby itself fixed image of God.'[6] Any contrast between Sinaitic and Davidic covenants should not, on this view, be overdrawn.[7] Israel's self-understanding remains that of a migrant people; any 'concession' to temple and palace retains the marks of this wandering. To this contention add a Christian theme: the ubiquity of the risen Christ in the Spirit seems further to recommend the view that places, including even the place of Jerusalem, are secondary to God's word.

However, although attractive, such a sceptical position should not be accepted too easily. There is a sustained ambivalence within Christianity, as also in Judaism, on the theological significance of place. Sheldrake understands this ambivalence in terms of a 'balance' that needs to be struck between particularity and universality. The Incarnation, he argues, requires the view that God is committed to particularities. However, a commitment to particularities is accompanied by a sense that God is not bound by such particularities: 'God's revelation is in the particular' is accompanied by the view 'that God's place ultimately escapes the boundaries of the localized'. The Resurrection is for Sheldrake the transgression of place in which the body of Jesus Christ is unbounded.[8] We should go further still: in Jesus Christ we have not a recommendation of balance between the universal and the particular but instead an understanding that, in this particular Christ of God, the universal is also given.

Sacramental Place

A different way of exploring the issue of place is by reference to sacrament: 'the event of a sacrament defines a place,' writes Robert Jenson, 'and at that place *is* the divine reality that the sacrament communicates to the world.'[9] According to Jenson, Scripture is replete with reference to sacramental places: 'God takes location from which to act in his creation by taking on created body: by riding the cherubim-storm, by filling the Tabernacle and then the Temple, by walking about Palestine, by suffering in the flesh, by taking bread and cup as body and blood.' To make the point for Judaism, in a footnote Jenson quotes Jewish thinker Michael Wyschogrod: 'There is no place in which God is not present. But this truth must be combined with the insistence that God also has an address ... He dwells in Number One Har Habayit Street [Jerusalem].'[10] Kenneth Cragg makes an almost identical point, attributing the following remark to Abraham Heschel: 'Yahweh has an address on earth' (see p.3).

We must be a little cautious here. Talk of sacramental places should not be sentimentally extended to some general sacramentality. 'The fallen creation is no longer the creation of the first creative Word,' argues Bonhoeffer. Therefore 'The creation is not sacrament.'[11] Not all parts of creation, in Christian tradition, should be seen as sacramental; instead, sacraments refer to particular signs, such as the Eucharistic bread and wine. Yet the reference should not be construed too narrowly: the capacity of the bread and wine to mediate the presence of God turns upon the orientation of all creaturely order on God, in the unity of God's acts in creation, liberation and redemption.[12] In that we are speaking here of the consummation or finishing of creation in God, the appropriate theological control is therefore eschatological.

If the primary protocol against seeing all places as sacred is eschatological, then that protocol is also Christological, for Jesus Christ is the 'firstborn of all creation ... the firstborn from the dead' (Col.1:15, 18 NRSV). The incarnation of God in Christ defines a place, and that place includes ancient Jerusalem. In affirming the missionary programme that Jesus requires – which is mandated by the explosion of praise that constitutes the response to this Jesus freed from the no-place of death – the *place* of the Incarnation cannot be overlooked. Why not? Because the Incarnation is not some principle of God's immanence but rather identifies this carpenter as the Christ of God. In other words, what is affirmed is not some general notion of the presence of God or some message to be beamed to the ends of the world, but instead the struggles of a Jewish body, Jesus Christ, referring all matters, including his own life and death, to his Father's 'Kingdom'. To argue that in Jesus the importance of the place of Jerusalem is denied or overcome is to fail to attend to Jesus as the incarnate One who struggles with and against his own people, against some of the religious and political authorities and, finally, for and against the God of Israel. Moreover, these struggles have a central 'venue': Jerusalem. It is one thing to argue that the covenant with Israel is concentrated and extended in Jesus Christ. It is another to overlook the precise ways (by struggle and death) that this Messiah renews the covenant. To put the matter one more time, yet differently: any tendency to separate the salvific presence of Jesus of Nazareth from his career and thereby from his place would once have been called Docetic.[13]

In framing the issue in such fashion, I am trying to guard against an unhappy tendency in Anglican theology, identified by Rowan Williams, that construes the Incarnation abstractly, as an *image*. This image of incarnation has been employed to articulate 'the fusion of heaven and earth, the spiritualising of matter'. What, however, is lost, on this view, is 'that element underlying the history of the incarnational definition that is to do with the radical testing of human "sense" before the tribunal of Jesus, which is the tribunal of the last days'.[14] If Williams is right, it would be better to speak of the incarnate One rather than the Incarnation. To attend to the Gospel narratives that relate the drama of the incarnate One is to attend to the span of Jesus' life, passionate death and lively presence, precisely to his comings and goings. In addition, to attend to these comings and goings is to be confronted by 'the realities of truthfulness and finality, encounter and judgement, in the presence of the entirety of Jesus' story'. To speak of the incarnate One is thereby not to gaze at a picture of the marriage of heaven and earth but rather to try 'to grasp how *this* story begins to speak of the decisive work of God in its specific historical setting'.[15]

The significance of this conclusion for a theology of place in a Christian account of pilgrimage is considerable. To go on pilgrimage to Jerusalem is not thereby to try to catch a glimpse of a marriage between heaven and earth, to visit the site of the union and to catch something of the atmosphere. The fundamental concern here is thereby not the validation of interior religiosity or ecclesiastical order (the latter permits the laity to go on pilgrimage, accompanied by the priest). Instead, the matter is more troubling, even threatening: to visit Jerusalem in the steps of the incarnate One is to try to discern one more time the pattern of Christian discipleship that is concerned fundamentally with what Williams calls the movements of 'reversal and renewal' that structure the Gospel narratives. These movements include the betrayal of Jesus, his death and return from death. Even this formulation is too abstract: reversal and renewal are always to be discerned by reference to the actions of Christ. As such, James Alison has properly argued, this Christ is fundamentally associated with the gratuitous action of forgiveness, 'the presence of gratuity as a person'.[16] The approach of the pilgrim to Jerusalem is thereby one marked by 'judgement and repentance ... with conversion and transformation' before the tribunal of the incarnate, eschatological Judge.[17]

From the perspective I have been sketching, which we may with appropriate caution call 'sacramental', the claim that mission towards the new Jerusalem either permits or requires a detour around Jerusalem cannot be sustained. Why not? On this false detour, Jesus is always behind the Christian, and behind the mission. That is, Incarnation is employed as a settled *datum*: we know who Jesus Christ is, we know what Jesus Christ wants, and we know that salvation in Christ supersedes the covenant with Israel. The conclusion inexorably follows: next stop, the ends of the earth. On this view, Christ is at the Christian's back, like some divine movie director, demanding more missionary action. What, however, becomes of the matter of facing Christ, of being judged and liberated? Moreover, if there is no place for judgment and liberation and thereby for repentance and conversion, can the freedom of God, the otherness of God be meaningfully maintained? The conclusion is inescapable: on this missionary view, the freedom of Christ in the Spirit to judge and forgive is radically abridged.

To criticize such missionary supercession of Jerusalem is not however in any straightforward way to affirm Jerusalem as a site of pilgrimage. In a somewhat unhappy formulation, Sheldrake argues that 'The Christian doctrine of the Incarnation offers an image of God's irrevocable commitment as *remaining*'.[18] What is intended by such a formulation? Certainly, the language of 'image' is disconcerting. Moreover, the themes of judgment and conversion are lost as Incarnation is here construed in abstraction from the career of the incarnate One. However, the emphasis on the dwelling of the Word as *remaining* seems right, if the particularity of Jesus' body is to be maintained. What must be emphasized is that the renewed presence of the resurrected Christ in the Spirit does not cancel or obliterate the particularities of Jesus' comings and goings. In my view, this 'remaining' of Jesus is secured by reference to his ascension (Luke 24:50–51; Acts 1:9–10; Mark 16:19; Hebrews 4:14).[19] The 'departure' of the resurrected Jesus is from a particular place. *This* Messiah's body departs from *that* specific place. In Acts, that place is the Mount of Olives. The pilgrimage to Jerusalem gains validity from the affirmation that Jerusalem or its environs are the place of Jesus' withdrawal.

Attempts to deny such validation are in my view rooted in a lack of theological attention to ascension. Such lack of attention is all too common in theological discourse today and yet, as Douglas Farrow shows, the ascension is a central aspect of Christianity, as the Nicene creed makes clear.[20] The particular body that is veiled at the ascension is the same body that is universally available in the Eucharist. The body of Christ is not dissolved into resurrection but, in an anti-Gnostic move, maintained through it.[21] Christ is not resurrected as spiritualized presence but as bodily presence, accessible, so to say, in the Eucharist. Jesus' resurrection, in other words, is completed by his ascension. Furthermore, by reference to ascension, the pilgrimage to Jerusalem is to be understood as a journey of preparation: to repent and be converted in order to attend more fully to the particularities of the pilgrim's own place.

However, I am getting ahead of the argument and anticipating my conclusion. Through these two opening sections I have argued that what must be avoided is on the one hand the denial of Jerusalem and on the other hand the affirmation of Jerusalem in such a fashion that the ways of repentance and conversion are bypassed. Sacramental event, we may conclude, always has a place. The place of the incarnate One is the place of the self-identification of YHWH through a drama of reversal and renewal. In this drama, there are no spectators, only participants. To develop this point, in the next section I turn to a more detailed consideration of a theology of place.

Placing Jerusalem

How is the place of Jerusalem existentially significant for Christian pilgrims? If you visit the Church of the Holy Sepulchre in the old city of Jerusalem, you will meet queues of pilgrims waiting to visit the tomb that marks the attested place of Christ's resurrection. Pilgrims also queue to kiss the spur of rock considered to be the rock of Golgotha. Perhaps most striking is the sight of the pilgrims who kneel and make the sign of the cross at the Stone of Unction where, tradition maintains, Jesus' body was laid or where it was anointed after being taken down from the cross. This spot, at the entrance of the church, is marked by a limestone slab laid on the floor, and is covered in a perfumed oil and sometimes strewn with petals. Pilgrims kneel, cross themselves, and prepare for entry into the main body of the Church of the Holy Sepulchre. Here on display is a profound desiring to attend Jerusalem's holiest Christian site. Indeed, here we encounter the richness and sensuousness of pilgrimage. Jerusalem, it appears, is the place that Christians (as well as Jews and Muslims) cannot not desire.

It is not the purpose of this chapter to defend such actions of pilgrims. However, nor do I think that these actions can be overlooked. These are the outward manifestations of matters of the heart that support pilgrimage to Jerusalem. Doubtless dictators through the ages would have killed to secure such heartfelt devotion; indeed, they did kill, but without securing the devotion. In an age which privileges as its creed a utilitarian individualism in conjunction with the maximization of efficiency through technique, we are here confronted by a different 'structure of feeling' embedded in the 'uselessness' of pilgrimage. In making this comment, I am not claiming that the desire to go on pilgrimage to Jerusalem is a private affection of the heart. Our desires are rooted in social conditions; our most liberating preferences do not have solely personal origins.[22] Contrary to first appearance, the attachment to the place of Jerusalem is not fashioned by the individual pilgrim directly but is always mediated through the operations of liturgy. How should this be thought?

In a highly interesting comment, Michel de Certeau offers the following account of how Christianity 'works':

> However it is taken, Christianity implies a *relationship to the event* that inaugurated it: Jesus Christ. It has had a series of intellectual and historical social forms which have had two apparently contradictory characteristics: the will to be *faithful* to the inaugural event: the necessity of being *different* from these beginnings.[23]

For the moment, I shall concentrate on the meaning of being faithful. Faithfulness to the inaugurating event of Christianity, Jesus Christ, is, we might say, a liturgical act. The affective connection made by Christians with Israel–Palestine cannot be separated from Scripture and liturgy. In other words, Jerusalem is always associated in the Christian imaginary with God's summons of Israel and Jesus. As Robert Jenson notes, 'God is whoever raised Jesus from the dead, having before raised Israel out of Egypt.'[24] Thus the memory of Jesus' comings and goings in a determinate place is *not* the same as, say, my memory from childhood of walking on Wenlock Edge. I shall always associate my childhood with this escarpment. However, walking on Wenlock Edge precedes my memory of that place.

Jerusalem, for most Christians, is a different case: 'memory' precedes the place. In other words, the memory of Jerusalem is a liturgical memory that precedes our first-hand knowledge of the modern city of Jerusalem. Christians do not remember Jerusalem in the way that I remember Wenlock Edge from my childhood. That is, first, the location and, second, association with place by memory. Rather, the invocation of Jerusalem is always liturgical: 'This is my body, This is my blood' invokes, by the actions of the Spirit, the risen Christ whose particularity cannot be understood except by way of Jerusalem and Israel.

In understanding place, memory is clearly important. That much is evident. How then shall we think of place in a more systematic fashion? Philip Sheldrake argues that 'The hermeneutics of place progressively reveals new meanings in a kind of conversation between topography, memory and the presence of particular people at any given moment.'[25] A critical theological hermeneutics of place, we should add immediately, will enquire whether such new meanings function in liberatory or oppressive ways. There needs to be, as Sheldrake opines, 'an ethical emphasis in any reflection on the relation between place and the sacred'.[26] I regret the term 'emphasis'. It seems to me that there needs to be a permanent ethical moment in any hermeneutics: a testing of the memory of a people by an orientation on peace, justice, freedom and truth.[27] In such fashion, a critical hermeneutics may engage with Jerusalem as a site of conflict.

The basic contours of a theory – but not yet a theology – of place are already evident. Differing little from Cragg's position, Sheldrake argues that place is best understood through the interaction of a people or relationships; a land or environment; and a history or memory. 'Place,' he argues, 'depends on relationships and memories as much as physical features.'[28] Place emerges, we might say, in and through an historical or dramatic process by which a people remembers and renews its history in a specific location. Place is thereby always temporal, social and environmental. Rightly, Cragg calls such an account of place 'indifferently a *human* charter' (p.4) in that human life is not conceivable without a community's existence through time in a particular locale. Put bluntly, this account is not fascist or even sectarian, but just universal. History, land and society are thereby a transcendental condition of human life. Such a condition is enacted in particular, contingent ways that we may then name as 'place'.

An account of human identity emerges in dialectical relation to this consideration of place. The identity of any human social group cannot be grasped except by way of that group's construal of place, in which its history, social relationships and location are active. If place, as suggested here, indicates an identification with a specific environment together with attention to the quality of a community's relationships and the retelling of a community's history, then the community's performance of place is also a point of access to the identity of a community. To be in a place is to be a particular people with a particular identity. In this perspective, place cannot be opposed to identity, nor can place be separated from the history of a community. Sheldrake does, I consider, make this mistake in arguing that 'place has three essential characteristics – it engages with our identity, with our relationships and with our history'.[29] In my view, place does not engage identity but rather constitutes it. In other words, place is a summary of the interactions between community, land and memory. Place offers access to a community's identity and operates as a summary of a community's history and relations in a particular environment. Place, we may conclude, is summative of identity.

It follows that place is also a *normative* concept. The place of a people, and thereby their identity, offers an account of how that people considers that its life should be ordered. The ways in which it owns and disowns, remembers and forgets, shapes and reshapes its past; the ways in which it uses its land, and corrects misuses, and whether and how it opens its land to others; the ways in which a community understands how its common life should be governed (should the weakest be protected, is the stranger to be made welcome?) – all these indicate normative elements. That place is always a normative concept and actuality is of vital importance when the meanings of a place are contested (as in Jerusalem) and, as contested, are a source of conflict. Of course, we must note straight away that such normative principles are not always morally just in practice.

This is not yet a *theology* of place, however. The problematic status of identity for Israel and Christianity serves here as a clue in the development of a theology of place. The identity of Israel and the identity of churched Christians are not constructed in straightforward fashion out of the interplay of memory, land and people. Instead, that place and that identity are received as *gift*. Israel and the Church are the consequence of God's prior choosing. We have seen this already in the previous section: Jewish and Christian Scripture records the ways in which God gives a land and gives a Son. The polity of Israel and the polity of the churches are attempts to offer a response in social form to these gifts.[30] As Rowan Williams puts the matter:

> This deliverance [from Babylonian Exile], decisive and unexpected, is like a second Exodus .... Out of a situation where there is no identity, where there are no names, only the anonymity of slavery or the powerlessness of the ghetto, God makes a human community, calls it by *name* (Is. 40–55), gives it or restores to it a community. But this act is not a *process* by which shape is imposed on chaos; it is a summons, a call which establishes the very possibility of an answer.[31]

Even when Israel feels unable to make the response in an appropriately social form, as during the Exile, Israel's self-understanding, as recorded in its Scripture, is to consider itself still as sought out by YHWH.

The status of the Church is not substantively different: in Christ, there is a renewal of the community of the disciples and the establishing of the Church. As the witness of Scripture makes clear, this new identity of Christian Jewry and, later, Gentile Christianity is given by the action of God in Christ and is thereby part of God's purposes: 'though he was rich, yet for your sakes he became poor' (IICor.8:9) and so 'emptied himself, taking the form of a slave' (Phil.2:7). With this emptying comes God's calling of the Church from 'what is low and despised in the world' (ICor.1:27). The radical nature of this gift of identity needs to be grasped fully. As Daniel Hardy has recently argued, the New Testament does not present us with a linear sequence: Christ, then Church, and then Mission. Instead, quoting John Knox, Hardy argues that 'One will not say that God acted in Jesus and *then* created the Church. To speak of his action in and through Jesus and of his action in creating the Church is to speak of the same action.'[32] The action of God is thereby social:

the creation of community through death in which the community understands its identity as given in Christ, that is, kenotically. The identity of the Christian Church is thereby peculiar: this identity is both received and given away in service.

For Christian churches the primary mode in and through which the Church learns of its identity, and Christians of their identity as participants in that body of Christ, is liturgical; and the primary operation is the Eucharist. It is not adequate to argue, as Cragg does, that the commitments to land, people and history are somehow cancelled 'in Christ'. Instead, we must attend to the way in which the liturgical memory, one source of the desire to travel to Jerusalem, construes place. In other words, to argue that sacred space, *ethnos* and language are neutralized, to use Cragg's terminology (p.5), in the New Testament is, in my view, to disregard the way in which the Eucharist construes place liturgically. Does such liturgical invocation drive us towards the particularity of Jerusalem or away from that place? An answer to that question must turn upon an account of the way liturgical invocation construes place, including the place of Jerusalem.

Eucharistic Place

What is required is a liturgical concept of closeness to Jerusalem. By careful adherence to the rigours of such closeness, pilgrims may renew their sense of Christian identity as gift at Jerusalem. What is this liturgical concept of closeness as displayed in the Eucharist? Kenneth Cragg rightly argues that 'any Christian "theology of pilgrimage" has to be consistent with the re-enacting in any and every local scene of "the night in which he was betrayed"' (p.8). How is such consistency to be understood?

Eucharistic practice is embodied practice: it refers to actual congregations in specific places. Christian communities are not resident aliens in the sense of being rootless; Eucharist can only be celebrated in places. *This* bread and *this* wine in *this* place present Jesus Christ. However, the Church does not seek to create, protect or nurture ecclesial place. Rather, it responds and witnesses to an eschatological event: the Church 'has a place, but that place has its centre of gravity in the church's home towards which it remains on pilgrimage'.[33] In the Eucharist, the Church remembers the liberating action of God through embodied word, crucifixion and escape from death, discerns once more its context in the created order and looks forward in expectation to the return of Christ.[34] Situated in a particular environment, the gathered Church invokes the memory of the gift of the Son, crucified and risen, acknowledges in gratitude the creaturely blessings that it has received and looks forward to the return of the Son whose eschatological gift will be judgment. There is here an important sense in which the Church does not originate a concept of place. Rather, in the

Eucharist it receives, by its remembrance and the invocation in the Spirit of the presence of Christ, a notion of place. As such, the Church seeks neither to organize nor to dispose of its place.

The three elements of place identified earlier (history, environment and community) are all present, yet transformed. In the Eucharistic pedagogy outlined here, the sense of the past begins from and refers to Golgotha, and in the recalling of the crucifixion of a Jew encompasses the history of Israel. That history is, furthermore, an eschatological history: bearing witness to the true *polis* from its context of a *polis* that is passing away, the Church is 'between the times' and thereby is not required to defend any particular space.[35] Furthermore, the construal of environment as place cannot be thought except in thankfulness for the goodness of the created order and within an eschatological orientation. It is true that the Christian Old Testament presents the deliverance of Israel to a land of fecundity and justice but, as H. Paul Santmire argues, that deliverance is accompanied by the blessing of all the earth by the Creator.[36] Such blessing thus resists restriction to a particular people and a particular place. As Cavanaugh notes, the Church 'is a gathering, but it is not therefore marked by a "fascist" binding – a homogeneous exclusion of otherness – precisely because the church must constantly renew itself as a gift of God who is Other in the Eucharist'.[37] Land is thereby rendered always excentric because of such Eucharistic otherness: that is, related to others. The community of the Church understands itself to be in movement outwards: this 'society' of the Eucharist is radically inclusive and provocative, embodying 'the challenge of how there might be a social order in which the disadvantaged and even the criminal could *trust* that the common resources of a society would work for their good'.[38]

True Eucharistic place is thereby responsive, not originative. It is responsive in a double sense. First, the placed Church receives its identity through the sacrifice of the Eucharist: 'the Eucharist performs the Church,' as Cavanaugh notes.[39] Second, it responds to that response sacrificially, in the *kenosis* of service.

In searching for a way of articulating this Eucharistic position for a theology of pilgrimage, care must be taken not to fall into the trap of affirming a general principle of sacramentality. Sheldrake warns against this error. To argue that discipleship requires 'placedness' together with a 'continual movement beyond each place' is surely correct.[40] By such means, the contingencies of history are affirmed but not sealed off from one another. There cannot be, as Sheldrake rightly notes, protected places. However, in arguing that 'the catholicity of a community is the demanding call to manifest God's own act of making space for all particular realities in their interdependency ... and of transcending the boundaries of time and place as well as natural or cultural divisions between people',[41] the matter of *how* that calling bestows an identity is raised. Sheldrake comments that 'The Eucharist is ... the enactment of the special identity of the

Christian community.'[42] Therefore we must enquire how the Eucharist operates a liturgical performance to *grant* the Church its identity. What is it, in other words, to participate in the construal of place that is the Eucharist, in which the identity of the Church is granted?

In focus here are the transitions enacted and demanded by the drama of the Eucharist, by which identity is bestowed. The result of these transitions is, as Rowan Williams argues, a new social identity given by a Eucharistic process.[43] The primary transition is the matter of real presence in the Eucharist in which Jesus gives himself, by reference to the Last Supper, in the bread and the wine. In the rite, the participants also effect a transition, are covenanted to God and others, and are thereby able to trust in the faithfulness of God. By his 'surrender' into the elements of bread and wine, Williams argues, Christ anticipates his betrayal; by offering the signs of hospitality to his betrayers, their faithlessness is negated ahead of time. This social movement Williams calls God's 'guarantee of hospitality': despite their faithlessness, this hospitality turns the disciples from betrayers into guests.

Furthermore, we should see the Last Supper as a summary of the practice of table-fellowship evident through Jesus' ministry. Writes Cavanaugh: 'In the Eucharist, the poor are invited now to come and feast in the Kingdom.'[44] The faithless are not those only of Jesus' immediate entourage but all those to whom Jesus directed his ministry. Latin American liberation theology has memorably summarized that direction as God's 'preferential option for the poor'. In a particular situation in which the bread and wine are consumed, participation in the rite invokes the passion of Jesus, the pouring away of Jesus' life, and the restoration of community: of Jesus with God, with his disciples and with the marginalized. The Eucharist is thereby a social action in which distortions and breaks in sociality are consistently corrected and renewed. A social action through betrayal and death, the Eucharist thereby constitutes the Church as a social form *sui generis*.[45] The Eucharist is a social action in which the faithless make the transition to faithful by way of God's guarantee of hospitality sealed in the giving up of a life. The identity of the Church given in the Eucharist is the transition into a place of hospitality. This identity is given despite the fact that those who are to be hospitable will have failed and will fail in their efforts at hospitality.

Overcome through this transition is what Sheldrake rightly describes as 'a selective way of being social'.[46] That is, the social form of the Church interrogates the regnant forms of social organization from the perspective of its sacramental practice. And that interrogation, to borrow again from Williams, takes the form of a social vision or embodiment 'in which almost the only thing we can know about the good we are to seek is that it is no one's possession, the triumph of no party's interests .... The Church declares ... that there is a form of common human life [in which] the status of an invited or desired guest is accessible to all'.[47] The Church in its social form, and through its concrete 'political' actions as social form, seeks to serve the regeneration of society towards such a sacramental substance. 'A Christian practice of the political is embodied in the Eucharist,' Cavanaugh argues.[48] He is right, and that practice is sacramental. This means, in turn, that the Church's sacramental labour *ad extra* is towards the God-given social identity that enacts hospitality for all.

'The Eucharist must not be a scandal to the poor,'[49] writes Cavanaugh, by which he means that the Eucharist demands the enactment of the guarantee of hospitality. Failure in such enactment subverts a material politics into a 'political statement'. The Eucharist is a social action with social 'consequences', a material action that requires material changes. How shall pilgrimage to Jerusalem be articulated so as not to be a scandal to this Eucharist? In what ways shall a theology of pilgrimage be developed that is consistent with such a sacramental perspective?

The Place of the Pilgrim

Earlier, I discussed the desiring of pilgrims to attend Christian holy places in Jerusalem. In the perspective of the sacramental practice being advanced here, we should, I suggest, be suspicious of the sort of desire that wants to attend to the echoes of Jesus' actions as if modern Jerusalem is somehow still the setting of the Christ drama. The moral identity of a Christian *pilgrim* is different from that of a *tourist*. Of course, one hears deeply heartfelt tales: the pilgrim who watches a storm brewing on the Sea of Galilee and makes the connection with the Gospel episode of Jesus calming the storm (Mark 4:35–41; Matthew 8:18, 23–7; Luke 8:22–5); the pilgrim who sees mist gathering on the Sea of Galilee and pictures her Lord walking on the water (Mark 6:45–52; Matthew 1:22–3; John 6:16–21).

A desire to gain a sense of Jesus' place may be justified, but this kind of desire for some sort of encounter with Jesus is misplaced. Why is this so? To hope for such an encounter is to express an ' "ontological need" for wholeness, unity and immediacy'[50] in which Christianity does not traffic. Instead, a sacramental account of place stresses, as we have seen, a transition into hospitality and an excentric orientation on others. Furthermore we should note that the pilgrim's demand for immediacy is problematic: such desiring, although deeply felt, obscures the social processes which inculcate such desires. Such desires are best understood as profoundly mediated, and thereby open to manipulation, not least by tourist operators and of course by the pilgrim herself.[51] As Williams recommends, we should keep to a sacramental perspective: 'They [the sacraments of baptism and eucharist] are too important as reminders, to believers and non-believers, of the need to put to death corrupt attachments to a false anthropology', of which, I would argue, such desires are a part.[52]

However, there is no doubting the importance of journeys in Judaism and Christianity: Exodus and Exile have already been mentioned; Paul's peregrinations are discussed elsewhere in this volume. Philip Sheldrake reflects 'on the importance of roots, of a sense of belonging "somewhere", but also on the transformative power of extended journeys away from home to an elsewhere'.[53] However, such transformative power of pilgrimage needs to be governed by a liturgical memory: Jesus is the Christian's praise. The moral economy of pilgrimage should be structured by such praising in which the Christian hopes to leave her old identity and receive another 'in Christ'.

Such identity is, as we have already seen, social. That reference to sociality urges the wisdom of returning to an earlier view of pilgrimage as a journey to visit holy *people*. According to Sheldrake, through the Patristic period 'Places could be said to be sacred by association with human holiness' to the extent that 'One of the earliest recorded Christian pilgrimages to Palestine was specifically to visit the *monks* as much as the Holy Places.'[54] Jerusalem is attractive to pilgrims when it is associated with the holy presence of Christian people. A Christian holy place may be understood as holy by reference to the presence of Christian people, that is, by association. By extension, a certain 19th-century development, reported by Burrell, which sought for archaeological purposes to separate holy *places* from holy *sites* needs to be resisted.[55] What is required is the renewal of the earlier tradition that did not separate holy sites from holy places.

Furthermore, we may also note that some of the early Christian pilgrimages (3rd to 6th centuries CE) in the western Mediterranean were, according to Peter Brown, journeys to tombs, to encounter the holy presence of a martyr at the site of his or her burial. Holiness is here associated with the place of a saint's tomb: 'The holy was available in one place, and in each place it was accessible to one group in a manner in which it could not be accessible to anyone situated elsewhere.'[56] There is some historical evidence, therefore, both for the importance of pilgrimage for early Christianity and for the association of *praesentia* – holy presence – with particular places. This sensibility of Latin Christianity needs reviving in the consideration and performance of present-day pilgrimage to Jerusalem. The ascension of Christ insists on the particularity and the resurrection of Christ requires the universality of his body. Sacramental pilgrimage invokes a liturgical memory to participate in the Eucharist at the place where the body dwelt: the resurrected body of Christ remains the crucified body, and that body was crucified at Jerusalem. Of course, the means of participation in that resurrected body remains at all times liturgical.

From being attentive to Jerusalem as holy place rather than site, it is possible to honour the way that 'the actions of Jesus redefined the nature of what was "centre"'.[57] Pilgrimage to Jerusalem must therefore be understood as a movement away from the centre in that the journey to Jerusalem is ecclesial: to join with those Christian communities whose presence in that holy place makes it holy over again. To be, in other words, the Eucharistic form of Christ in the place where Jesus was. The most important Christian, political act that Christians can engage in during a pilgrimage to Jerusalem is participation in the Eucharist with Arab Christians.[58] That is, following de Certeau, to be *faithful* to the inaugural event yet also to be *different* from these beginnings. Such a Eucharistic framework for pilgrimage to Jerusalem is opposed to Burrell's suggestion that Jerusalem should be regarded as iconic, by which 'untapped potential within us' will be awakened so as 'to engage our very persons'.[59]

If the discussion of transition in the Eucharist in the previous section is correct, it is from our 'potential' that we need rescuing. In addition, the practice of Eucharists 'to go' should be resisted: fixed altars should be sought rather than makeshift ones in which a Eucharist is performed at, say, the Sea of Galilee to enhance a pilgrimage. The Eucharist is not a spiritual variation on mood music. Furthermore, if the primary political act will be participation in the Eucharist with Christian peoples at Jerusalem, this will be more difficult to achieve than seems obvious at first sight: according to figures cited by Burrell, the majority of Christians in Palestine–Israel live in the Palestinian territories, away from the 'holy sites'.[60]

Moving away from the centre of holy sites to participate in the rite of the Eucharist is to make the Church visible, as Cavanaugh makes clear, in its transition to a God-given identity founded on hospitality. The Christian community gives itself away in support of peace, justice, freedom and truth following the pattern of the Eucharist. What Jerusalem gives to the pilgrim is therefore a transition: a Eucharistic segue into the creative liberty of God, in communion with those Arab (and other) Christians by whose presence Jerusalem is associated over again with the holiness of the incarnate One. In other words, pilgrims to Jerusalem enter the holy place by joining those Christians *in situ* who are through the Eucharistic rite invoking the memory of the incarnate One who died in that place.[61] That is, pilgrimage to Jerusalem is always a journey of transition. To repeat an earlier comment: the pilgrimage to Jerusalem is to be understood as a journey of preparation; to repent and be converted in order to attend more fully to the particularities of the pilgrim's own place;[62] to learn, in other words, of the unity of the Church by participation in the Eucharist at Jerusalem, and of the fullness of salvation that is displayed and enacted in service. In such unity we learn of the divisions of the world and the requirement of service in opposition to such divisions: to transform places of need and loss into those of hospitality and care. That much is suggested by sacramental vision.

Such a sacramental and trinitarian approach seems to me to be theologically preferable to the approach recommended by David Burrell which, stressing Christianity's credentials as a monotheism, argues for the proper 'humility and thanksgiving' that should be the response to 'radical dependence on the source of all being and every gift'.[63] In that such humility and gratitude are shared by Islam, Judaism and Christianity as monotheisms, there are here, so Burrell's argument goes, grounds for hope. However, such a view fails to identify why it is that Jerusalem is important to Christian pilgrims: not, that is, for the sake of the Creator God but for a Son of Israel, the Christ of God, who tabernacled there. If Jerusalem is the *triune* God's address, at that address you will also find the Eucharist, and after that non-violent direct actions against Israeli 'state terrorism'.[64] In ways unknown, yet known in the purposes of God, such peacemaking in the way of the incarnate One, 'to guide our feet into the way of peace' (Luke 1:79 NRSV), may renew the Psalmist's tradition of Jerusalem. In that tradition, as Haddon Willmer summarizes, 'the city is called to realize a justice which is more than giving each person his due: it is to give God his due, by building the city that his peace, presence and forgiveness make possible, so that all his people may share it together'.[65]

The pilgrimage ends: the pilgrim returns to his or her own place. How should we think of that return? In 'The Journey of the Magi', by T.S. Eliot, the speaker of the poem, on return from giving gifts to the Christ child, says, 'We returned to our places, these Kingdoms/But no longer at ease here, in the old dispensation/With an alien people clutching their gods/I should be glad of another death.'[66] This is connected with what I mean by pilgrimage to Jerusalem as sacramental: after the encounter of Jerusalem, we return to the starting place of our journey 'no longer at ease here'. We are thereby better placed to confess the ways in which in pilgrimages in our place we fail to be hospitable. Pilgrimage to Jerusalem is not therefore about a journey to manipulate God's blessing but is concerned with a return to our place – an environment, history and community – in which our faith, hope and love are deepened. We need not look to Jerusalem to tell us of our identity because in God 'humanity is faithfully kept for us'.[67] Christians are not first citizens of contemporary Jerusalem. Instead, Christians are first of all citizens of the *new* Jerusalem. Our access to that new Jerusalem is the Eucharist. The new Jerusalem activates and governs our engagement with contemporary Jerusalem. Pilgrimage to Jerusalem, the site of the Passion and the first Eucharist, may dramatize that access, as Christians meet at the altars of Christians living in Jerusalem. That is the liturgical point I have been making throughout this chapter.[68]

Notes

1   In my view, in his essay 'Jesus, Jerusalem and Pilgrimage Today' (Chapter 1 of this volume), Cragg separates the matters of Jerusalem as educating in the faith and as a site of conflict. In the final part of the present chapter, I seek to draw these matters together.

2   Sheldrake, *Spaces for the Sacred*, 61. Such Protestant sensibility may value pilgrimage, but in the specific sense of a Christian individual's journey or way rather than a journey to, say, Jerusalem, Santiago de Compostela or Lourdes.

3   Ruether, 'Ecofeminism', 19.

4   Jenson, *The Triune God*, 67.

5   Ibid., 68.

6   Jenson, 'Eschatology'.

7   Cf. McConville, Chapter 2 of the present volume: 'The OT texts are unanimous in their witness that the God of Israel might not be imaged … Here is a fundamental difference between Israel's pilgrimages and those of the other nations.'

8   Sheldrake, *Spaces for the Sacred*, 30.

9   Jenson, *The Works of God*, 123.

10   Ibid.

11   Bonhoeffer, *Christology*, 53.

12   Pannenberg, *Systematic Theology*, II, 137–8.

13   Cf. Burrell, 'Jerusalem after Jesus', 257.

14   Williams, *On Christian Theology*, 85.

15   Ibid., 82.

16   Alison, *Knowing Jesus*, 16.

17   Williams, *On Christian Theology*, 83.

18   Sheldrake, *Spaces for the Sacred*, 29; italics in original.

19   This would be the basis of my response to the fine essay by Lincoln, 'Pilgrimage in the New Testament' (Chapter 3 of the present volume).

20   Farrow, 'Confessing Christ Coming', 134–5.

21   Ibid., 137.

22   Bookchin, *The Philosophy of Social Ecology*, xviii.

23   Michel de Certeau, 'How is Christianity thinkable today?', 142.

24   Jenson, *The Triune God*, 63.

25   Sheldrake, *Spaces for the Sacred*, 17.

26   Ibid., 63.

27   See McDonagh, *The Gracing of Society*, esp. 8–18.

28   Sheldrake, *Spaces for the Sacred*, 8.

29   Ibid., 9.

30   This is a central theme of O'Donovan's *The Desire of the Nations*.

31   Williams, *On Christian Theology*, 67–8.

32   See Hardy, *Finding the Church*, 26, citing John Knox, *The Church and the Reality of Christ* (London: Collins, 1963), 88.

33   Cavanaugh, *Torture and Eucharist*, 271.

34   Here I am drawing on O'Donovan, *The Desire of the Nations*, Ch. 5.

35   Cavanaugh, *Torture and Eucharist*, 14.

36   Santmire, *Nature Reborn*, 31–5.

37   Cavanaugh, *Torture and Eucharist*, 271.

38   Williams, *On Christian Theology*, 220.

39   Cavanaugh, *Torture and Eucharist*, 235.

40   Sheldrake, *Spaces for the Sacred*, 64.

41   Ibid., 70.

42   Ibid., 75.

43   Williams, *On Christian Theology*, 214–17.

44   Cavanaugh, *Torture and Eucharist*, 263.

45   Ibid., 271.

46   Sheldrake, *Spaces for the Sacred*, 89.

47 Williams, *On Christian Theology*, 119, 220.
48 Cavanaugh, *Torture and Eucharist*, 2.
49 Ibid., 263.
50 Floyd, 'The Search for an Ethical Sacrament', 188.
51 See Clark, 'Municipal Dreams', 166. I appreciate that this runs counter to some justifications of pilgrimage: see, for example, the discussion of the encounter with God by Martin Robinson in Chapter 10 of the present volume. The sacramental approach I am proposing is opposed to such experientialism.
52 Williams, *On Christian Theology*, 221.
53 Sheldrake, *Spaces for the Sacred*, vii.
54 Ibid., 38, 39.
55 Burrell, 'Jerusalem after Jesus', 258.
56 Brown, *The Cult of the Saints*, 86.
57 Sheldrake, *Spaces for the Sacred*, 69.
58 I set aside here problems of inter-communion.
59 Burrell, 'Jerusalem after Jesus', 259.
60 Ibid., 256.
61 The invocation is thereby doubled: these Christians invoke the memory of the actions of Golgotha at the place of Golgotha.
62 According to McConville, who writes of the 'ethical accompaniment to pilgrimage' in Chapter 2 of the present volume, such an orientation is not alien to consideration of pilgrimage in the Christian Old Testament.
63 Burrell, 'Jerusalem after Jesus', 262, quoting Marcel Dubois.
64 As suggested by Ateek, 'Newsletter of the Sabeel Ecumenical Liberation Theology Center'.
65 Willmer, 'Images of the City and the Shaping of Humanity', 37. Willmer cites Psalms 48, 127 and 137.
66 Eliot, 'The Journey of the Magi', *The Wasteland and other poems*, 66.
67 Willmer, 'Images of the City and the Shaping of Humanity', 46.
68 Warm thanks to Bill Cavanaugh for a very helpful set of critical comments on a draft of this essay.

References

Alison, J., *Knowing Jesus* (London: SPCK, 1993).
Ateek, N., 'Newsletter of the Sabeel Ecumenical Liberation Theology Center', Jerusalem, Christmas 2001, electronic version, no page numbers.
Bonhoeffer, D., *Christology* (London: Fontana, 1971).
Bookchin, M., *The Philosophy of Social Ecology: Essays on Dialectical Naturalism*, 2nd edn (Montreal, New York and London: Black Rose Books, 1996).
Brown, P., *The Cult of the Saints: Its Rise and Function in Latin Christianity* (Chicago: University of Chicago Press, 1981).
Burrell, D.B., 'Jerusalem after Jesus', in M. Bockmuehl (ed.), *The Cambridge Companion to Jesus* (Cambridge: Cambridge University Press, 2001), pp.250–64.
Cavanaugh, W.T., *Torture and Eucharist: Theology, Politics and the Body of Christ* (Oxford: Blackwell, 1998).
Clark, J., 'Municipal Dreams', in A. Light (ed.), *Social Ecology after Bookchin* (New York: Guildford Press, 1998), pp.137–91.
de Certeau, M., 'How is Christianity thinkable today?', in G. Ward (ed.), *The Postmodern God: A Theological Reader* (Oxford: Blackwell, 1997), pp.142–55.

Eliot, T.S., *The Wasteland and other poems* (London: Faber & Faber, 1972).

Farrow, D., 'Confessing Christ Coming', in C.R. Seitz (ed.), *Nicene Christianity: The Future for a New Ecumenism* (Grand Rapids: Brazos Press and Carlisle: Paternoster, 2001), pp.133–48.

Floyd, W.W., 'The Search for an Ethical Sacrament: From Bonhoeffer to Critical Social Theory', *Modern Theology*, 7(2) (1991), 175–93.

Hardy, D.W., *Finding the Church: The Dynamic Truth of Anglicanism* (London: SCM Press, 2001).

Jenson, R.W., *Systematic Theology I: The Triune God* (New York and Oxford: OUP, 1997).

——, *Systematic Theology II: The Works of God* (New York and Oxford: OUP, 1999).

——, 'Eschatology', in W.T. Cavanaugh and P. Scott (eds), *The Blackwell Companion to Political Theology* (Oxford: Blackwell, 2004).

McDonagh, E., *The Gracing of Society* (Dublin: Gill and Macmillan, 1989).

O'Donovan, O., *The Desire of the Nations* (Cambridge: Cambridge University Press, 1996).

Pannenberg, W., *Systematic Theology*, vol. II (Edinburgh: T&T Clark, 1994).

Ruether, R.R., 'Ecofeminism', in Carol J. Adams (ed.), *Ecofeminism and the Sacred* (New York: Continuum, 1993), pp.13–23.

Santmire, H.P., *Nature Reborn: The Ecological and Cosmic Promise of Christian Theology* (Philadelphia: Fortress Press, 2000).

Sheldrake, P., *Spaces for the Sacred: Place, Memory and Identity* (London: SCM Press, 2001).

Williams, R., *On Christian Theology* (Oxford: Blackwell, 2000).

Willmer, H., 'Images of the City and the Shaping of Humanity', in A. Harvey (ed.), *Theology in the City* (London: SPCK, 1989), pp.32–46.

CHAPTER 10

Pilgrimage and Mission

Martin Robinson

In the 1960s the name Lindisfarne was almost entirely connected in the popular imagination with the pop group of the same name. Today, the name Lindisfarne almost always translates as Holy Island and resonates much more with themes of spirituality. Particularly during the summer months, hundreds of visitors make the daily pilgrimage to tread where holy feet have trod, to view and touch the ancient sites of Christian mission. In Chapter 1, Kenneth Cragg makes the point that the rationale of pilgrimage contains the themes of 'blessing by proximity and access by contact'. Some of those who cross the causeway to Holy Island, to sit where Celtic saints have prayed, wish not only to connect with ancient holiness but also to be inspired imaginatively in their own conception of mission in the western world today.

Very few books dedicated to the subject of pilgrimage make an explicit connection between pilgrimage and mission. By the same token it is extremely unlikely that a text on the subject of mission will devote significant space to pilgrimage.[1] There is sometimes an implied or suggested connection in that pilgrimage can renew the spiritual vigour of the believer and hence equip them for the challenges of their Christian witness in the world. Pilgrimage can be understood as a motif that stands for mission as a journey of faith. But a necessary or integral connection is rarely explored. Is it the case that there is merely a tangential or secondary relationship between these two themes in the Christian life, or is it that each requires a profound understanding of the other to remain healthy? This chapter will explore the idea that pilgrimage and mission are intimately and importantly connected.

But why should these vital elements of the Christian faith have become so distanced? Why is there not an obvious and immediate connection between pilgrimage and mission? Firstly, it is clear that however popular pilgrimage may have become in medieval Christianity, it is not a uniquely Christian activity. *The New Catholic Encyclopaedia* reminds its readers that pilgrimage is an ancient practice that predates both Old and New Testaments. In one sense it is a borrowed concept.

> Pilgrimages have a long history in the ancient Near East among Semitic peoples; they are as old as the sacred shrines uncovered by archaeologists. To these various cultic centres the common man carried a part of the fruits of his land and livestock to offer it to the gods in homage and thanksgiving

... Some of the Canaanite open-air shrines were merely converted to the
use of the Yahwistic cult, e.g. Sichem, Bethel, and Mamre.[2]

The knowledge that pilgrimage is sometimes more deeply connected to the
practice of faiths other than Christianity possibly creates a deep sense of unease
in the missionary – the one who seeks to proclaim the unique claims of
Christianity. At best, for the missionary, the notion of pilgrimage can seem
esoteric, hardly core material for the seeker or the new convert. At worst it
might contain a hint of the impure, and even the syncretistic. It is easy to see
how the missionary might mistrust such talk just as the Reformation zealots
worried about the incorporation of motifs such as the Green Man in medieval
European Christianity.[3]

Secondly, such a concern is further heightened by the awareness that
pilgrimage does not feature significantly in the pages of the New Testament.
Andrew Lincoln deals with this same point in some detail. He makes the
explicit point that 'there are no NT documents that encourage Christians to
hold as normative for themselves the notion of pilgrimage to Jerusalem or to
any other particular place that is to be regarded as sacred' (p.40).

Certainly Jesus went on pilgrimage to Jerusalem in fulfilment of his religious
duties. We may assume that those followers of the Way whose self-identity was
still distinctly Jewish continued to visit the Temple, but Gentile believers were
no more expected to practise pilgrimage to Jerusalem than they were expected
to keep the Old Testament food laws or indeed to be circumcised. The very
connection of pilgrimage with Jewish faith and practice at least suggested a
radical discontinuity for a community for whom the temple could now be seen
as a dispersed reality.

The reality of persecution, of trials and difficulties tended to cause Christians
to reinterpret the physical pilgrimage to Jerusalem by means of an
eschatological vision. In the light of this spiritualization of pilgrimage, a
physical pilgrimage was no longer necessary and indeed might detract from the
urgency of preaching the Gospel at a time when the eschaton was perceived as
imminent. An Orthodox writer reminds us of this tendency:

> One of the most powerful features of early Christianity was its deep sense of
> the transitoriness of the present age and its eager waiting for the age to come.
> 'Here we have no lasting city, but we are looking for the city that is to come'
> (Hebrews 13:14). We are only pilgrims on the way to 'the Jerusalem above;
> she is free, and she is our mother' (Galatians 4:25–6). The vision of a new
> heaven and a new earth symbolized by the Holy City, the new Jerusalem,
> coming down out of heaven from God (Revelation 21:1–2) kept the hope
> aflame in the hearts of the pilgrims amidst the earthly trials and persecutions.[4]

Thirdly, the origins of a specifically Christian interest in pilgrimage do not
immediately suggest an intimate connection with mission. The early records of

Christians visiting the Holy Land in the first few centuries of the Christian church suggest curiosity rather than either personal devotion or mission. The first recorded Christian pilgrim to Jerusalem was Melito of Sardis, who travelled to the city around 170AD.[5] His stated motive was to confirm that which he had read in Scripture. Jerome expressed a similar concern, believing that a visit to the Holy Land would enable pilgrims to gain a better understanding of Scripture.

But the great growth in pilgrimage as an activity amongst Christians dated from the attempts by Helena and Constantine to identify, restore and honour the sites of importance for Christians in Jerusalem. However sincere the devotional motivation of those who pioneered such efforts, the linkage with mission is difficult to see. Indeed, it would be possible to argue that it was a post-missionary obsession, given that the Church had achieved a position in the Empire which previous generations of Christians could scarcely have imagined.

Fourthly, the act of pilgrimage is often thought to mirror the interior journey of the spiritual life rather than the exterior activity of mission. A pilgrimage is not a crusade in any evangelistic sense of the word. Even when pilgrimage has a social ingredient, travelling along the road with others, the companionship envisaged is not intended to divert the individual pilgrim from the intended spiritual benefits of the experience. Increasingly, in modern Europe, the pilgrim may not claim to be a believer, but only a seeker after God; pilgrimage does not seek to instruct or convert or indeed to change the world at all. Even for seekers as contrasted with believers, it is the priority of the inner life that motivates the pilgrim act. As one source puts it:

> Three movements of the soul, those of repentance, faith and love, characterize the Godward journey. They are inner attitudes which express themselves in aspiration and action. They are all present and operative throughout the pilgrimage but at different stages one or other will tend to predominate. It is normal in the early stages of the pilgrim's journey for repentance to be of especial importance. Later the deepening and enlarging of faith commonly becomes a major concern. Later still the progress of the spiritual pilgrim is measured chiefly by growth in love for God and one's fellows.[6]

Fifthly, pilgrimage necessarily drives the pilgrim to an awareness of their solitude, whereas mission seeks to build community: the Church, not as an ultimate goal but as an essential vehicle through which the Kingdom of God is brought into being. Even though pilgrims in medieval times often travelled in groups, especially, as Jonathan Sumption claims, for safety on the route, the presence of others is not a necessity but a convenience.[7] Certainly the company of others can be enjoyed and valued. As Chaucer illustrates, entertainment can come from within the fellowship of others: humour and drama to lighten the journey. But, as many writers testify, the presence of others can be a problem and the individual pilgrim needs also to consider the time that he or she travels alone even if in the company of others.

> After plying me with preliminary questions, she moved into the diagnosis. 'And are you walking alone?' 'Yes,' I said. 'Perhaps Monsieur prefers being alone to being with people,' she suggested hopefully. 'No, I enjoy both being alone and being with people.' A shadow of disappointment swept across her face, but she was a determined student. 'I see,' she said after a pause, 'when you are alone you want to be with people, and when you are with people you want to be alone.' 'That is partly true,' I replied, 'solitude helps me to appreciate company and company helps me to appreciate solitude, but there's a time for speaking and a time for being silent.' She looked puzzled and disappointed and I was dismissed with a curt 'Bon Voyage'.[8]

Mission, as with Paul's missionary band, not only calls community into being, it relies upon the diversity of gifts found within the Church for a proper expression of missionary activity.

Sixthly, pilgrimage at the level of popular piety is often motivated by personal need, the desire to obtain something from God, to bargain with God by acts of extreme devotion. Mission, on the other hand; is usually characterized by the call to meet the needs of others, to share in partnership with God in the Missio Dei. Indeed the extent to which personal sorrow, sadness and loss impels the desire to go on pilgrimage can become a concern for the keepers of the particular shrine that is visited. Many writers have attempted to discover why people visit particular places. One writer concludes:

> Many pilgrims, then, decided to go to a particular shrine because they heard about its reputation from neighbours or from others passing through their villages or because they had received dream-admonitions. Others, however, wandered from one shrine to another in search of health, until they felt sufficiently cured. Many English pilgrims went first to Becket's tomb, an indication of his popularity. Sometimes these perambulations in search of health took pilgrims well beyond the coasts of England. An Attenborough man went to Compostela in early 1201 for a cure. He felt some relief while there but after his return in mid-May his condition deteriorated and he spent the next few months 'shrinehopping'. Things grew worse until someone recommended Sempringham, where on 29 September he was cured by the relics of St Gilbert.[9]

Shrine officials stand in constant need of drawing the distinction between genuine devotion that arises properly from Christian faith and the desperate hope for a miracle which can lead pilgrims to a preoccupation with the shrine as a source of magical power.[10] There can be a fine line between an interest in the mystical and a fascination with the magical, between a genuine search for God and a bad case of shrinehopping.

So is there any essential and important connection between pilgrimage and mission, or should we see these activities as entirely separate preoccupations that attract entirely different kinds of people with very different agendas? Is it the case that an individual might only happen to be drawn to both agendas because of some peculiar quirk in their experience or personality? I have already suggested that I am convinced of an intimate and necessary connection, so how might that relationship be expressed?

The Call of God

Traditionally mission has been understood as a 'sending out'. One missiologist in responding to his own question 'What really is Mission?' offers as his first answer, 'The pattern of "being sent out" is the first biblical idea behind the concept and reality of mission.'[11] That is not an adequate definition. Before being sent out, the believer and indeed the Church is 'called out'. The call out from amongst the world, out of the familiarity of home and culture is the necessary prerequisite to a new orientation that endows the sending out with its proper meaning. To be sent out without first being called out suggests that the one who is being sent is already adequate and has no need of personal conversion and change. The calling out by God, the invitation that comes to us from God, is as important as the sending by God. It is that invitation that ties our mission and our subsequent sending to a journey that is not certain. One writer puts it this way: 'The road is an unknown road, walked in faith. While not strictly pilgrimage, the stories of Abraham's call, the exodus wanderings and the return from exile are biblical themes which Christian devotion has linked with actual and spiritual pilgrimages.'[12]

The calling out is that which makes us homeless and defines our new life of faith as a perpetual journey or wandering. The life of faith begins with an invitation to participate in the Missio Dei. It is necessarily a journey or a pilgrimage. The metaphor of pilgrimage to describe the Christian life is well rooted in the Scriptures. Like Abraham and Jesus we are wanderers. This is not our home, we are looking for the heavenly city, for another country. An actual pilgrimage offers a spiritual and psychological space to review that broader call, but from the perspective of mission what matters is not a single particular pilgrimage but what one writer has called 'the pilgrim principle'. The missiologist Andrew Walls explains such a principle in this way:

> Not only does God in Christ take people as they are: He takes them in order to transform them into what He wants them to be. Along with the indigenizing principle which makes his faith a place to feel at home, the

Christian inherits the pilgrim principle, which whispers to him that he has no abiding city and warns him that to be faithful to Christ will put him out of step with his society; for that society never existed, in East or West, ancient time or modern, which could absorb the word of Christ painlessly into its system.[13]

It is the pilgrim principle that keeps the church which is engaged in mission properly focused on its future hope. As Brother John of Taizé notes:

Our word 'parish' comes from the Greek paraikos, which means precisely 'pilgrim, passing stranger'. Is not every Church, in fact, called to be the 'pilgrim's house', centred on prayer and sharing ... the Church gives us a glimpse of the goal of pilgrimage, the future city (Hebrews 13:14), already breaking into our life.[14]

Mission, conducted in the light of the pilgrimage principle, is always centred on the coming Kingdom and cannot be content to centre on the aggrandisement or expansion of the Church. Pilgrimage, conducted in the light of mission, can never be satisfied with a purely personal fulfilment, the immediate end of a particular journey. Pilgrimage in the light of mission points to a more final end and so a more compelling present.

The Encounter with God

Both pilgrimage and mission carry within their true call a desire to express a genuine encounter with God. These encounters may at times seem very different but both seek for an authentic experience of God. It might be possible to think of these encounters as different aspects of the breath or Spirit of God. Just as in breathing we must both inhale and exhale, so in encountering God there is a time to breathe in and a time to breathe out. Both dimensions of breathing are important.

It could be argued that the Church passes through periods when it has exhausted itself from too much exhalation. In such times it is important to learn again how to inhale deeply. Many observers in the field of mission suggest that the Church in the western world finds itself in just such a moment. Having given of itself energetically in the expansion of Christianity around the globe in the modern era, the Church in the west seems to many to be suffering from a crisis of confidence, unsure of its direction, uncertain of its mission. Reflecting on the situation of the North American Church, one writer offers a view that stands for most churches in the western world:

This is a time for a dramatically new vision. The current predicament of churches in North America requires more than a mere tinkering with long-

assumed notions about the identity and mission of the church. Instead, as
many knowledgeable observers have noted, there is a need for reinventing
or rediscovering the church in this new kind of world.[15]

The challenge of mission in such a new landscape does not call merely for new
techniques but for a complete re-imagining of the mission of the Church and
what it means to be the Church. The Church in the west is being called to a new
kind of pilgrim journey, one in which many new discoveries will need to be
made. Pilgrimage, breathing in, becomes a call to reflection, to asking
profound questions, to using the journey to consider again our origins and our
destination. The need for the Church in the west to begin a pilgrimage of
discovery concerning its true vocation is urgent. The missionary imagination of
the Church is best engaged when journey lies at its heart. As one writer puts it,
'The ship is safest when it's in port. But that's not what ships were made for.'[16]

  True pilgrimage always has a missionary end in mind. It sees that encounter
with God is not an end in itself but an act of mission. One young pilgrim to
Rocamadour commented:

> Here you feel that the pilgrim people are on their way to the promised land:
> two hundred young people, who only yesterday were strangers to each
> other, are about to pray together and to share what constitutes their life.
> Together, they'll feel joyful in Jesus Christ. Here we shed our prejudices;
> friendship and esteem are born of this new view of life. Hands stretch out to
> each other; the guitars sing of hope, joy, reconciliation. Like Jesus, we've
> walked all the way; we've dropped our masks and discovered truth.
> Tomorrow we'll build a Church open to everyone. That's what the
> pilgrimage is about.[17]

Building a Church that is open to everyone goes to the very heart of the God
encounter. It expresses well the true goal of pilgrimage and mission.

The Beckoning God

As we have seen, both pilgrimage and mission contain the sense of call and
encounter, but something deeper yet calls both pilgrim and missionary along
the way of pilgrimage, the way of mission. The invitation of God that
constitutes an initial call never ends but continues as a perpetual beckoning or
encouraging along the way. We gain a sense of the nature of that perpetual
beckoning from the post-resurrection encounter that Jesus has with his
disciples, recorded in Matthew's Gospel: 'Then Jesus said to them, "Do not be
afraid. Go and tell my brothers to go to Galilee; there they will see me."'
(Matt.28:10).

From the very earliest moment of the resurrection experiences we gain a picture of a Church that is being beckoned to journey. Why could they not meet Jesus in Jerusalem? That is where he was crucified and buried. That is where the women first met him. Why do they need to travel all the way to Galilee to see what they could just as easily encounter where they were?

As the disciples obeyed and made the journey to Galilee, in fact to a particular mountain, there they were given what has become known as the Great Commission contained in Matthew 28:18–20. This has been seen as the sending mandate and as such is probably the most important foundational scripture for the modern missionary movement and possibly for mission through all ages. It describes the missionary heart of the Church but it was given by Jesus to those who responded to his divine beckoning along the way.

Curiously, the mandate was given to a group that were willing to respond, to journey at least as far as Galilee, but who were far from certain about what they were seeing. This was not a group of doubt-free fanatics but a strange assortment of missionary pilgrims. Matthew tells us, 'When they saw him, they worshipped him; but some doubted' (Matt.28:17). It was to this whole group of pilgrims that the mandate was given, not just to the doubt-free element.

As we can see from the accounts in John's Gospel of the doubt expressed by Thomas, the element of exploration, the desire to discover, so important to pilgrimage, is able to use the element of doubt creatively. Pilgrimage is not for the faithful who have nothing to discover. The element of uncertainty, which lies at the heart of both pilgrimage and mission, is nourished by the beckoning of God which calls us on, not just to the whole journey, but to the next stage, to the metaphorical 'Galilee' along the way. Basil Hume wrote these words about the questions rightly experienced by the pilgrim:

> While on the road we cannot help wondering about God. What is He like? What does He want for us? What does He expect of us? And sometimes we ask whether He exists at all. So many of our fellow pilgrims have decided that there is no God; others just go through life doubting or not knowing. But the important questions still require answers. What happens after death? Nothing? Has life no meaning? Are we only part of an absurd situation devoid of sense and meaning?[18]

These are exactly the questions that face both missionary and pilgrim. God beckons us along the road not only to discover answers, but also to discover him in whom the answers reside. As Basil Hume also points out, in pilgrimage it is not just we who are in search of God but also God who is in search of us. The perpetual beckoning is as much about the action of God as our response to that whispered encouragement from the one who has gone before us.[19]

The uncertainty that faces the western Church, the lack of confidence about its life and future, do not need to induce despair. As mission embraces pilgrimage and pilgrimage embraces mission, the element of uncertainty forces us to listen all the more carefully to the voice of the one who beckons. He does not reveal every contour, twist and turn of the journey ahead, but He does at least call us to the next stopping place, to Galilee from Jerusalem, having first gone on ahead to meet us there.

Travelling for Christ

It is hoped that these brief reflections indicate that, at their heart, pilgrimage and mission not only have a common root but also are inextricably bound together. These dimensions of the journey of faith need each other in order to remain hopeful and healthy. But is it possible to point to some actual examples of that intertwining in the history of the Church? Precisely because pilgrimage and mission are at their most creative when uncertainty is present, the times in Church history when we might most easily see a clear connectivity between pilgrimage and mission are precisely those times of crisis when the Church has necessarily engaged in a re-invention of its life and witness. The missiologist David Bosch has drawn from the writings of Hans Kung in suggesting that there have been a number of key crisis points during which times the Church has left one paradigm and formed another.[20]

One of those crisis points for the western Church took place in the period that historians call 'the Dark Ages'. As the Roman Empire faded in Western Europe, new pagan tribes, who became the new rulers, overwhelmed the formerly substantial Christian populations in the various provinces of Rome. In recent times there has come a growing recognition of the importance of the Celtic saints in the reconversion of Western Europe. One Irish–American author expressed this in the memorable title of his book, *How the Irish Saved Civilization*.[21] Particularly in the late 6th and early 7th centuries, hundreds and probably thousands of missionaries from Celtic shores found their way along the river valleys of Europe, founding communities of believers wherever they went.

The Celts were clearly missionaries but, fascinatingly, they also saw themselves as pilgrims of a particular kind. The term *peregrinatio* has been used to describe their self-understanding. The term can mean 'pilgrimage', but it was not travel to a single and particular destination so much as a perpetual journeying for Christ. It was not an aimless wandering with a devotional motif. Still less was it an escape from home or indeed a leaving of the Church. Rather, the specific intention of the wandering was to establish communities of the faithful: it was to found the Church. The communities that they formed looked very different from the Church that had existed in earlier times. There is a good deal of evidence that suggests that, when Celtic missionaries established new communities, relationships with the existing Christian churches that had survived from an earlier time were not always convivial. Columbanus, in particular, managed to enrage a good number of local bishops by his refusal to recognize their existing authority and to work under their auspices.

For the Celtic saints the linkage between pilgrimage and mission came through their understanding of martyrdom. For the Celts, there were three kinds of martyrdom. The first, the red martyrdom, involved an actual physical death for the cause of Christ. Interestingly there were very few, if any, recorded red martyrs in the period that we are considering. There were certainly many in a later period, especially in relation to the encounter between the Vikings and Irish Christian communities.

The second martyrdom was the green martyrdom. Green martyrdom was denoted by a strong penitential element in which the martyr did not die physically but died to self and to sin in a long exile from home. The intention was to purge sin by this form of death by absence from all that is loved and familiar, from hearth and home.

The third martyrdom was the white martyrdom. This form of martyrdom was very similar to that of green martyrdom in that the individual left home and probably went overseas. The motivation however, was not to do penance so much as to serve Christ. It is at this point that pilgrimage and mission became one and the same activity. In actual practice there probably was not much effective difference between green and white martyrdom. For example, Saint Columba is thought to have left Ireland for Scotland, in part as a punishment or penance for wrongdoing, but mission quickly became the dominant theme. That partly explains his very unusual behaviour when he did have to return to Ireland to help settle a dispute, in that he wore clods of turf on his feet brought with him from Scotland, so that his own feet would not touch Irish soil.

The linkage between perpetual pilgrimage and continuous mission is of great importance. The Irish emphasized that kind of pilgrimage and were sometimes suspicious of pilgrimage to a particular place. In part, they may have shared the worries expressed by their contemporary and sometime adversary, Boniface. But as the following extract demonstrates, they certainly had their concerns about pilgrimage per se:

> One consequence, as Boniface complains, of Roman pilgrimages is that everywhere in 'Lombardy, Gaul and France' he comes across Anglo-Saxon prostitutes. It was, in fact, a kind of mass migration on the spiritual plane, and it was in vain that the Irish set themselves against this development: 'Going to Rome means great toil and brings little profit. The (heavenly) king whom thou dost miss at home, thou wilt not find there if thou dost not bear him with you. Great is the folly, great the madness, great the senselessness, great the lunacy. For it is surely entering upon death to draw on oneself the anger of the Son of Mary.[22]

Their worry was that this kind of pilgrimage was unrelated to the call of Christ, it was not conducted pro Christo but to satisfy other more personal longings. It did not necessarily result in the building of the Church or even in the virtue of the individual. The Celts were not engaged in a grand tour of the continent so much as a passionate re-imagining and reconstruction of the Church.

The strange fusion of mission and pilgrimage practised by the Celts seems to have flowed from a kind of extravagant passion and boldness that characterized their sense of Christian vocation. Indeed it is possible to argue that it is precisely the interaction between mission and pilgrimage that allows such extravagant passion to be maintained.

The Challenge Today

Just as the Celts needed to employ their extravagant passion in order to create a new paradigm for the Church in a time of crisis, so the western Church needs the same kind of boldness to recreate the Church for our times.

Many writers describe the Church as anaemic, a pale shadow of the radical movement that Jesus initiated. One temptation in such a situation is to do what many thousands are doing and that is to abandon the Church and attempt to live as Christians outside its walls. The New Zealand researcher Alan Jamieson has documented just such a trend.[23] The comedian Lenny Bruce reflected this trend in his comment, 'Every day people are straying away from church and going back to God.'[24]

The temptation therefore is to see such churchless Christianity as a kind of personal pilgrimage that features spirituality but rejects institution. However understandable such a response might be, that kind of pilgrimage, unrelated to mission, will never refound the Church and ultimately fails to see the value of true pilgrimage. Equally a mission that does not take seriously the spiritual longings of the multitudes, that attempts only to adjust the Church at the margins, to keep things rather safe and only make necessary concessions to meet people's 'felt needs' as a kind of marketing approach to mission, to opt against being a pilgrim people, will totally fail. To reinvent the Church, to discover a new paradigm for its life and witness, will require the kind of extravagant passion that only comes when mission and pilgrimage are bound together in an embrace of expectant hope.

It is precisely at this point that the Celts can inspire our missionary enterprise. The creative Celtic linkage between pilgrimage and mission produces something more than aimless wandering, the addictive search for endless stimulation, suggested by Zygmunt Bauman's image of the tourist. But equally it avoids Bauman's notion of the pilgrim as one who is on a fixed path 'resisting all temptations to deviate from the path, slow down on the road or, worse still, give up' (see Chapter 11). The Celtic saints were on an open path. For them the road was not a highway on dry land but the unpredictable behaviour of the waves, the winds and the currents. It was the seas and rivers that provided monastic motorways and not the existing straight lines of the Roman roads of Europe. Their journey had purpose but it was also subject to the activity of the Spirit interpreted through the winds and the waves. They knew the 'why' of their journey but the 'where' and the 'what' were not always so clear.

Such a combination produces a kind of hopeful openness which can take account of the profound concerns of this present generation, so eloquently expressed in postmodernity, whilst avoiding the contradictory traps that the image of the tourist expresses. As Bauman acknowledges, the tourist has little contact with the indigenous peoples or cultures that he temporarily inhabits. In postmodernity, all cultures are apparently valued, but at the same time the failure to connect significantly with any of them reveals a hidden arrogance. Cultures which are temporarily surfed for their passing interest and stimulation are secretly despised.

A missionary and pilgrim Church does desire to take all cultures seriously, but at the same time invites every culture to join a journey of discovery. The Celtic pilgrim did stop along the way. The intent in halting for a time was to create a community of pilgrims in a given culture and a particular situation and to interpret the Christian story for that time and place.

Almost by definition the pilgrim operates at the margins of a given culture. That is significant both for mission and for cultural renewal. Arguably, most significant changes in cultural life do not begin at the centre but on the margins. When the activity of the margins becomes irresistible then the centre is redefined. The missionary pilgrim acts subversively at the margins to initiate change. From the perspective of Christian mission, change does not come from the exercise of a dominating power so much as from the power of an unknown but glimpsed future.[25] While in one sense the end may be certain, the shape of that yet to be visited destination is still unknown. It exists in the present much more as a hope that acts powerfully on the imagination to give meaning and shape to that which we temporarily inhabit.

There are increasing signs across the western world that experimental communities of this kind are emerging. They are not merely initiating new missionary methodologies so much as re-imaging what a pilgrim Church might look like. They are in feel and shape much closer to the Celtic model of pilgrim missionary communities than they are to the kind of missions that the west has traditionally sent to other continents.

It is of course too early to say what the long-term impact of such new forms of the Church might be. It is possible that they will merely represent failed experiments that will not reshape the mainstream. A number of missiologists are beginning to tell the stories of these new expressions of the Church. This is not the place to document these emergent forms, but it is important to ask whether we can genuinely think of them as epitomizing pilgrimage. In describing them as 'pilgrim communities', is it possible to be accused of merely using pilgrimage as a metaphor unrelated to its historic expression?

The example of the Celts suggests otherwise. Indeed it is possible to argue that it is only when pilgrimage loses its connection with mission that the very idea of pilgrimage creates a problem for Christians. Personal devotion, however intense and sincere, which is not related to a desire to see a changed world, betrays historic Christian spirituality and does indeed take on something of the character of spiritual tourism. The road to Jerusalem, or Lourdes or Santiago, can never be a substitute for a lifelong journey for Christ and towards Christ. The true purpose of a single pilgrimage is only ever to enhance the journey towards the eternal city.

Notes

1   It is, however, the case that the journal *An Evangelical Review of Missions* does contain a regular feature in which leading mission scholars or practitioners reflect on their personal pilgrimage in mission.

2   Polan, 'Pilgrimages', *New Catholic Encyclopaedia*, 362.

3   The Green Man is thought to be an older pagan theme which can be found reflected in carvings in some medieval churches.

4   George, *The Silent Roots*, 46.

5   Lincoln also refers to the origins of Christian pilgrimage (p.44).

6   Jones, Wainwright and Yarnold, *The Study of Spirituality*, 566.

7   Sumption, *Pilgrimage – An Image of Medieval Religion*, 196f, makes the point that pilgrims needed to travel together for reasons of safety.

8   Hughes, *In Search of a Way*, 83.

9   Finucane, *Miracles and Pilgrims*, 85.

10   Eade and Sallnow, in *Contesting the Sacred*, 64, quote from a guidebook at Lourdes thus: 'This water is not magical: it is drinkable, chemically pure, similar to other springs at Lourdes, lacking in therapeutic or radioactive qualities. It sometimes heals but its role is primarily to remind us that we should turn to Him who is the source of eternal life.'

11   Spindler, 'The Biblical Grounding and Orientation of Mission', 127.

12   Ellis, *Together On The Way*, 136.

13   Walls, *The Missionary Movement in Christian History*, 8.

14   John of Taizé, 'Pilgrimage Seen through the Bible', 393.

15   Guder, *Missional Church: A Vision for the Sending of the Church in North America*, 77.

16   Frost and Hirsch, *The Shaping of Things to Come*, 223.

17   Coehlo, *The Pilgrimage*, 22.

18   Hume, *To Be A Pilgrim*, 25.

19   Ibid., 22.

20   Bosch, *Transforming Mission*, 181f.

21   See Cahill, *How the Irish Saved Civilization*.

22   Von Campenausen, *Tradition and Life in the Church*, 247.

23   Jamieson, *A Churchless Faith*.

24   Cited in Frost and Hirsch, and quoted from a Lenny Bruce website.

25   See also Andrew Lincoln's references to the impact of the heavenly Jerusalem in the concluding arguments of Chapter 3.

Bibliography

Antier, J., 'Pilgrimages in France: Religious Tourism or Faith in Action?', *Lumen Vitae*, 39 (1984), 367–79.

Bosch D., *Transforming Mission* (New York: Orbis, 2000).

Cahill, T., *How the Irish Saved Civilization: The Untold Story of Ireland's Heroic Role from the Fall of Rome to the Rise of Medieval Europe* (Anchor, 1996).

Eade, J. and M. Sallnow (eds), *Contesting the Sacred* (London: Routledge, 1991).

Ellis, C., *Together On The Way: A Theology of Ecumenism* (London: British Council of Churches, 1990).

Finucane, R., *Miracles and Pilgrims* (London: J.M. Dent, 1977).

George, K., *The Silent Roots: Orthodox Perspectives on Christian Spirituality* (Geneva: World Council of Churches, 1994).

Guder, D. (ed.), *Missional Church: A Vision for the Sending of the Church in North America* (Grand Rapids: Eerdmans, 1998).

Hirsch, A. and M. Frost, *The Shaping of Things to Come: Innovation for Mission in the Twenty-First Century* (Peabody MA: Hendricksons, 2003).

Hughes, G., *In Search of a Way: Two Journeys of Spiritual Discovery* (London: DLT, 1994).

Hume, B., *To Be A Pilgrim* (London: SPCK, 1984).

Jamieson, A., *A Churchless Faith* (Wellington: Philip Garside Publishing, 2000).

John of Taizé, Brother, 'Pilgrimage Seen through the Bible', *Lumen Vitae*, 39 (1984) 380–93.

Jones, C., G. Wainwright and E. Yarnold (eds), *The Study of Spirituality* (London: SPCK, 1986).

Polan, S., 'Pilgrimages', *New Catholic Encyclopaedia* (Washington: The Catholic University of America, 1967), pp.362–3.

Spindler, M., 'The Biblical Grounding and Orientation of Mission', in F.J. Verstraelen (ed.), *Missiology: an Ecumenical Introduction* (Grand Rapids: Eerdmans, 1995), pp.123–43.

Sumption J., *Pilgrimage – An Image of Medieval Religion* (London: Faber & Faber, 1975).

Von Campenausen, H., *Tradition and Life in the Church: Essays and Lectures on Church History* (London: Collins, 1968).

Walls, A., *The Missionary Movement in Christian History: Studies in the Transmission of Faith* (Edinburgh: T&T Clark, 1996).

CHAPTER 11

The Pilgrim and the Tourist: Zygmunt Bauman and Postmodern Identity

Derek Tidball

Thomas Wilson, born in 1764, was a man whose mind 'was gradually impressed with the supreme value and paramount importance of eternal realities'.[1] He became a significant figure among the Congregationalists of his day, especially after retiring as a prosperous businessman from the silk industry at the age of 34, in order that he might 'promote more actively and efficiently the cause of God'.[2] In the biography of his father, Joshua Wilson wrote,

> My father was enabled to avoid a great error into which persons retiring from business often fall. They are too apt to consider themselves at liberty to live in a desultory, irregular manner without a fixed plan, a determined scheme of action – the consequence of which is, they have no practical aim – no definite object of pursuit. My father formed his purpose advisedly, and arranged his plan deliberately. The object selected by him is the greatest that can engage the attention or occupy the faculties of man, to which he had in previous years devoted a considerable part of time, and to which he now determined to devote the whole of his remaining life. That object was USEFULNESS, which has been well designated 'the very excellency of life'.[3]

Retirement, for Thomas Wilson, meant involvement in the Gratis Sunday School Society, the Religious Tract Society, chapel building activities, the British and Foreign Bible Society, the Congregational Union, the Hibernian Society, the Irish Evangelical Society, the London Missionary Society, the Colonial Missionary Society, the Home Missionary Society, the Metropolis Chapel Fund Association and the Council of London University.

I was reminded of Thomas Wilson when I read Zygmunt Bauman's reference to the word 'Forward' which is chiselled into the stonework of Leeds Town Hall. Bauman draws attention to the way in which this motto epitomizes life under modernity.[4] Life was lived through a given time and space with purpose, knowledge and determination. It had structure. It provided security. It added one achievement to another until the life project was completed and the destination reached. And, it was useful, just as was the life of Thomas Wilson.

By contrast, today, living in the culture of postmodernity, we are 'living without guidebooks'.[5] Life is a collection of fragments without any sense of direction or commitment to a destination. Above all else, the postmodern man or woman seeks to resist structures. 'The hub of postmodern life,' writes Bauman, 'is not identity building but the avoidance of being fixed.'[6]

No one has monitored these changes in personal identity formation more than Zygmunt Bauman. In a stream of books and articles, which are even more prolific now that he has retired as the Professor of Sociology at the Universities of Leeds and Warsaw, he has recorded his observation of and participation in this cultural shift. He has both advocated it and agonized over it. He has established himself as postmodernity's prophet. One looks in vain, in Bauman, for the carefully researched statistical evidence which characterizes much of English sociology. Instead he falls within the tradition of the French social philosophers who engage in painting the grand picture, meditating on the underlying issues and inventing the apposite metaphor. Yet he does so with increasing *angst* at the uncertainty with which he is surrounded, giving rise to Dennis Smith's comment that 'he transformed himself from a navigator into a weather forecaster – a role more immediately useful for a refugee who has lost confidence in all destinations'.[7]

One cannot help but believe that Bauman's personal story has a major influence on his view of postmodernity.[8] He was born into a poor Jewish family in Poland and suffered much from anti-Semitism. Fleeing to Russia, he fought in the Polish army against the Germans in World War II, rising, after the war, to the rank of captain. He was a member of the Polish Workers' Party and a communist. Summarily dismissed from the army in an anti-Semitic purge, he became a lecturer in Philosophy and Social Science at the University of Warsaw and developed a strong belief in the role of intellectuals in guiding the course of public affairs. Perhaps not surprisingly in view of this, in 1968 he was to lose his job for a second time when he was summarily dismissed as a dangerous influence on Polish youth. He travelled to Israel, Canada and America before settling in the United Kingdom, eventually becoming Professor of Sociology at Leeds in 1971.[9]

His life story is one of transitions and fragments. More significantly still, it is one of losing confidence in Marxism which, to him, was the most powerful metanarrative of modernity. He even lost confidence in his own ability to ask the right questions, and certainty was increasingly replaced by doubt. Faced throughout his life by massive and unpredictable historical changes, he can write now only provisionally and incompletely. As his recent biographer states, 'It is this *particular mixture* of involvements, ruptures and transitions, and their *complex interweaving* through three careers, that makes Bauman's own perceptions, his particular "take" on the world, so fascinating.'[10]

In that 'take' Bauman has some particularly fascinating things to say about our understanding of our identity as postmodern persons. This chapter will set out three preliminary considerations of the question of identity, then explore his central metaphor of postmodern identity, before engaging in a critique of his views.

Three Preliminary Considerations

The first consideration is that by the postmodern, Bauman essentially means postmarxism.[11] While his perception is not confined to the postmarxist world, this undoubtedly colours his perspective. It is the failure of the grand metanarrative of Marxism which has led to the world of diversity, fragmentation and uncertainty of which he writes. This contextual factor has importance for the way he sees, or perhaps more accurately, fails to see, the significance of religion in today's world, of which more later.

The second preliminary consideration is that Bauman argues that the question of personal identity is a particularly recent question, a modern invention.[12] It is only as community collapses that identity is invented.[13] In former days people's lives were scripted for them in secure communities and the question of 'Who am I?' was not one which individuals needed to ask of themselves. Their role and identities were prescribed, obvious and to a large degree unquestioned. They only needed to ask 'What should I do?' and 'How should I act?'. But with the growth of individualism and the unmaking of communities (which cannot be remade in the way they were) the question has inevitably risen to the surface. So searching for identity is 'today's talk of the town and the most commonly played game in town'.[14] He argues:

> Identity entered the modern mind and practice dressed from the start as an individual task. It was up to the individual to find escape from uncertainty. Not for the first and not for the last time *socially* created problems were to be resolved by *individual* efforts, and *collective* maladies healed by *private* medicine.[15]

It is this journey of uncharted individualism which makes a whole industry of counsellors, personal trainers, coaches and spiritual directors. For, in the absence of community wisdom and guidance to which all consent, the individual has to make his or her own way, leaning on whatever private support they can arrange.[16] Rejecting the traditional priests of modernity, 'postmodern men and women do need the alchemist who is able, or claims to be able, to transmogrify base uncertainty into precious self-assurance, and the authority of approval (in the name of superior knowledge, or access to wisdom closed to others) is the philosophical stone these alchemists boast of possessing'.[17]

Such lives, Bauman states, 'are full of sound and fury'. For '"Identity" means standing out: being different, and through that difference unique – and so the search for identity cannot but divide and separate'.[18] We are faced, he claims, with a choice. We can either have the security of community life, with the rigidity that goes with it, or we can reject that because we do not want to be fixed, and face the uncertainty and self-imposed exile of being uprooted.[19]

The third preliminary consideration is a doubt as to whether the quest to construct meaningful identity can ever be carried out successfully. Building identity is not easy. It gives rise to anxiety, especially about things and people we regard as strange.[20] But in postmodernity it is a deeply paradoxical quest. On the one hand it is encouraged by the cultural media. On the other hand,

> *having* an identity solidly founded and resistant to cross-waves, having it 'for life', proves a handicap rather than an asset for such people as do not sufficiently control the circumstances of their life itinerary; a burden that constrains the movement, a ballast which they must throw out in order to stay afloat.[21]

Bauman's Central Metaphor of Postmodern Identity

The sense of life as a journey dominates Bauman's thinking about both modernity and postmodernity[22] and leads him to his central metaphor of postmodern identity, namely, that of the tourist. We are all, he claims, on the move constantly, with the majority (but not by any means all) demonstrating the sort of mobility one associates with the tourist. He expounds the metaphor in a number of places,[23] most notably in *Postmodernity and its Discontents*, which includes a lecture entitled 'Tourists and Vagabonds: the heroes and victims of postmodernity', delivered at the University of Virginia in 1995. But the metaphor had already been put to good use, especially in his earlier work on *Postmodern Ethics*, where he applied it to the moral debates and ambiguity generated by postmodernity.

Bauman's Fourfold Typology

While the picture of the tourist is pre-eminent in his thought, the tourist does not journey alone. In his fuller picture tourists share the space they occupy with vagabonds, strollers and players. These three companions of (or perhaps variations on) the tourist may be more briefly described and dismissed.

Vagabonds[24] move not by choice but of necessity. If they were free agents they would probably choose to stay put, but others dictate that they must move and consequently the world is an inhospitable place for them. Bauman terms them 'involuntary tourists', recognizing that this is a contradiction in terms. They are the tourist's *alter ego*. They are, he explains, 'the waste of the world which has dedicated itself to tourists' services'.[25] In other respects (passing through other people's space without a sense of belonging and without a purposeful destination) they have characteristics in common with tourists. They are, in fact, tourists without money.

The second image is that of the stroller,[26] who is most frequently encountered today in the shopping mall. Strollers live on the surface, engaging in a series of fleeting encounters, none of which has any depth or makes any impact. They just move on to the next encounter. In a perceptive comment, Bauman points out that the most recent form of 'strolling' is to be found in people who never even get up out of their armchairs. Couch potatoes are strollers when they surf the telechannels: 'The ultimate freedom is screen-directed, lived in the company of surfaces, and called zapping.'[27]

The third image is that of the player,[28] who sees life as a succession of games in which disbelief has to be suspended as risks are engaged and intuition and caution are exercised in equal measure. Bauman's verdict is that 'The mark of postmodern adulthood is the willingness to embrace the game wholeheartedly, as children do'.[29]

The Dominant Type: the Tourist

It is the tourist, however, that Bauman explores most fully and uses most creatively as a metaphor of postmoderns. The tourist is curious, in search of amusement, living through novelty and pleasure, travelling through other people's space, while prepared to pay for the privilege of doing so. Other features of the tourist may be outlined briefly as follows:[30]

- They do not belong to the place they visit. They are both in and out of the place at the same time.
- They keep their distance. 'It is as if each of them was enclosed in a bubble.' Inside the bubble the tourist feels safe.
- They travel lightly, with just enough to insure themselves against the inclemency of alien places.
- They may set out on the road again at a moment's notice, as soon as they are threatened or their potential for amusement seems to have been exhausted, or still more exciting adventures beckon from afar.
- 'Mobility is the name of the game.' They need to move as soon as new dreams call.
- This is what they call freedom, independence or autonomy.
- The most frequent cry they utter is 'I need more space.' No one is allowed to question their right to move out of the space currently occupied.
- The length of their stay is not planned in advance, nor is their next destination. 'The point of the tourist life is to be on the move, not to arrive.' Unlike pilgrims, they have no goal or ultimate destination.

- Any logical itinerary is only discovered retrospectively.
- Stopovers are campings, not domiciles.[31]
- 'Only the shallowest of roots, if any, are struck. Only skin-deep relations, if any, are entered with the locals.' Locals are just accidentally 'bumped into'.
- The company they keep has no claim to loyalty: they are an unanticipated consequence of travelling.
- What makes the tourist 'feel in control' is not the old-fashioned control of making one's life and shaping one's world, but 'situational control'. Their world seems infinitely pliable. 'Shaping the world in this way is effortless, but it is also, for the world, at least, inconsequential.'
- Life is made up of 'episodes', self-enclosed events that do not last beyond their own duration. 'Not to be continued' is written all over them. But there is 'a nasty fly in the otherwise tasty ointment of a life lived at every moment as an episode', since the past may pop up and revisit you.
- So there is a price to be paid. 'The tourist's way of doing away with uncertainties brings about uncertainties of its own.'
- Tourists embark on their travels by choice – or so they think.
- They can always return home if they feel homesick or get fed-up with their hotel rooms. But once they do get home they discover their view of home was merely a mirage. The home quickly becomes a prison again. 'The tourist has acquired the taste for vaster, and above all open, spaces.'

The Implications of the Metaphor

Bauman's point is that tourism is a metaphor for all postmodern life and applies widely to those who live in the postmodern habitat, regardless of whether they literally travel or not. 'The world is the tourist's oyster.' As such, 'The world is there to be lived pleasurably – and thus given meaning.'[32] Work, no less than holidays, has to be approached with the mentality of the tourist and must produce the constant stream of excitements and satisfaction which the tourist derives from travelling, or else it will not be tolerated. Tourism's lifestyle is seductive. 'Ideally, one should be a tourist everywhere and everyday.'[33] Consequently, one's career is not carefully constructed or logically unfolded but is episodic, maybe even with long spaces in it for escape purposes. This is what postmodern people consider to be true freedom, to provide meaning and to be the means of forming personal identity.

Earlier, Bauman had used the tourist when exploring the nature of postmodern ethics. Beilharz neatly summarizes his position:

> There is a hole in the heart of modernity. It is called ethics. Moderns fill this hole with order, with rules and with regulations. Ethics was a chance given to moderns, who have been unable largely to take on the challenge, for they

are traditionalists at heart, creatures of habit, for whom the prospect of autonomy is simply too much; easier to just follow the rules.[34]

In contrast, postmoderns believe that people can be neither exclusively good nor exclusively bad, and contend that all life is morally ambiguous. If this is so, there can be no moral universals. Rules and regulations will not do. Unlike their predecessors they welcome freedom and the ability to construct their own moral lives on an intuitive foundation rather than a rational one.[35]

Traditional moral responsibility, then, is certainly not part of the baggage which tourists carry with them. In fact, being tourists makes them even less concerned to work through the moral ambiguities they face than they might otherwise do. They just live indifferent to the ambiguities. This works out in a number of ways, as can be illustrated from observing overseas tourists. Since they have paid for their freedom, tourists assume the right to 'disregard native concerns and feelings' and to reconstruct the world in their own image or to their own liking.[36] They can observe other people's customs and cultures from a little distance and return instantly to their own, as when they demand their own ethnic food and to speak their own language (usually loudly). Immoral customs, such as child prostitution, are viewed as local problems – the way the natives do things – and not the business of the tourist. Any concern which is voiced is met with the response that 'everybody does it' and 'it's none of my business'. Other illustrations of this point could have been added by Bauman. The pitiful wages paid to those employed in the tourist industry; the pollution caused by the excessive commitment to cleanliness, soap and shampoo, in tourists' bathrooms; the use of energy for jet planes and jacuzzis; and the oppression of the poor who are kept out of sight of the tourist – these are all common experiences which continue to let injustice flourish and contribute to the further degeneration of the environment. No wonder Bauman concludes, 'The tourist is bad news for morality.'[37]

The Metaphor the Tourist has Displaced

The metaphor of the tourist which Bauman believes epitomizes the postmodern context has displaced the metaphor of the pilgrim which was more familiar within the modern context. Bauman's view of the pilgrim is constructed upon the work of Max Weber,[38] and his study of the way in which the Reformation, particularly in its Puritan phase, shaped generations to live life as if it were a project to be advanced. The project was to be pursued with alacrity, resisting all temptations to deviate from the path, slow down on the road or, worse still, give up. Life was serious and to be lived seriously before God. Weber was the one who wrote, 'this (Puritan) asceticism turned with all its force against one thing: the spontaneous enjoyment of life and all it had to offer'.[39] Bauman acknowledges, of course, that the idea of the pilgrim is as old as Christianity itself (perhaps missing out, curiously, its even older roots in the Jewish faith) but he believes that it was modernity that gave this metaphor of life special prominence and a new twist.[40] As with the tourist, it is important to realize that people can be pilgrims without ever leaving home. In fact, he comments that, ironically, the Puritan pilgrim was probably always too busy to leave home and waste time at the seaside. Protestants invented the idea of 'inner-worldly pilgrims'.[41]

There are some striking contrasts between the tourist and the pilgrim.[42] Pilgrims set their hearts on reaching a destination. They are aware that much might conspire to distract them, lead them astray or prevent them reaching their goal. Determination and zeal are necessary to ensure that they avoid being lost. The focus on the future destination (Bauman believes) leads to a devaluing of the present.[43] Earthly life becomes but an overture of heaven. The further one is distant from one's goal the greater the dissatisfaction with one's life. The pilgrim connects time and space into a structured coherence. He or she moves through space making the most of the time to ensure the goal is reached. So, typically, the pilgrim does not spend resources on instant satisfaction (as the tourist would do) but saves for the future and commits him/herself to delayed gratification. The present world which they inhabit spatially only makes sense in the light of the future destination.

Pilgrims were identity-builders. They made their way through life leaving a coherent story behind them.

> The world of pilgrims – of identity-builders – must be orderly, determined, predictable, insured; but above all, it must be the kind of world in which footprints are engraved for good, so that the trace and the record of the past travels are kept and preserved.[44]

But, in Bauman's view, 'the world is not hospitable to pilgrims anymore'.[45] He assumes rather than justifies his verdict at this point, although a number of possible reasons for the change are intimated. He argues that pilgrims 'dug their own graves'. They did indeed, he says, plant footprints in the desert, transforming the barren places of the world into a place for pilgrims, but the trouble with the desert is that the winds blow and sand soon covers the tracks of those who have been there before. People rejected the fixedness required to be pilgrims in a search for greater freedom and the living of extemporary lives. Freedom of choice enticed people out of the fatalism of the fixed life of the pilgrim. Elsewhere, as we have seen, Bauman mentions the importance of the rise of individualism and the collapse of community. And he concurs with Antony Giddens[46] in seeing the collapse of time and space as a major contributor to the change.[47]

More likely, however, the displacement of the metaphor of pilgrimage is the result of the widespread loss of faith, for pilgrims need something bigger than themselves to sustain their pilgrimages. Without a transcendent dimension there is no point – one might as well become a tourist.

Whatever the reason, the destination seeking of the pilgrim has given way to the aimless meanderings of the tourist. The structured and fixed life of the pilgrim, as exhibited so perfectly by Thomas Wilson, has given way to the fluid avoidance of all fixedness on the part of tourists who 'are masters supreme of the art of melting the solids and unfixing the fixed'.[48] The moral responsibility of the pilgrim which transformed his/her world for the better has given way to the moral indifference of the tourist who just leaves his/her litter behind. The pilgrim who created has given way to the tourist who recycles. The community experience and spiritual bonding of the pilgrim has given way to the individualism and inability to engage with others of the tourist. The coherent life project of the pilgrim has given way to the incoherent, episodic and fragmentary way of living of the tourist.[49] The pilgrim's sense of vocation has given way to the tourist's quest for excitement.

Bauman seems convinced that pilgrims have had their day and cannot be resurrected. With the passing of modernity, it was inevitable that the pilgrim, the arch symbol of modernity, should pass as well.

Is this an Improvement?

It is hard to tell whether Bauman is approving of the changes and is actively advocating them or whether he is merely commentating on them. Some of our difficulty in interpreting him may stem from the passing of time, for he is certainly less enamoured of postmodernity now than ten years or so ago, as shown by the choice of his more recent book titles, such as *Postmodernity and its Discontents*.[50]

His writing is always passionate and warm, and he never gives the impression of being a disinterested observer. Indeed, throughout his life he has been anything but a disinterested observer. It seems truer to say, with Dennis Smith, that he is a 'prophet of postmodernity' in the sense of an astute observer who sees below the surface, unmasks the pretentious and diagnoses the sickness that lies at the heart of society. One cannot read him without believing there is a degree of censure or dis-ease about the way things are going, particularly in regard to the poor. How else can one read the final pages of his chapter on 'Broken Lives, Broken Strategies' in *Life in Fragments*?[51] He quotes Baudrillard as saying, 'This easy life knows no pity. Its logic is a pitiless one.'

Next he quotes with approval the words of Stjepan G. Mestrovic when he wrote,

> genuine morality, the habits of self-abnegation and love of neighbour, diminish in intensity ... Meanwhile, the poor have become poorer, and the rich have become richer, while the media refer to 'compassion fatigue' in

order to explain why hardly anyone really cares about starvation and other suffering in the world.

He then adds his own comments which also surely call into question the direction in which postmodern men and women seek to find their identity. 'Overdrawing the picture, but only slightly, one may say that in the popular perception the foremost, perhaps the sole duty of the postmodern citizen ... is to lead an enjoyable life.' And is there not a wistfulness in his statement that 'momentary explosions of solidary action which may result' (for example in protests regarding planning) 'do not alter the essential traits of postmodern relationships, their fragmentariness and discontinuity, narrowness of focus and purpose, surface-deep shallowness of contact'? Surely it is not possible to build a satisfying personal identity on such a flimsy foundation?

Perhaps it is not fair to ask Bauman to move beyond his uncertainty and provide us with surer moral guidance. As Beilharz comments in relation to his writing about globalization, 'Bauman's hope is not to solve all the problems, but to act as one messenger among others who bring mixed news.'[52]

Bauman: an Evaluation

Bauman's insightful analysis of the postmodern condition has much to offer, not least in understanding how we approach forming our personal identities and, therefore, our understanding of personhood today. The metaphors he proposes are evocative, full of rich insights and observations. We instantly recognize them and simultaneously are provoked by them. Like a good preacher using a telling illustration, he engages the reader. If he never writes dispassionately, we can never read him dispassionately.

But there are a number of criticisms which cause us not to accept his picture of postmodern identity without qualification. They arise from the methodological, logical, moral and religious questions he provokes.

Methodological Considerations

There is a tendency in Bauman's writing about postmodern identity to overstate the case. As one reviewer says, 'Adorno once remarked that truth resides in exaggeration. Bauman may concur. In any case, he too often overstates his boldest ideas.'[53] Insightful as the metaphor of the tourist is and recognizing that the mentality of the tourist does powerfully affect all of life – life in the office as well as life on the beach – is it true that its impact is as extensive as Bauman implies? There needs to be at least another category of people between the tourist and the vagabond, for the world is not yet divided between the rich who can afford to travel and the impecunious who are moved on by others.[54] There are gradations of wealth and poverty in between which Bauman ignores. Many would long to travel (and to that extent are affected by the tourist mentality) but can only afford to do so under limited conditions or by proxy through the television. The stroller and the player do not adequately cover the mundaneness of the lives of many. His picture needs to be more carefully nuanced.

Similarly, whilst work (and education) is changing and the tourist mentality is infiltrating territory where it would previously have been strictly forbidden, the idea that work has been widely transformed into an extension of tourist activity suffers from being an academic's limited perspective on life. Higher education in the UK, as we know to our own cost, is only now belatedly suffering from the imposition of the driving force of modernity upon it; a driving force which was felt much earlier and more fully in industry and commerce. Now everything has to be measured, calculated, objectified, checked and justified, in a way which was unthinkable even ten years ago. Productivity reigns and so must be calculated. The university is now less the domain of the tourist than it has ever been before. I doubt whether those working in the health service, schools, the police and other public sector occupations would agree that 'the world is a tourists' oyster'.

This does not so much undermine Bauman, since his perspective contains many recognizable elements of truth, as suggest that reality is more complex – ambivalent, perhaps – than he allows. The criticism perhaps exposes the weakness of his methodological approach. He rests content with the impressionistic picture, after the manner of the philosophic artists, rather than striving for the more carefully researched or detailed architect's drawing of contemporary culture, which, while more boring, represents social reality more faithfully.

Conceptual Ambiguities

One reviewer of his work on *Postmodernity and Its Discontents* suggests that the fundamental flaw of Bauman's work is that it is 'built upon a "modernist" notion of the social', as is evidenced by his understanding of morality[55] and his criticisms of Communitarianism. He is left, Best argues, with 'a notion of the social built upon universal foundations, which is always the very opposite of the postmodern'.[56] Much of what Bauman writes, Best concludes, could have been written about modernity and belongs to the mainstream, and has no particular postmodern referent to it.

It is very difficult for one schooled deeply in modernity to escape the modernity trap altogether and enter truly into the postmodern perspective. One may adjust one's lenses to bring the postmodern world into a better focus but perhaps ultimately one needs to discard the idea of wearing glasses altogether and somehow see in an entirely different way. Bauman clearly does share the fragmentariness, uncertainty and ambiguities of the postmodern, but perhaps has not entered into it sufficiently to interpret it adequately.

However, it might be said in defence of Bauman against Best that in adopting his conceptual framework Bauman is being a better interpreter of our times than Best believes. We do not live wholly in a postmodern world yet, even if we will do one day, which is to be doubted. The doubt arises from the fact that postmodernity defines itself as a reaction to modernity, rather than having positive cultural foundations of its own. It is better at asking questions than answering them and, after a time, as Beilharz explains, the shine goes off postmodernity because it is difficult to keep 'living without an alternative'.[57] Modernity is not yet completely 'post', consequently much of our interpretation must still lie within the 'mainstream'.

Moral Ambivalence

For all the insight in Bauman's work, he seems to stop short of satisfactorily answering the most crucial question about postmodernity and identity, namely, whether postmodernity is an adequate basis on which to build a satisfactory personal identity. Does the tourist, the consumer, the visitor to Disney have enough about him/her, enough depth, enough foundation, to answer the question he or she is asking: 'Who am I?' Bauman has some faith in our intuitive wisdom and therefore some hope that we will be able to shake off the superficial attractions of the tourist world and to learn to find more adequate building materials elsewhere with which to construct satisfying identities.[58] But it is not a confident hope.

His dismissal of the pilgrim is too hasty. Part of his difficulty lies in the understanding of the pilgrim. While he acknowledges that pilgrims have a long history in Christianity, it is the particular type of 'inward' pilgrim who was formed by the Puritan era and who enjoyed a particularly close relationship with modernity, which Bauman dismisses. The pilgrim, however, is older than this and even older than Christianity. The Israelites were a pilgrim people. From Abraham onwards they were on a journey in response to the call and command of God towards a destination.[59] After the Exodus they made a pilgrimage to the land of promise. Once settled in the land, they celebrated pilgrimages to the great festivals in Jerusalem in response to the Lord's command. Under the new covenant, as Kenneth Cragg's chapter argues, the living reality of Christ made geographical pilgrimage unnecessary. Jesus became the radical centre of faith, replacing the city and the temple.[60] Being 'in Christ', whatever one's geographical location, rendered a pilgrimage to Galilee or Jerusalem 'in no way imperative'. So physical pilgrimages soon ceased, at least for a time.[61] Pilgrimage, for Christians, essentially became inward, long before the advent of the Puritan pilgrim who travelled hand-in-hand with modernity. Hebrews sets out the pattern and encourages believers to imitate the faith of Abraham, who looked forward to an unseen 'city with foundations, whose architect and builder is God'.[62] They were advised not to long for a country on earth but to make progress towards 'a better country – a heavenly one'.[63]

The essential marks of the pilgrim, however differently they are worked out in different cultural contexts, are these: pilgrims are on a journey, in response to a transcendent authority as well as to fulfil an inner desire, towards a definite destination, transforming the world for the better as they go. Each of these aspects is found in Psalm 84. The notes of longing to appear before God and of the determination needed to get to the destination of being in his presence are particularly evident. But note too that, 'as they pass through the valley of Baca (the valley of barrenness), they make it a place of springs'.[64] When tourists go home they leave their litter behind for someone else to clear up. When pilgrims pass through, they transform the world for the better.

All this has implications for the industry which produces pilgrimages, in the more literal sense, today. Using Bauman's grid one cannot help but feel that many modern pilgrimages partake much more of the ethos of religious tourism than they do of the Biblical understanding of pilgrimage. The same search for experience, transience, spectatorship, non-engagement with the local culture and moral irresponsibility are often evidenced in the package tour that visits Jerusalem, Galilee, the Seven Churches of Asia or Patmos as in the package tour that visits Corfu, Bali or Florida. Modern pilgrimages may simply be a way of salving the consciences of religious people and allowing them to participate in tourism by another name.

Perhaps the world needs fewer tourists and more pilgrims after all. Bauman can never quite bring himself to say so, but everything he writes points in that direction. Possibly the reason why Bauman feels so ill-at-ease with the pilgrim lies in his failure to understand the crucial role of religion down through history, to which we now turn.

Religious Inadequacies

Perhaps it is a reflection of Bauman's upbringing and training under a communist regime, with its aggressive rejection of religion, but, according to James Beckford, his writings demonstrate a 'failure to appreciate the *continuous* importance of religion throughout history, including the modern period'.[65] Beckford's comments are justifiably provoked by Bauman's exposition of the role religion plays in postmodernity.[66] In postmodernity there is an opening for religion if it is of the attractive consumerist variety (which explains why fundamentalism becomes attractive in a context of moral ambiguity). Given this, it is not inconsistent that we are witnessing the revival of religious movements. But, for Bauman, religion belongs to the 'residual realm of little importance'.[67] His failure to treat religion, and its contribution to moral and ethical formation, adequately in previous cultures leads him to argue that its role today is recent and, even, aberrant. But many have had recourse to religion as an authoritative source of moral values. Beckford points out that Bauman's neglect of the place of religion enables him to overdraw the contrast between 'the universalising aspirations of everything modern and the neo-tribal thrust of everything postmodern'.[68] Of course religion has undergone change. But Bauman underestimates what it was, as well perhaps as its recreative, reinventive power, that is, what it can be.

Bauman speaks of the pilgrims of old leaving footprints in the desert sand, footprints which eventually were obliterated, removing the evidence of the pilgrim way of life. If modernity was a desert that needed shaping, postmodernity is just as much a desert. The question is not only whether the tourists of today will leave any footprints in the sand, but what kind of footprints they will be. Unless people can define their identity by reference to something beyond themselves the likelihood is that they will leave footprints which indicate they have meandered round and round in circles and left traces which will be obliterated even faster than those of the pilgrims who constructed a world which was better than the one they entered.

The fact that the world is inhospitable to pilgrims should not concern us. Being faithful to God's call should. His people are frequently called to be nonconformists. But it is the nonconformists who have so often shaped (and rescued) the world. Who knows but that we might do so again? And, in doing so, we may discover the wisdom of God who knows that it is only those who lose their lives who can find them,[69] only those who submit to his rule who find freedom and only those whose lives are shaped by an eternal destiny who can mostly truly be at home in this world. The question 'Who am I?' cannot be answered without reference to 'Who is my God?' The answer we give to the latter question determines whether or not we can ever adequately answer the former one, which is currently, as Bauman says, 'the talk of the town'. Postmoderns may like being tourists. But believers of any age will tenaciously hold to being pilgrims.

Notes

1 Wilson, *Memoirs*, 62.
2 Ibid., 159.
3 Ibid., 163.
4 Bauman, *Discontents*, 86.
5 Smith, *Zygmunt*, ch.1.
6 Bauman, *Discontents*, 89.
7 Smith, *Zygmunt*, 27.
8 The impact of one's biography on one's academic work is frequently acknowledged within sociology. Many have speculated, for example, on whether the concept of alienation is central to

Karl Marx because he grew up as a Jew whose family had converted, for the sake of commercial expediency, to Protestantism while living in a community dominated by Catholics.

9   A fuller account can be found in Smith, *Zygmunt*, 32–47.
10   Ibid., 43.
11   Beilharz, *Zygmunt*, 122.
12   Bauman, *Fragments*, 81.
13   This paraphrases a quotation of Jock Young cited with approval by Bauman, *Community*, 15.
14   Bauman, *Community*, 15.
15   Bauman, *Fragments*, 82.
16   Ibid.
17   Bauman, *Discontents*, 178. The place of religion more generally in postmodern society is discussed on 165–85. Bauman sees the need for the alchemist as consistent with the consumer-oriented nature of postmodernity in contrast to the producer-oriented nature of modernity.
18   Bauman, *Community*, 16.
19   Ibid., 52.
20   Bauman, *Discontents*, 27.
21   Ibid., 26
22   Beilharz, *Zygmunt*, 129.
23   In addition to those cited, see also Bauman, *Globalization*, 77–102.
24   The concept of the vagabond is expounded in Bauman, *Discontents*, 92–4, *Fragments*, 94–5 and *Ethics*, 240–42.
25   Bauman, *Discontents*, 92.
26   The concept is expounded in Bauman, *Fragments*, 92–3.
27   Bauman, *Fragments*, 93.
28   Ibid., 98–9.
29   Beilharz, *Zygmunt*, 123; Bauman, *Fragments*, 99.
30   The features summarized can be found in Bauman, *Discontents*, 89–93.
31   This is one of the reasons why he rejects the nomad as a more appropriate and less provocative metaphor. The nomad belongs in the wilderness even while camping in it. The nomad's life, unlike the tourist's, is formed by habitual patterns of behaviour and the nomad knows where he is going. See Beilharz, *Zygmunt*, 126, 129.
32   Bauman, *Ethics*, 241.
33   Ibid., 243.
34   Beilharz, *Zygmunt*, 123.
35   Ibid.
36   Bauman, *Ethics*, 241.
37   Ibid., 242.
38   Most notably, *The Protestant Ethic and the Spirit of Capitalism*. But see also his other works which address the theme of rationality, such as his study of bureaucracy, the world religions and *Economy and Society*.
39   Weber, *The Protestant Ethic*, 166.
40   Bauman, *Fragments*, 82.
41   Ibid., 84.
42   The following paragraph is largely based on Bauman, *Fragments*, 83–8.
43   It can be argued that a sense of destination has, in fact, the exact opposite effect, filling this life with significance.
44   Bauman, *Fragments*, 87.
45   Ibid., 88.
46   Giddens, *Modernity*, 14–23.
47   Bauman, *Discontents*, 80–86.
48   Ibid., 86.

49   A classic example of this was noted in a recent article in *The Sunday Times* (22 April 2001) which referred to the reinvention of the life of Jane Fonda as a religious convert. She was previously and sequentially the 1960s sexpot Barbarella, an anti-Vietnam war activist and then an aerobics guru in the 1980s, before becoming 'a millennial Baptist'.

50   For fuller details, see Beilharz, *Zygmunt*, 131, who argues that 'the shine has disappeared off the postmodern' which was once a confident enterprise of modernity. It now however seems somewhat 'tawdry' and difficult to cope with 'after a decade of living without an alternative'.

51   The quotations which follow are taken from *Fragments*, 102–3.

52   Beilharz, *Zygmunt*, 154.

53   Vetlesen, 'Review', 173.

54   Best, 'Review', 707, states that 'Bauman suggests that the postmodern world can be plotted on a continuum from tourists to vagabonds', but he offers no evidence for the continuum and I am not aware that Bauman makes such a view evident. The dominant picture is rather of two distinct (albeit obviously extreme) types of postmodern person.

55   Defined by him as doing something for another person and not taking into account one's self-interests.

56   Best, 'Review', 709.

57   Beilharz, *Zygmunt*, 131.

58   Ibid., 126.

59   In Abraham's case the destination was not revealed to him beforehand but was known by God (Gen.12:1).

60   Acts 7:48–53.

61   Granted that Paul goes on pilgrimage to Jerusalem (Acts 21:17ff), but after the city was destroyed no such pilgrimages were possible for a time.

62   Hebrews 11:10.

63   Hebrews 11:16.

64   Ps.84:6. The valley of Baca is the valley where balsa wood grew and was considered therefore to be barren and dry.

65   Beckford, 'Postmodernity', 33.

66   Bauman, *Discontents*, 165–85.

67   Beckford, 'Postmodernity', 2.

68   Ibid., 33.

69   Matthew 10:39, 16:25; Luke 9:23–5.

References

Bauman, Z., *Postmodern Ethics* (Oxford: Blackwell, 1993).

——, *Life in Fragments* (Oxford: Blackwell, 1995).

——, *Postmodernity and its Discontents* (Cambridge: Polity Press, 1997).

——, *Globalization: the human consequences* (Cambridge: Polity Press, 1998).

——, *Community* (Cambridge: Polity Press, 2001).

Beckford, J., 'Postmodernity, High Modernity and New Modernity: Three Concepts in Search of Religion', in K. Flanagan and P.C. Jupp (eds), *Postmodernity, Sociology and Religion* (London: Macmillan, 1996).

Beilharz, P., *Zygmunt Bauman: Dialectic of Modernity* (London, Thousand Oaks and New Delhi: Sage Publications, 2000).

Best, S., 'Review of "Postmodernity and its Discontents" ', *The Sociological Review* 45 (4) (1997), 706–9.

Giddens, A., *Modernity and Self-Identity: Self and Society in Late Modern Age* (Cambridge: Polity Press, 1991).

Smith, D., *Zygmunt Bauman: Prophet of Postmodernity* (Cambridge: Polity Press, 1999).

Vetlesen, A.J., 'Review of "Postmodern Ethics"', *The Sociological Review*, 43 (1) (1995), 170–73.

Weber, M.,*The Protestant Ethic and the Spirit of Capitalism* (London and New York: Routledge, 1930/1992).

Wilson, J., *Memoirs of the Life and Character of Thomas Wilson* (London: John Snow, 1849).

CHAPTER 12

Journeying on: a Concluding Reflection

Craig Bartholomew

Introduction

The relevance and fecundity of theological exploration of pilgrimage are clear from the essays in this volume. Our aim throughout has been to open up the key issues in a modern theology of pilgrimage without trying to force a premature consensus among the contributors. In this final chapter, my concern is to mull over what I see as the issues at the heart of this endeavour, not least as a means of highlighting areas where work still needs to be done.

The Importance of 'Pilgrimage' for the Church Today

Church leaders are much exercised about the future of Christianity in western culture. Missiologists like Lesslie Newbigin have argued that western culture is *the* mission field today and stress the need to contextualize the Gospel in the secular west. Newbigin tells the story of a conversation with an Indonesian general at the WCC Bangkok Conference 'Salvation Today' in 1973, in which the general said to him, 'Of course the number one question is: Can the West be converted?'[1] According to Newbigin, while mission 'has sought to explore the problems of contextualization in all the cultures of humankind from China to Peru, it has largely ignored the culture that is the most widespread, powerful, and persuasive among all contemporary cultures – namely, what I have called modern Western culture'.[2]

Contextualization evokes the dual stories that the Church inevitably indwells, namely the Scriptural or Christian story and the cultural story.[3] The Church lives at the crossroads of these two stories, and effective mission emerges from the tension between them as the Church seeks to avoid the pitfalls of both irrelevance on the one hand and syncretism on the other. As Kraemer comments, 'The deeper the consciousness of the tension and the urge to take this yoke upon itself are felt, the healthier the Church is. The more oblivious of this tension the Church is, the more well established and at home in the world it feels, the more it is in deadly danger of being the salt that lost its savour.'[4]

Such a perspective illumines the importance of the discussion in this book. Mainline church attendance is in serious decline in the secular UK and Europe, but Christian pilgrimage and religious tourism are booming.[5] In our postmodern context the experiential, visual, communal nature of pilgrimage is attracting Christians and others in a way that the mainline churches are not. 'Pilgrimage sites offer stories of saints and of God interacting with ordinary people; they provide an intensely visual environment; they draw the pilgrim into an atmosphere of corporate spirituality which yet allows infinite scope for individual response.'[6] It is to phenomena like pilgrimage that Christians will have to attend as they seek afresh to make the Gospel incarnate in western culture again. To ignore the phenomenon is to risk irrelevance. To embrace pilgrimage and religious tourism uncritically is to risk syncretism of the worst sort. Contextualization requires careful *theological* reflection on the phenomenon of pilgrimage and its resurgence with a view to creative ways in which Christians can and should appropriate its practice. That kind of reflection is what this book is about.

Reading Scripture *for* Pilgrimage

Theological reflection requires detailed engagement with the Bible as the Church's authoritative text. There is clearly no shortage of engagement with the Bible in this volume. However, our explorations of a Christian theology of pilgrimage soon bring up the issue of *how* we are to read Scripture for pilgrimage today. In the Old Testament God is particularly present in Jerusalem, and pilgrimage there is mandatory. The New Testament contains a lot about pilgrimage.[7] Consider:

- Jesus and his disciples are pictured as pilgrims to Jerusalem;
- the Gospels are structured around the pilgrim festivals, especially the Passover;
- the Ethiopian eunuch went on pilgrimage to Jerusalem (Acts 8:26–40);
- the converts at Pentecost were pilgrims;
- St Paul hurried up to Jerusalem to be there for the feast of Pentecost (Acts 20:16);
- presumably many of the trips to Jerusalem reported in the Acts and epistles were in connection with the festivals.

However, on most accounts (Cragg, Walker, Lincoln and Motyer agree on this) the particularity of Jerusalem is radically altered by its fulfilment in Jesus. How does one read the relationship between Old and New Testaments in this respect and what are its theological implications? Are the pilgrimages of the disciples hangovers from pre-resurrection practices or are they models for post-resurrection Christians? The different ways of relating the biblical data theologically are apparent in the contributions to this volume from the New Testament scholars, namely Walker, Lincoln and Motyer.

How does one construe Scripture as a unity such that one can make the theological connections with pilgrimage? What *discrimen* will facilitate this move and where does it come from?[8] These are the sort of questions requiring exploration if we are to relate Scripture authoritatively and creatively to pilgrimage today. We cannot explore these in detail here, but suffice it to note that it is important in this respect to take seriously the multifaceted way in which Scripture may function authoritatively.[9]

On the one hand it is clear to me that in the Bible as a whole Christians can no longer regard Jerusalem as God's 'address' now that Christ is risen from the dead. God in Christ is now universally available in and through the risen Christ. In *this* sense the New Testament 'neutralizes', to use Cragg's word, the Old Testament.[10] O'Donovan relates this aspect of the New Testament fulfilment of the Old Testament to 'an apophatic tradition in Christian thought with regard to all the concrete structures of Old Testament society',[11] and he finds support for this approach in the Epistle to the Hebrews in which the patriarchal hopes for an inheritance are transcended by their eschatological fulfilment. O'Donovan is quite clear about the difference between the Old Testament and the New Testament as regards holy place. He argues that in the New Testament we have a 'theological desacralisation' of special places: 'The revelation to Israel had been a situated revelation, in a land which Yahweh had hallowed, and in a city where he had chosen to dwell. But the revelation in Christ broke down the elective particularity, not only of race but also of place.'[12] He rightly asserts: 'I take it that this represents one fixed point around which our thought about the concept of land must move. I do not see how Christian thought could pretend to dispense with the apophatic approach (our hope is *not* earthly, *not* temporal) even if we felt at liberty to do so.'[13]

But does such fulfilment mean that the Old Testament now has nothing to teach us about land, politics, ritual and so on? Surely not. However, theologians often fail to go on from this apophatic aspect of the Old Testament–New Testament relationship to explore ways in which the Old Testament continues to instruct the church. O'Donovan argues that an apophatic approach to the Old Testament is complemented by a cataphatic or positive one which continues to find instruction in the concrete structures of Israel:

This line of argument in relation to Old Testament institutions is by no means unfamiliar: the Catholic tradition has followed it with regard to the priesthood, the Protestant tradition with regard to the Sabbath. And without affirming or denying what has been made of these examples, I take it that the general line of thought has some validity. We can at least try to

> learn about place from the Old Testament theology of the land without
> flying in the face of all that the New Testament has done with it.[14]

It is such a cataphatic approach that is vital, in my opinion, if we are to
construe Scripture rightly in relation to pilgrimage.

In the Old Testament we witness God's involvement with a nation, and thus
the way in which the life of that nation as a whole is structured may have much
to say to us on a variety of issues that the New Testament does not directly
address. Think, for example, of Israel as a polity. For the Church, the concept
of the people of God as a nation, let alone an ANE one, has been superseded
by an understanding of the people of God scattered throughout the nations of
the world. Nevertheless, O'Donovan rightly asserts in his *The Desire of the
Nations* that *Israel herself* is the hermeneutic principle that shapes a Christian
political reading of Scripture: 'the governing principle is the kingly rule of God,
expressed in Israel's corporate existence and brought to final effect in the life,
death and resurrection of Jesus.'[15] The New Testament has much to say about
politics, but the Old Testament witness is fundamental in this respect in its
depiction of God's involvement in the life of a nation, Israel. When it comes to
a theology of place, O'Donovan naturally turns again to the Old Testament,
where particular place receives more attention than in the New Testament.

A further example of the importance of reading the Old Testament
apophatically *and* cataphatically is the controversial issue of ritual. Protestants
have been cautious of ritual because of the apophatic tradition in this respect in
the New Testament, and once again not least in the Epistle to the Hebrews.
This is then often taken as the last word on ritual of any sort. No doubt
Catholics and Protestants will disagree on the extent to which the apophatic
line in the New Testament does close down church ritual, but either way what
is often lost sight of is the rich Old Testament insight into the role of ritual in
human society generally. Humans embody their most important values in
solemn rituals, such as the opening of parliament or the marriage ceremony,
and Israel is no exception to this. The anointing of a new king, the offering of a
sacrifice, the keeping of Sabbath, the conduct of a court case – there is a ritual
for all these and many other aspects of the life of Israel in the Old Testament.
Apart from the question of how these rituals are superseded in the New
Testament, and all Christians would agree that many are in one way or
another, at a positive level the Old Testament alerts us to the place of ritual in
human society and God's concern with the values and perspectives embodied
in such ritual. Thus it has often seemed to me that Christians would do well to
develop rituals and public art that embody appropriate values and perspectives
for our societies.

In Israel pilgrimage is akin to ritual. Pilgrimage to Israel was ritualized in
that it was mandatory (see Psalms 122:4; it is *decreed* that the tribes go up to
Jerusalem regularly) and formalized; the place of pilgrimage is fixed, as are the

times of pilgrimage and the activities involved. How does this ritualized pilgrimage embody the values and beliefs central to Israel? There are many ways of approaching pilgrimage in the Old Testament, but a fruitful way is to examine the Psalms of ascent in Psalms 120–34. This group of psalms share the title, 'A Song of Ascents'. They were probably designed to be sung on the way to Jerusalem as a sort of 'pilgrim hymnal'.[16] The songs, like the journeys, are designed to centre the life of God's people in the great realities on which its life is built. Commenting on the instruction in Psalm 122 for the pilgrim to pray for the peace of Jerusalem, McCann perceptively notes that such prayers

> amount to the recognition of God's reign and his or her commitment to live under God's reign. As in Psalm 48, this commitment is not facile optimism nor mere wishful thinking. This commitment is eschatological. For the psalmist, to enter Jerusalem *really does* mean to enter a new world. The joy is real … To live for God's sake … and for the sake of others … is to experience, embody, and extend the justice God intends for the world. This life-style, this commitment *is* reality.[17]

It was a constant challenge for Israel to live as the people of God it had become. The danger, to which Israel regularly succumbed, was to think of itself as 'like the other nations'. Pilgrimage was a major means by which Israelites would take time out from their daily activities to recentre their lives in the reality of their being a royal priesthood with the LORD living in their midst (cf. Exod.19:3–6). In this way pilgrimage functioned as ritualized practice designed to embed in the consciousness of the Israelites their identity as *God's* people.

How can this help us today, particularly in the light of the 'neutralization' of Jerusalem as God's 'address'? Nolan and Nolan point out that 'the urge to identify certain places and things as especially significant, indeed sacred, seems a deeply rooted human need, as is the desire to go as pilgrims to such places'.[18] My way of expressing this would be to say that God has made humans such that they need rituals in which they embody their highest values. These rituals function as a means of keeping their lives centred on these values and narratives. In a fallen world such rituals become more, not less, important. Pilgrimage is one such practice. As Eugene Peterson notes, 'We necessarily live much of our lives in exile, so to be able to spot the people and places that re-establish our true identity is *so* important.'[19] Thus, while in the light of the New Testament pilgrimage to Jerusalem or to anywhere else cannot and should not be regarded in any way as mandatory, this does not pre-empt the need for and role of Christian pilgrimage. The need for ritual and pilgrimage will remain, and I see no reason why Christians should not take seriously the task of developing pilgrimages as one means of recentring our lives around the Christian narrative.

Thus Peterson seems to me quite right to distinguish, in his elaboration of a Christian spirituality, between the basic, non-negotiable practice of daily praying with the Psalms, Lord's day worship with one's community and recollected prayer through the day, and the various spiritual disciplines that are not compulsory but on hand when we need them.[20] He asserts, 'There are popular presentations of the spiritual life that set prayer and worship in a series with the "disciplines". This is wrong. It suggests, if not actually invites, a consumer approach to the spiritual life, as if we have all these options placed out on the table from which we can pick and choose according to appetite and whim. The basic Rule of Common Worship/Psalms–Prayer/Recollected Prayer is where we start from and return to – always.'[21] Peterson describes the disciplines, of which he lists 14, as a tool shed, well stocked for use when required but otherwise left alone. The tools include spiritual direction, journaling, retreats, confession and pilgrimage. This, I suggest, is precisely the right place to position pilgrimage theologically: a useful discipline, but not compulsory.

The Development of Christian Doctrine and Pilgrimage

A striking feature of the discussion in this book is the *historical* aspect of Christian involvement in pilgrimage. There is much pilgrimage in the New Testament but it is unclear whether it was a hangover from the past or a legitimate expression of Christian life. It is possible that Christian pilgrimage goes back very far. Many historians think that Hadrian built pagan temples over the Temple Mount and Holy Sepulchre, because they were places of pilgrimage for Jews in the first place and Christians in the second.

However, as Peter Walker shows in Chapter 5, Christian pilgrimage really got going when Constantine became emperor. In the course of this historical development, a theology or theologies of pilgrimage emerged.[22] This means that any assessment of a Christian theology of pilgrimage will have to wrestle seriously with the way in which Christian doctrine develops. This is the topic that Newman famously discusses in his *An Essay on the Development of Christian Doctrine*. Under the theme of the sacramental principle, Newman defends the 4th-century appropriation by the Church of many outward rites that were taken over from their culture and became a means of grace.[23] In this context Newman asserts, 'In like manner the Sign of the Cross was one of the earliest means of grace; then holy seasons, *and holy places, and pilgrimages to them*; holy water; prescribed prayers, or other observances; garments, as the scapular, or coronation robes; the rosary; the crucifix.'[24] Pilgrimage to holy places has often been connected with the relics of saints and, intriguingly, Newman relates this development theologically to the materiality of Christianity; it is anti-gnostic and takes the body seriously.

It is fascinating to note that, when Tom Wright describes how he has changed his mind about pilgrimage, he says:

> A lot has to do with the slow turning away from various forms of dualism, to which evangelicalism is particularly prone, and towards a recognition of the *sacramental* quality of God's whole created world. ... With the incarnation itself being the obvious and supreme example, and the gospel sacraments of baptism and eucharist not far behind, one can learn to discover the presence of God not only in the world ... but through the world.[25]

Wright goes on to note that the cult of relics can itself be explained in relation to the grace of God at work in the embodied person. Wright is not persuaded by this argument, but it is very interesting to see how he connects pilgrimage to the same doctrines as Newman: creation, incarnation and sacrament.

Many Protestants would, of course, find Newman's apologia for High-Church practices altogether unconvincing. Indeed, within Roman Catholic and High-Church circles there is much difference of opinion about Newman's approach to doctrinal development.[26] The fact is, though, that doctrines do arise and develop historically,[27] and Christian pilgrimage presents us with a classic case of early Church development of a practice and a theology of pilgrimage. It is too easy simply to dismiss this as the spin-off of a perverse Christendom. Christendom was a major attempt to take the Christian mission seriously,[28] and as we noted at the beginning of this chapter, pilgrimage ought to be taken seriously by the Church today if it is a missional church.

Modern pilgrimage thus presents the Church with a challenge as to how to relate Christian doctrine to life today. Doubtless Catholics and Protestants will do this differently, but any fresh engagement with the issue of pilgrimage will have to think through the doctrines of creation, incarnation and sacrament. Indeed a major issue underlying all pilgrimage is the *theology of place*. Here again the need for theological reflection is apparent. In the Old Testament, Jerusalem is 'the place of the name'; in the New Testament this particularity is neutralized. However, a theology of place cannot simply be read off the Biblical narrative: as O'Donovan's discussion of apophatic and cataphatic ways of reading the Old Testament indicate, theological construction is a complex business.

Among some Evangelical scholars there is a renewed interest in the theology of place. In *The Wisdom of Each Other*, written as letters to a friend and recent convert, the leading Evangelical authority on spirituality, Eugene Peterson, writes,

> Your delight in coming across that monastery isolated out there on those austere plains, 'miles from nowhere', and finding a community of praying brothers there is contagious. I am more and more convinced that holiness

does indeed infiltrate *place*. In such places, I have always a sense of homecoming – *heaven*-coming.[29]

Tom Wright affirms Peterson's theology of place in his experience of visiting a school building in Canada that had been a church:

> I walked in and sensed the presence of God, gentle but very strong. I sat through the loud concert wondering if I was the only person who felt it, and reflecting on the fact that I had no theology by which to explain why a redundant United church should feel that way. The only answer I have to this day is that when God is known, sought and wrestled within a place, a memory of that remains, which those who know and love God can pick up.[30]

Wright, as we noted in the Introduction to this volume, specifically connects this experience of place with pilgrimage to the Holy Land.

What are we to make of Peterson's and Wright's experientially shaped reconsideration of place? Does not the New Testament rule this out of court? Possibly, but even the Biblical narrative is more complex than sometimes meets the eye as regards place. Thus the temple is above all else where Yahweh dwells and is thus quintessentially a holy place. But, even within the temple there are degrees of holiness. And even while the temple occupies a special status within Israel, the Old Testament depicts the land of Israel as a whole as holy. And at other places in the Old Testament the whole of the earth is 'mine', according to Yahweh, thus making it holy too. These clues may indicate that we need not assume that to call one place holy is to imply that other places are irrelevant and 'secular'.

A more nuanced understanding of place is required. Place is not just a geographical concept, but also a historical and thus storied one. Place, with its timed and storied aspects, is a central element in human life and identity.[31] To understand place is to 'grasp the reciprocal relation between nature and culture: geographical space mediating a possibility for human life in community; human inhabitation elevating a dead space into the character and distinctiveness of place'.[32] And of course there are different types of places as there are different types of stories. Brueggemann uses the phrase 'storied-place'[33] and perhaps this can help us distinguish different types of places in terms of the different stories associated with them.

For God's people in the Old Testament the story of Jerusalem was unique: God lived there and this made Jerusalem special or holy in a distinct way. For Christians Palestine is also special but for different reasons: it was there that God established his Old Testament people from whom came Jesus, who lived, died and rose again in Palestine. As an inscription found in Amaseia in Pontus in western Asia Minor delightfully puts it, Palestine is a 'God-trodden' land.[34] The difference between these approaches is important and will shape pilgrimage to Jerusalem in a significantly different way.[35] The effect of this is that, while Christians ought no longer to regard Jerusalem as 'the place of the name', this does not dispense with the need or responsibility to take place seriously as part of God's good creation. Healthy pilgrimage, not least to Palestine and Jerusalem, is one way to do so.

As a way of affirming place, pilgrimage may be particularly important at this time in western culture. Place, as discussed above, is not a static concept but is deeply shaped by culture. And it can be argued that, in our late-modern culture, we have lost that very human sense of place amidst the time–space compression[36] characteristic of 'postmodernity'. O'Donovan relates this loss to the demographic mobility in modernity and to the communications highway which threatens to make the city itself redundant.[37] Place has become something that one moves through, and virtual reality is no replacement.[38] As David Lyon perceptively notes of cyberspace, 'There is no place to this space.'[39] In South Africa I heard recently of young adults employed for the first time who are flown from Durban to Johannesburg each Monday by their employers, set up for the week in a hotel room which also functions as their office from which they work, before returning home to Durban each Friday. The *place* of work is here radically altered and disconnected from any social, geographically proximate community. This loss of place in our (post)modern context may be a reason why so many within and outside the Church find pilgrimage so attractive. It should, at least, encourage Christians to reaffirm place, and healthy pilgrimage is a means to that end.

Pilgrimage and Politics

A pilgrimage can be thought of as a micro-journey by means of which one explores the macro-journey of one's life. Thus Christian pilgrimage to Israel would be aimed at helping one to live out the Gospel more comprehensively when one returns to one's daily life. It is vital that this connection with the whole of life is present in pilgrimage: the *journey in*, as it were, becomes the foundation for the *journey out*. And this should be true not just at a personal level but at a communal and societal one too.

It is a scandal, and pilgrimage of a very distorted sort, when so many Christians visit Jerusalem without a second thought about the Church in Israel and the suffering in the Middle East. In his fascinating *From the Holy Mountain*, William Dalrymple exemplifies a healthier type of pilgrimage in the Holy Land. In the context of his arrival in Jerusalem he is attentive to the change in the fortunes of Christians in the old city. In 1992, 52 per cent were Christian; now Christians make up fewer than 2.5 per cent of the population. In the context of his pilgrimage in Jerusalem, Dalrymple connects the ancient Christian sites to present-day oppression of Christians in Israel by the Israeli government. 'All this is part of the most dramatic decline in a Christian population to have taken place anywhere in the modern Middle East, with the single exception of Turkish Anatolia.'[40] And Dalrymple insightfully asserts that this makes a significant difference to the pilgrimage sites in the Holy Land: 'All this matters very much. Without the local Christian population, the most important shrines in the Christian world will be left as museum pieces, preserved only for the curiosity of tourists. Christianity will no longer exist in the Holy Land as a living faith; a vast vacuum will exist in the very heart of Christendom.'[41]

If Christians are genuinely concerned to follow the Jesus who was born and died in Israel, then, like him, they will need to take the whole of life, including politics, seriously. The Old Testament prophets were deeply concerned for justice in Israel and, while human bombs are immoral and unacceptable, so too is Israeli oppression of the Palestinians. Part of all Christian pilgrimage to Israel ought as a matter of principle to connect with these issues.

On the Journey

According to Lesslie Newbigin,

> The Bible begins the story of salvation by telling how God called Abraham to leave his home and his people, and apparently also his ancestral gods, and to become a pilgrim, and how he promised that through Abraham and his descendants blessing would come to all the nations. ... The true sons of Abraham ... know themselves to be a pilgrim people who have here no permanent quarters. ... The Church ... has understood itself more as an institution than as an exhibition. Its typical shape ... has been not a band of pilgrims who have heard the word 'Go', but a large and solid building which, at its best, can only say 'Come'.[42]

It is a moot point whether or not 'we have here no permanent quarters'. If one regards the new heavens and the new earth as the destiny of this creation, then there is a sense in which our quarters are permanent, albeit subject to healing and serious transformation. Indeed Abraham's call is about becoming the means for blessing to all nations such that God's destiny for his creation will be achieved. So, in this sense, I am not sure that pilgrim as a metaphor for the Church is helpful.[43]

However, as a metaphor reminding the Church of its dynamic journey in which it has to learn ever anew how to live the story of Jesus in different times and places in its between-the-times context, pilgrimage is powerful and evocative. As was suggested at the start of this chapter, such a missional ecclesiology provides an imperative for a theology of pilgrimage today. In my opinion Christian involvement in pilgrimage is legitimate and important in our postmodern context. The real challenge, however, is *how* to shape the practice of pilgrimage so that Christians' identity as God's people is deepened in their day-to-day lives, and so that those unfamiliar with the narratives associated with sites of pilgrimage will have ample opportunity to connect with them. At our conference on pilgrimage referred to in the Introduction, there were two fine discussions of such creative shaping of pilgrimage.

Robert Trimble, then of McCabe Pilgrimages, addressed the important topic of tourism and pilgrimage. This is an important interface that needs to be worked at in the context of a theology of pilgrimage. Trimble made the point that pilgrimage has always had its facilitators, its tour operators, as it were. Many, of course, were unscrupulous.[44] But the point is well taken: someone has to plan for the journey and make it happen. The important thing is that the plans facilitate *healthy* pilgrimage rather than just tourism of a consumerist sort. The Muslim thinker Ziauddin Sardar describes tourism as 'consumerism writ large, naked and unashamed, and to feed the insatiable need of tourists whole nations are converting themselves into vast emporia, havens of everything under the sun that can be bought'.[45] It is too easy for Christian pilgrimage to become an extension of western consumerism so that we bring back souvenirs rather than blessings.

An excellent example of the way pilgrimage can be shaped along healthy lines was the plans McCabe Pilgrimages made in the year 2000 for links between churches in the UK and church projects in Israel. This ensured that Christian pilgrims from the UK made contact with the living stones[46] in the Holy Land. As Trimble noted, 'The connections between a church in Durham and an orphanage in Bethany help to ground the experience of pilgrimage.'[47]

The second example was that of Tewkesbury Abbey. The Revd Canon Michael Tavinor, formerly vicar of the Abbey, spoke about the importance of making such churches places of pilgrimage rather than just tourist attractions. A visit to Tewkesbury Abbey highlights the serious attempts made there to connect visitors with the Christian faith. Inter alia, in a small room near the entrance a short video runs continually, welcoming visitors and introducing them to the Abbey – in the process, clear connections are made with the living faith the Abbey stands for.[48] In our secular societies thousands continue to visit cathedrals and abbeys; it is a creative challenge to find ways of making such visits a means to connect with the Christian story as embodied in such places.[49] At the very least it means that these places need to continue to be steeped in prayer and worship, otherwise, as Dalrymple pointed out, they will simply become museum pieces to be seen by curious tourists.

Conclusion

As someone in the Protestant, Anglican tradition, I have been surprised and fascinated by the issues that arise from theological reflection upon pilgrimage then and now. There are huge Biblical, historical, theological, anthropological and sociological dimensions to this discussion. This collection of essays draws attention to the vital importance for Christians today of theological reflection upon Christian pilgrimage. The essays make that case decisively, in my opinion, wherever one arrives in one's view of pilgrimage. It is clear too that none of these essays exhausts the discussion. Taking the Biblical area, for example, there is a mass of Old Testament and New Testament data to attend to and complex hermeneutical issues about how to read Scripture authoritatively. And so too with the historical debate: it whets my appetite to discover the debate Christians have engaged in about pilgrimage through the ages. Gregory of Nyssa discusses pilgrimage with real sophistication at several places in his writings. After the Reformation his views were heatedly discussed once again, largely because of the translation of a letter of Gregory's by the Calvinist scholar Pierre du Moulin (1551). In response a Swiss Jesuit, Jacob Gretser, wrote a lengthy tome defending pilgrimage (1606). Later, in 1620, the Calvinist theologian Johan Heidegger joined the debate with an equally erudite tome against pilgrimage.[50] In all the areas we raise in this volume, more work remains to be done. Our hope is that these essays will contribute to and stimulate that further discussion.

Notes

1   Newbigin, *A Word*, 66.
2   Newbigin, *Foolishness*, 2–3.
3   See Goheen, 'Scholarship'.
4   Kraemer, *The Communication*, 36.
5   For UK church attendance see Brierley, *The Tide*.
6   Dyas, 'Pilgrimage', 94.
7   I am grateful to Gordon Wenham for alerting me to the abundance of these data.
8   *Discrimen* is the word Kelsey, *Uses*, 158ff, uses, from Jenson, for the imaginative construal the reader brings to the Bible so that it functions theologically as Scripture. See Vanhoozer's useful discussion of Kelsey in his *First Theology*, 28ff.
9   Cf. here Vanhoozer's critique and development of Kelsey, *First Theology*. Vanhoozer stresses that many things can be done with language. My approach here stresses the multifaceted authority of Scripture along different lines.
10   Peter Scott takes a different view on this issue. See Chapter 9 of the present volume.
11   'Loss', 49.
12   Ibid., 44.
13   Ibid., 49.
14   Ibid., 50.
15   *The Desire*, 27.
16   McCann, *Theological Introduction*, 152.
17   Ibid., 154.
18   Nolan and Nolan, *Christian Pilgrimage*, 338
19   *The Wisdom*, 85.
20   Peterson, *Under the Unpredictable Plant*, 104–9.

21 Ibid., 107.
22 A useful text on the development of Palestine into the 'Holy Land' is Wilken, *The Land*.
23 *An Essay*, 365ff.
24 Ibid., 374 (italics mine).
25 Wright, *The Way*, 4 (italics mine).
26 On Newman and development see Lash, *Newman*.
27 For an Anglican perspective on doctrinal development see McGrath, *The Genesis*.
28 See O'Donovan, *The Desire*.
29 *The Wisdom*, 85.
30 Wright, *The Way*, 5.
31 See Norris, *Dakota*, for a fine expression of this reality.
32 O'Donovan, 'Loss', 47.
33 Brueggemann, *The Land*.
34 See Wilken, *The Land*, 192.
35 See, for example, Wright's (*The Way*, 9–11) explanation of how he sees Christian pilgrimage to Israel.
36 See Harvey, *The Condition*, and Lyon, *Jesus*, on this theme.
37 See O'Donovan, 'Loss', for the three elements O'Donovan singles out as feeding into the universalist emphasis in western (including Christian) thought whereby place is undermined: the Platonic tradition of the spirit as transcending spatial definition, the concern of Christian theology to desacralize holy places in the light of Christ's resurrection, and the legacy of 19th-century economic doctrine whereby land is regarded as a resource for industrial production.
38 I am indebted to my friend Bob Walker for alerting me to the relevance of theology of place to the current discussion of 'new urbanism' in North America, as North Americans have become aware of the problems with urban sprawl. See Katz, *The New Urbanism*, Kunstler, *The Geography of Nowhere* and *Home From Nowhere*, and Duany *et al.*, *Suburban Nation*.
39 *Jesus*, 124.
40 Dalrymple, *From the Holy Mountain*, 316.
41 Ibid., 317.
42 Newbigin, *Honest Religion*, 100–101.
43 Here, no doubt, I betray my Reformed leanings. A research student, Robby Holt, helpfully pointed out to me that, while Reformed thinkers stress creation and stewardship, the Anabaptist tradition makes much of pilgrimage as a metaphor for the Christian life. Hays, *The Moral Vision*, 258, notes that 'The metaphor of pilgrimage emerges again and again in Hauerwas's work as the most apt description of the church's experience.' On the relationship between the Reformed and the Anabaptist traditions in Newbigin's ecclesiology, see Goheen, *As the Father*, 403–10.
44 See Sumption, *Pilgrimage*, for the realities of medieval pilgrimage.
45 *Postmodernism*, 249. It is important to note that not all tourism is consumerist. For a fascinating discussion of tourism from a Christian perspective, see Aay, 'Tourism'. An important topic not explored here is the nature of healthy tourism and its relationship to pilgrimage.
46 'Living stones' is a metaphor for the Christians in the Holy Land. See, for example, Hilliard and Bailey, *Living Stones*.
47 From Trimble's notes.
48 See also Tavinor's pilgrim guide, *Tewkesbury*.
49 This discussion raises the question of church architecture and the handling of space in not just well-known historical churches but the local church too. For a fascinating discussion of space in a church and such intriguing topics as place and the stations of the Cross, see Visser, *The Geometry*.
50 On this discussion see Wilken, *The Land*, 118.

214 *Theological Perspectives on Pilgrimage*

Bibliography

Aay, H., 'Tourism With the Eye of the Heart: Arie Van Deursen's Guiding Vision for the Dutch
   Christian Travel Association', in J.H. Kok (ed.), *Marginal Resistance: Essays Dedicated to John
   C. Vander Stelt* (Sioux Center, Iowa: Dordt College Press, 2001), pp.25–50.
Brierley, P., *The Tide is Running Out* (London: Christian Research, 2000).
Brueggemann, W., *The Land* (Philadelphia: Fortress, 1977).
Dalrymple, W., *From the Holy Mountain: A Journey in the Shadow of Byzantium* (London:
   Flamingo, 1998).
Duany, A., E. Plater-Zyberk and J. Speck, *Suburban Nation: The Rise of Sprawl and the Decline of
   Nation* (New York: North Point Press, 2000).
Dyas, D., 'Pilgrimage, Medieval to (Post) Modern: the Journeying Goes On', *Australian Folklore*,
   August 2000, 88–99.
Goheen, M., *'As the Father Has Sent Me, I am Sending You': J.E. Lesslie Newbigin's Missionary
   Ecclesiology* (Utrecht: Boekencentrum, 2000).
——, 'Scholarship at the Crossroads: Exploring Lesslie Newbigin's Missionary Model of
   Contextualization', *EJT*, 10 (2) (2000), 131–42.
Harvey, D., *The Condition of Postmodernity* (Oxford: Basil Blackwell, 1989).
Hays, R., *The Moral Vision of the New Testament* (San Francisco: HarperSanFrancisco, 1996).
Hilliard, A. and B.J. Bailey, *Living Stones: Pilgrimage With the Christians of the Holy Land*
   (London: Cassell, 1999).
Katz, P., *The New Urbanism: Towards an Architecture of Community* (New York: McGraw-Hill,
   1994).
Kelsey, D.H., *The Uses of Scripture in Recent Theology* (London: SCM, 1975).
Kraemer, H., *The Communication of the Christian Faith* (Philadelphia: Westminster Press, 1956).
Kunstler, J.H., *The Geography of Nowhere: The Rise and Decline of America's Man-Made
   Landscape* (New York: Touchstone, 1993).
——, *Home From Nowhere: Remaking Our Everyday World for the 21st Century* (New York:
   Touchstone, 1996).
Lash, N., *Newman on Development: The Search for an Explanation in History* (London: Sheed and
   Ward, 1975).
Lyon, D., *Jesus in Disneyland: Religion in Postmodern Times* (Cambridge: Polity, 2000).
McCann, J.C., *A Theological Introduction to the Book of Psalms: The Psalms as Torah* (Nashville:
   Abingdon, 1993).
McGrath, A.E., *The Genesis of Doctrine* (Oxford: Basil Blackwell, 1990).
Meek, D.E., *The Quest for Celtic Christianity* (Edinburgh: Handsel Press, 2000).
Newbigin, L., *Honest Religion for Secular Man* (London: SCM, 1966).
——, *Foolishness to the Greeks: The Gospel and Western Culture* (London: SPCK, 1986).
——, *A Word in Season: Perspectives on Christian World Missions* (Grand Rapids: Eerdmans and
   Edinburgh: St. Andrews Press, 1994).
Newman, J.H., *An Essay on the Development of Christian Doctrine. The Edition of 1845* (London:
   Penguin, 1973).
Nolan, M.L. and S. Nolan, *Christian Pilgrimage in Modern Western Europe* (Chapel Hill and
   London: The University of North Carolina Press, 1989).
Norris, K., *Dakota: A Spiritual Geography* (Boston and New York: Mariner Books, 1993 and
   2001).
O'Donovan, O., *Resurrection and Moral Order: An Outline for Evangelical Ethics* (Leicester: IVP
   and Grand Rapids: Eerdmans, 1986).
——, 'The Loss of a Sense of Place', *Irish Theological Quarterly*, 55 (1989), 39–58.
——, *The Desire of the Nations: Rediscovering the Roots of Political Theology* (Cambridge: CUP,
   1996).

Peterson, E., *Under the Unpredictable Plant: An Exploration in Vocational Holiness* (Grand Rapids: Eerdmans, 1992).

——, *The Wisdom of Each Other: A Conversation Between Spiritual Friends* (Grand Rapids: Zondervan, 1998).

Sardar, Z., *Postmodernism and the Other: The New Imperialism of Western Culture* (London: Pluto, 1998).

Sumption, J., *Pilgrimage* (London: Faber & Faber, 1975).

Tavinor, M., *Tewkesbury* (Norwich: Canterbury, 1998).

Vanhoozer, K., *First Theology: God, Scripture and Hermeneutics* (Leicester: IVP, 2002).

Visser, M., *The Geometry of Love: Space, Time, Mystery, and Meaning in an Ordinary Church* (Toronto: Harper Flamingo, 2000).

Wilken, R.L., *The Land Called Holy: Palestine in Christian History and Thought* (New Haven and London: Yale UP, 1992).

Wright, N.T., *The Way of the Lord* (London: Triangle, 1999).

Index

DATE DUE

SEP 1 0 2007	
SEP 1 8 2007	
OCT 1 1 2007	
NOV 1 3 2007	
DEC 0 7 2007	
24/01/2013	
JUL 2 4 2012	

BRODART, CO.   Cat. No. 23-221-003